PRAYER PRAISE & PROMISES

A daily walk through the Psalms

AF798058

PRAYER PRAISE & PROMISES

A daily walk through the Psalms

Warren W. Wiersbe

Good Shepherd
BOOKS
HYDERABAD

Prayer, Praise & Promises

by Warren W.Wiersbe

Copyright © 1992 by The Good News Broadcasting Association, Inc.
Originally published in the U.S.by Baker Books, a division of
Baker Book House Company, MI.

First Small Size Edition 2011
Twelve reprints 2012 - 2024
Reprint 2025

ISBN 978-93-6173-780-0

All rights reserved.
No part of this publication may be reproduced in any form or
by any means, electronic, or mechanical, including photocopying,
recording, or any information storage and retrieval system,
without permission in writing from the publisher.

Unless otherwise noted, all Scripture quotations are from
The New King James Version, Holy Bible. Copyright © 1979, 1980, 1982,
by Thomas Nelson Inc., Publishers. Used by permission.

Published by
Good Shepherd Books
Logos Bhavan, Suchitra Junction, Secunderabad - 500 067, Telangana.
www.gsmediaindia.com

Good Shepherd Books is an imprint of Good Shepherd Media,
the publishing division of OM Books Foundation.

Printed and bound in India by
Good Shepherd Media, Secunderabad - 500 067

FOREWORD

The Psalms have always held a special place in the affection of Israel. The people of God rejoiced and lamented together by singing the Psalms. The early Christians discovered the Psalms to be an integral link to their heritage as well.

A psalm was the expression of joy uttered by Augustine at his conversion, and a psalm was the consolation on his lips as he lay upon his death bed. Chrysostom comforted himself in exile by quoting the Psalms. John Hus had a psalm on his lips as he was burned at the stake. Reciting a psalm, Luther entered the Diet of Worms, prepared to defy the Church and stand by faith alone.

But the Psalms have meant much more to us than affection or motivation. They also have been a significant source of inspiration. A. C. Gabelein used to say, "A psalm a day keeps worry away." Many of us have found the Psalms to be an excellent source of comfort, of courage, of strength.

Strength and hope for our spiritual journey is the goal of Warren Wiersbe in this daily devotional on the Psalms, and he succeeds very well. Writing in his own practical and interesting style, Dr. Wiersbe brings us to the banquet table and serves a heaping portion of God's blessing and strength through each psalm. Every reader will be blessed, but more than that, every reader will be instructed, motivated, inspired and challenged.

Here you will find daily food in abundance—good food, tasty food, food to fuel your Christian life. If a psalm a day does keep worry away, who of us can afford to be without one? This devotional book will ensure that your minimum daily Psalms requirement is met. Bon appetit!

Woodrow Kroll

Read Psalm 1:1-6

DAY 1

Preface to
GOD'S HYMNAL

Have you ever read the preface to the hymnal used in your church? Few people ever do. The preface to God's hymnal (the Book of Psalms) is Psalm 1. It begins with a word we often use—*blessed*. Nowhere does Scripture tell us that God blesses programs or promotions. But it does teach that He blesses individuals. He blessed Abraham so he might be a blessing to others. And He blesses us so we might bless others.

What you delight in is what will direct your life, so be careful what you enjoy. The blessed person delights in the Law of the Lord (v.2). He delights so much in the Word of God that he *meditates* on it during the day. Meditation is to the soul what digestion is to the body. It means assimilating the Word of God.

The blessed person is like a tree (v.3). A tree has roots. The most important part of your life is your "root system." Don't be like the ungodly, who are like chaff (v.4). Chaff doesn't have roots. It is blown away by every wind that comes along. Your root system is important because it determines your nourishment. It also determines your stability and your strength when the storm comes and the wind starts to blow.

People can't see your root system, but God can. Praying and meditating on the Word of God will cause your roots to go down deep into His love.

God delights in blessing His children. But we must prepare ourselves for His blessings by first appropriating the resources He has given us. Delight in the Word of God and feed on it. But do more than occasionally read the Word; meditate on it constantly. Make it your source of spiritual nourishment, and God will bless you with strength and stability.

DAY

2

Read Psalm 1:1,2

SEPARATED AND SATURATED

Two of the most popular words in the Christian vocabulary are *bless* and *blessing*. God wants to bless His people. He wants them to be recipients and channels of blessing. God blesses us to make us a blessing to others, but He has given us certain conditions for receiving blessings.

First, *we must be separated from the world* (v.1). The world is anything that separates us from God or causes us to disobey Him. Separation is not isolation but contact without contamination. Sin is usually a gradual process. Notice the gradual decline of the sinner in verse 1. He is *walking* (Mark 14:54), *standing* (John 18:18) and then *sitting* (Luke 22:55). Becoming worldly is progressive; it happens by degrees. We make friends with the world; we become spotted by the world; we love the world, become confirmed to it and end up condemned with it. Lot is an example of someone who became worldly. He looked toward Sodom, pitched his tent toward Sodom, lived there, lost everything and ended in sin.

Second, *we must be saturated with the Word* (v.2). Whatever delights us directs us. We saturate ourselves with the Word by meditating on it. Meditation is to the spirit what digestion is to the body. When we meditate on the Word, we allow the Spirit of God within us to "digest" the Word of God for us. So not only do we delight in the Word, it becomes a source of spiritual nourishment for us.

Enjoy the blessings God has for you and allow Him to make you a blessing to others. (A third condition, being situated by the waters, is the topic of our next devotional.)

God desires to bless us, but we must meet His conditions for receiving blessings. By staying separate from the world and keeping saturated in the Word, we may expect God's blessings. Resolve to meditate on the Word of God and obey it. He will make you a blessing to others.

Read Psalm 1:3-6

Are You Situated

BY THE WATERS?

DAY

3

A tree is a blessing. It holds soil, provides shade and produces fruit. The godly are like trees, with root systems that go deep into the spiritual resources of God's grace (v.3). But sadly, many professing Christians are not like trees but are like artificial plants or cut flowers with no roots. They may be beautiful for a while, but soon they die.

A tree needs light, water and roots to live. We all have resources upon which we draw life. The question we need to ask ourselves is, Where are our roots? The person God can bless is planted by the rivers of water. We must be careful not to be like Christians who are dry and withered and depend upon their own resources. They are like tumbleweeds, blown about by any wind of doctrine.

To have the blessings of verse 3, we need to meet the conditions of verses 1 and 2. That is, we must first be separated from the world and saturated with the Word to be situated by the waters.

God desires to bless us, but we need to meet certain conditions to receive His blessings. We bear fruit only when we have roots, and we must draw upon spiritual resources to bring forth fruit in due season. To bear the fruit of the Spirit, we must allow the Spirit to work in us and through us.

In contrast to the believer, the ungodly are not like trees but are like chaff. They have no roots, produce no fruit and are blown about. The ungodly reject the Word of God and will perish without hope (v.6). As Christians we must not reject the ungodly but try to reach them. God blesses us so that we might be a blessing to others. His Spirit helps us bear fruit that can help win the lost.

Are you like a tree or like chaff?

We need God's resources to bear fruit. But where we place our roots is paramount. Only as we grow them deeply into the spiritual resources of God's grace will we produce fruit. Make the Bible your spiritual resource. Delight in it and feed your soul with its truth. God can use you to help win the lost.

DAY 4

Read Psalm 2:1-12

WHEN GOD LAUGHS

Are you surprised that God laughs? "He who sits in the heavens shall laugh; the Lord shall hold them in derision" (v.4). God has a sense of humor, but His laughter is the kind that is born of judgment. It's the laughter of derision, the laughter of irony. What is God laughing at? He's laughing at puny little kings and rulers who have united to shake their fists at His throne and tell Him they don't want Him to rule over them (vv.2,3). God laughs at them because He knows man cannot survive without submitting to His authority. Man is made in the image of God, and if he fights against Him, he fights against himself. Man, in his rebellion, tries to make God in his own image. He thinks God can be treated with disdain and disobedience. And God laughs.

We can laugh when we read the headlines or watch TV reports. We see a world in turmoil, a world united against God, but we laugh because He is still on the throne. "Yet I have set My King on My holy hill of Zion" (v.6). Jesus Christ is God's King, and He is on the throne. Therefore, we can look at the nations as they are in turmoil, as they unite against God, and we can smile—in fact, we can laugh. They are fighting a losing battle. Jesus Christ is on the throne of the universe, and we who are Christians are seated with Him on that throne.

As believers, we are to be witnesses for Christ. Reaching a world that rebels against God's authority can be difficult. Be encouraged, for your efforts will not be wasted. God is in control and one day will bring all governments and earthly powers into submission. Pray that He will use your life to reach others and glorify Himself.

Read Psalm 2:1-6

FOUR VOICES

PART - 1

DAY 5

The world is getting noisier. So many voices vie for our attention. The result is that many people are getting the wrong instructions. It is important that we have discernment in a noisy world filled with propaganda. We need the truth.

We need to distinguish the four voices of Psalm 2. The first is the *voice of defiance*—the nations of the world (vv.1-3). It is amazing that the nations would defy Almighty God. He has provided for them (Acts 14:17), guided them (I Tim.6:17) and determined their histories (Acts 17:26). Why do the nations rebel? They seek freedom without God. P. T. Forsythe said, "The purpose of life is not to find your freedom. The purpose of life is to find your Master." Authority demands submission (Matt.11:29).

The world is a mess morally, intellectually, socially, politically, economically and ecologically because it has defied God. Man is made in God's image. The irony is that when man rebels against God, he rebels against himself.

Second, we have the *voice of derision*—the voice of God the Father (vv.4-6). While there is tumult on earth, there is tranquility in heaven. God laughs because the Kingdom is secure; the King has been established. Jesus is God's King. Though the nations rebel, we don't need to worry, for the King is already enthroned in heaven.

Listen to the voice of God. He is laughing at the world's rebellion, and you can laugh with Him if Jesus is your King.

The world often tries to drown out the truth. Its voice of defiance is clear. The world's corruption is a result of its defiance. Take inventory of the voices you listen to. Are you part of the voice of defiance, or can you laugh with God at the world's rebellion?

Read Psalm 2:7-12

FOUR VOICES
PART - 2

A third voice we hear in the world is the *voice of declaration*—God the Son (vv.7-9). He runs the universe by decree, not by democracy. He knows everything, is everywhere and can do anything. God's decrees will succeed. Puny, foolish men with their godless living will not eradicate or hinder His decrees.

God decrees that Jesus Christ is His Son. Jesus is God, and He is King by nature, by conquest and by His Resurrection. He is reigning today, and we can reign in life through Him (Rom.5:17).

God also decrees that He will break the rebellious nations with "a rod of iron." When His scepter of righteousness goes forth in judgment, the nations will cry out, not in repentance but in rebellion. God already has given the nations to His Son (Matt.4:8-10).

The fourth voice is *the voice of decision*—the Holy Spirit (vv.10-12). He wants us to learn—to be wise, to be instructed. Many depend on philosophy, psychology and history. These disciplines are helpful, but Christians must rely first and foremost on the Spirit of God to reveal truth.

The Holy Spirit wants us to be *willing to serve*. We serve the Lord, not sin. There is joy with our fear because God is our Father. In searching for liberty, the rebellious crowd practices anarchy, for freedom without authority is anarchy. We are made in the image of God. To rebel against Him is to rebel against our own nature.

The Holy Spirit also wants us to be *reconciled*. God is reconciled to us through Christ (Acts 16:31). Jesus "kissed" us in His birth and death. Today He is the Lamb, but someday He will come as the Lion to judge. God is holy and will not allow sin and rebellion to go on forever.

Are you listening to the right voices? "Blessed are all those who put their trust in Him." We are saved by faith through the death of the Son of God. Are you saved? If not, hear His voice and trust in Him.

Read Psalm 3:1-8

Are You
SLEEPING WELL?

DAY
7

How well we sleep sometimes indicates how much we really trust the Lord. David said, "I lay down and slept; I awoke, for the Lord sustained me" (v.5). We may think we can do that anytime. But what if we had been where David was? He was fleeing from his son Absalom, who had turned against him and had driven him from Jerusalem. Now David was in the wilderness with his army. It would be difficult to lie down and sleep knowing that you are in a dangerous wilderness and that your own son is against you. Oh, it wasn't the physical danger that kept David awake. He knew God would protect him. It was the inner spiritual and emotional agony of having his own flesh and blood trying to seize the kingdom from him.

But David said, in effect, "Lord, You are able to give me peace in my heart, the protection I need, the perspective I need. You are able to help me in the midst of this difficult situation." The heart of every problem is really the problem in the heart. David knew that it was not *the army on the outside* that would keep him awake but *the agony on the inside.*

This psalm starts with David's cry, "Many are they who rise up against me" (v.1). He's pleading for help. The psalm ends with David's singing a song of praise (v.8). Your day might begin by your pleading for help. But if you are trusting the Lord, it could end by your praising Him for the help He has given you.

Difficult circumstances often rob us of our peace and our perspective. When you find yourself in adverse circumstances or in the face of frightening consequences, admit your trouble and affirm your trust in Him. Then be encouraged that God protects you and gives you peace in the midst of the storm.

DAY 8

Read Psalm 4:1-8

BIGGER AND BETTER

Sometimes God's people can be so discouraging! In Psalm 4 we find David listening to people saying, "Who will show us any good?" (v.6). David's own men were discouraged. They were going through a trial, and some were saying, "O David, this is the end. God is no longer going to help us." That's hard to take. It's rough when your associates or friends say to you, "Well, you've reached the end. Who will show us any good?"

But David called on the Lord, and God enlarged him. "You have relieved [enlarged] me when I was in distress" (v.1). Pressure on the *outside* should make us bigger on the *inside*. The trials of life will press against us and make us either midgets or giants—either smaller or bigger. But we have to start on the inside. "You have relieved me when I was in distress." How did this happen?

David cried out to God, "You have put gladness in my heart" (v.7). He started out with sadness and ended with gladness. He started with tears and ended with triumph. Once again he's sleeping beautifully. "I will both lie down in peace, and sleep; for You alone, O Lord, make me dwell in safety" (v.8).

David discovered that what was important was not *the circumstance around him but the attitude within him.* Let God enlarge you when you are going through distress. He can do it. You can't do it, and others can't do it for you. In fact, others may want to make things even tighter and narrower for you. But when you turn to the Lord and trust Him, He will enlarge you on the inside. You'll come out of your distresses a bigger person because you've trusted in the Lord.

There is a relationship between our attitude inside and our circumstances outside. If we maintain the proper attitude, God will use our trials to enlarge us. Are you going through a trial today? Give your circumstances to the Lord and trust Him to enlarge you.

Read Psalm 4:1-8

DAY 9

Rest in the
MIDST OF TRIALS

David was experiencing great difficulty. He was in a "tight corner." God permits tight corners (II Sam.12:10). He forgives but disciplines, and we reap what we sow (Ps.25:17).

Psalm 4 is encouraging because it tells us that God cares for us and gives us several blessings in the midst of our trials. First, He gives us *the blessing of enlargement* (v.1). *Relieved* means "enlarged." When God permits enlarged troubles, He enlarges His people; that is, we grow. Joseph is a good example of this (Ps.18:19,36). His difficulties revealed his character, and he grew. Enlarged troubles lead to an enlarged life, which leads to an enlarged place and enlarged paths. God had an enlarged ministry for David, but He first had to make him grow.

Second, God gives us *the blessing of encouragement* (vv.2,3). Eventually, all earthly causes will fail. Only the plan of God will succeed. The Lord is our shield, our glory and the One who lifts our head. In this life we will have problems, but God encourages us.

Third, God gives us *the blessing of enablement* (vv.4,5). Tight corners bring us face to face with trusting versus temptation (Matt.4:3,4). David had a right to be angry. Anger can be used of God to bring about righteousness, or it can be used by Satan to bring about sin (James 1:20). *Meditate* means "to discuss with yourself." It's so easy to brood when we're lying in bed, but God gives quietness when we meditate (Ps.46:10).

Fourth, God gives us *the blessings of enlightenment and enjoyment* (vv.6-8). David's people were discouraged. Are you a discourager or an encourager? As Christians, we should have the smile of God upon us (Num.6:25). We should exhibit gladness and joy in the Lord. God adds to this the blessing of peace and sleep. This is possible when Christ is Savior. So get your eyes off the enemy and on the Lord. The temptation to sin is great during difficulties, but trust in the Lord, and He will give you peace and joy in the midst of difficulty.

God's blessings are designed to do more than simply comfort us in our difficulties; they are to help us grow. Take strength from knowing that God is weaving His purposes into your life and that He will reward your trust in Him. "And we know that God causes all things to work together for good to those who love God, to those who are called according to His purpose" (Rom.8:28).

DAY
10

Read Psalm 5:1-12

A HEART PROBLEM

It's imperative for us to meet God in the morning if we want to have a good day. Jesus got up early in the morning to pray, according to Mark 1:35. Here we find the psalmist saying, "My voice You shall hear in the morning, O Lord; in the morning I will direct it to You, and I will look up" (v.3).

When I used to work the night shift, I would sleep in the morning. So when I got up in the afternoon, I would meet with the Lord. Meeting with God is not an appointment on a clock but an appointment in your heart. Does God hear your voice in the morning? When He looks on you at the beginning of your day, does He look on you as a priest who has come to offer Him sacrifices of praise? That's what direct means (v.3)—"to order my prayer." It means to arrange the sacrifice on the altar.

When you wake up in the morning, remind yourself that you are one of God's priests. How did you become a priest? Through faith in Jesus Christ. "To Him who loved us and washed us from our sins in His own blood, and has made us kings and priests to His God and Father" (Rev.1:5,6). You're one of God's priests. That means wherever you are is God's temple, because your body is His temple.

The first thing we do in the morning is the first thing the high priest used to do every morning. He laid the burnt offering on the altar. The burnt offering is a picture of total dedication to God. If you want to have a good day, start by giving yourself to the Lord as a burnt offering, a living sacrifice, holy and acceptable to God (Rom.12:1). A good day begins in the morning, and it begins at the altar.

Does your day begin with God? If not, decide to start each morning by dedicating yourself to Him as a living sacrifice and ask His guidance for the day's decisions and actions. He wants to direct your life. So view each day as a gift from God and determine to be a good steward of the day's resources. Make your time with Him a daily appointment.

Request, Reason and Response

IN THE MIDST OF TRIALS

What do you do in difficult situations? Many of the psalms were written during difficult, often painful, experiences. In Psalm 5 we find two sequences concerning trials. In the first sequence (vv.1-7), David is experiencing difficulty and makes his request—"hear me"(v.1-3). *Meditation* here means "sighing, murmuring, groaning"—a quiet expression of feelings. When our burden is beyond expression, all we can do is sigh and moan before the Lord. The Spirit hears our groanings and intercedes for us (Rom.8:26). David's meditation turns to a cry (v.2; Heb.5:7). Prayer is not always a quiet, joyful conversation with God. Sometimes it is a battle against the principalities arrayed against us.

David's reason for making this request is the holiness of God (vv.4-6). He cried to God because He is holy and stands against the wicked and boastful. Although He will judge the wicked, God does not always judge sin immediately. David's response is worship (v.7), individual and personal.

In the second sequence, David makes another request—"lead me" (v.8). He wants God's way, which is the righteous way. In the midst of difficulty, what we need most is wisdom to know the will of God (James 1:5). Notice that David asks to be led, not delivered. God has a straight way through every difficulty that will lead us to victory.

His reason this time is the wickedness of man (vv.9,10). Destruction means "a yawning, open abyss." An open tomb pictures defilement and death. Flattery is not communication; it is manipulation. Absalom fell by his own counsel. David did nothing. He let God do it all (Rom.12:19).

David's response (vv.11,12) is rejoicing in faith, love and hope. Joy comes from trusting in and loving the Lord. This kind of joy comes from God's work on the inside, not from circumstances on the outside.

The psalmist tells us to expect difficulty. We shouldn't run from our trials but bring to God our requests, our reasons and our response.

You need never be paralyzed by your difficulties. You have the privilege of praying to a loving, understanding Father, who knows your condition. He guides you through difficulty to victory. When your faith, hope and love are fixed on the Lord, you can face any difficulty or problem, and God will give you joy and peace within.

DAY

12

Read Psalm 6:1-10

WORSE THAN DEATH

All of us know what it means to sin and to confess our sin. Psalm 6 is the first of the seven penitential psalms. Occasionally God has to remind us to confess our sins.

In verses 1-5 David pleads for God not to rebuke him or to chasten him. God's chastening is not punishment. It builds our Christian character. Hebrews 12 talks about chastening, and the word used means "child training." It's the picture of a child learning how to be a good athlete. God chastens us, but He does so in love. David was afraid that God was going to chasten him in His hot displeasure (v.1). But our God is a God of mercy and grace. This doesn't mean, however, that we can minimize sin. This doesn't mean we should ever say, "Well, God is a forgiving God; therefore, I can do whatever I want to do, and He will forgive me." No, David was saying, "Lord, I've sinned. I'm weary with my groaning. Forgive me. I have done wrong." And God does forgive those who confess their sins to Him.

Sin is the Christian's worst possible experience. It's far worse than pain or suffering or even death itself. We are weak, and sometimes we fail. But let's never be afraid to come to our Father with our appeal for forgiveness. The tragedy is that all around us, enemies are waiting for us to fall. They want to point at us and say, "See, that Christian failed." But we can come before the Lord and ask Him for His forgiveness, and He will grant it to us. God will have mercy on us. "Whoever calls on the name of the Lord shall be saved" (Acts 2:21).

We must never treat sin lightly. Certainly, no Christian should ever harbor sin. But when we do sin, we may lean on God's mercy and grace and confess our sin to a loving Father. One of the great encouragements of the Christian life is that God forgives and restores. Are you living with unconfessed sin? Avoid God's chastening. Confess your sin and ask for His forgiveness.

Read Psalm 7:1-9

TESTED IN A TIGHT SPOT

DAY 13

This psalm was born out of a sad experience David had with Cush, a Benjamite (see I Sam.24-26). Cush was one of Saul's spies. And because of what David did, Cush caused the deaths of innocent men.

Whenever David had a problem with persecution or with people, he would run to God. "O Lord my God, in You I put my trust; save me from all those who persecute me; and deliver me" (v.1). David's enemies were pursuing him. But the first thing he did was examine his own heart. "O Lord my God, if I have done this: if there is iniquity in my hands" (v.3). He was saying, "If I have sinned, then let the enemy persecute me."

When we are persecuted or experiencing problems, the first thing we should do is examine our own hearts—not examine the enemy or even examine God by saying, "God, why did You allow such a thing to happen?" When you find yourself in a tight spot, look in the mirror and say, "Father, is there something in my life You are talking to me about? Is there some area in my life where I am not as yielded as I ought to be?"

You may ask, "What about my enemies? Who's going to take care of them?" That was David's question. The answer is that God will take care of the enemy. The wickedness of others will come to an end. Our righteous God will accomplish His purposes, but notice the end of verse 9: "For the righteous God tests the hearts and minds." Times of trial are not only times of testimony and trusting; they are also times of testing. When God tests you, He is showing you your own heart. You may say, "I know my own heart." But you don't. "The heart is deceitful above all things, and desperately wicked; who can know it?" (Jer.17:9).

God has a purpose for trials and testings. Do you find yourself in a tight spot today? Don't view this as something to endure. Rather, consider it an opportunity for growth. Use this time to examine your heart. Perhaps God wants to teach you something and develop an area of your life. Yield yourself to Him and trust Him to do a good work in you.

Read Psalm 7:10-17

Giving Birth to a MONSTER

This passage presents a frightening picture. We read about swords and arrows, pits, ditches and death. God is angry and is judging sin, and He hears David's petition about his persecutors: "O Lord, they are accusing me of something I didn't do. They are lying about me." That's tough to take. People lied about the Lord Jesus, too. And anyone who tries to live like Him is going to suffer this kind of persecution. David's enemies wanted to kill him. Some innocent men had been killed because of him. But David was praying that God would first cleanse his own heart. He said, "Examine me. Look at me. Test me. I want to be sure my life is ruled by integrity."

Sin brings its own judgment. "Behold, the wicked travails with iniquity, conceives trouble and brings forth falsehood" (v.14). This is a picture of pregnancy and birth. When a person conceives sin and then gives birth to it, he gives birth to a monster that will turn on him and destroy him. David changed the picture in verses 15 and 16: "He made a pit and dug it out, and has fallen into the ditch which he made. His trouble shall return upon his own head." That's a word of encouragement and also a warning. We can't give birth to sin without having to live with the baby, watching it grow up and create problems. Yes, God in His grace forgives. But God in His government says, "We must reap what we sow."

The warning here is don't give birth to sin. There's also an encouragement: If others are giving birth to sin, don't fret over it but pray for them.

What is your response when others do their worst to you? Be encouraged that God knows what is happening and will judge sin. If you take care of yourself and walk with integrity, you may be confident that God will deal with those who sin against you. Above all, don't give birth to sin yourself; rather, pray for those who persecute you. God will one day turn your persecution into praise.

Live
LIKE A KING

Psalm 8 deals with sovereignty. "O Lord, our Lord, how excellent is Your name in all the earth, You who set Your glory above the heavens!" (v.1). The first Lord means "Jehovah," the covenant-keeping God, the God who keeps His promises. The second Lord means "the Sovereign," the One who has not only the ability but the authority. "O Lord [the promise-making God], our Lord [the Sovereign, who has the power to keep His promises], how excellent is your name in all the earth."

When God saved you, He made you a king. You may not look like one or act like one, but you are one. Your day of salvation was a day of coronation. God put you on the throne through Jesus Christ. Then why do you live like a slave?

We discover in this psalm that God gave Adam and Eve the first crowns. But what did they do? They handed their crowns and scepters to Satan, because they wanted to become like God, to be sovereign. And they lost their dominion. Man today does not have dominion over beasts and fowl and fish. But Jesus does. He had dominion over the fowl: He told a rooster to crow when Peter sinned. He had dominion over the fish: He gathered them into the net when Peter was fishing. He even had dominion over the animals of the field: He rode on a donkey that no one had ever ridden before.

We've lost that dominion, but we've regained our spiritual dominion in Jesus Christ. You were saved to live like a king. Don't live like a slave.

Believers have a responsibility to live like kings. Our kingship securely rests on the authority and character of God. Are you living beneath your station? Determine to live like a king.

DAY 16

Read Psalm 8:1-9

WHAT IS MAN?

What is man? Charles Darwin said man is an animal. Sigmund Freud taught that man is a spoiled child. Karl Marx believed man is an economic factor. But the Bible says God has a much higher calling for man. God wants us to be kings; He wants us to reign in life. In Psalm 8 we see three different kings exemplified in Adam, Jesus and David.

First, God the Father created us to be kings (Gen.1:26-28). God gave Adam dominion over the earth. We are created in the image of God with a mind, heart, will and spirit. But sin has marred God's image in man. His mind can't think God's thoughts; his emotions are wrapped up in sin; his will is rebellious, and his spirit is dead.

Second, God the Son redeemed us to be kings. The tragedy of man's rejecting Christ as Savior is that he goes through life as a slave, not a sovereign. Because of his rebellion, man lost his dominion. But Christ's death, Resurrection and Ascension regained what Adam lost—and much more (Rom.5). Our Lord is reigning today, and we will someday reign with Him.

Third, God the Holy Spirit anointed us to live as kings. Our kingship comes from God. The power of His Spirit gave David the strength to kill Goliath. We are either a sovereign or a slave; either we will reign as kings, or sin will reign in our lives.

God never intended that we live like slaves but that we live like kings and reign over our circumstances and feelings. Trust Christ as Savior to reign in your life.

Do you find yourself a slave to a particular circumstance or emotion? Because of the sacrifice of Christ, we need no longer live as slaves in this world. Claim the power of God's Spirit and live as a king.

Read Psalm 9:1-6

YOUR SONG OF VICTORY

DAY 17

Psalm 9 is a great victory psalm. "I will praise You, O Lord, with my whole heart; I will tell of all Your marvelous works" (v.1). Notice the universals in that verse—"my whole heart" and "all Your marvelous works." I must confess that there are times when I don't praise the Lord with my whole heart. At times I've stood in church with the hymnbook in my hand, singing a great song of praise—but not with my whole heart. The best way to have victory is to praise the Lord wholeheartedly.

Granted, there are times when it's hard to praise Him. Think of Paul and Silas in prison (Acts 16:16-34). They had been humiliated. Their rights had been stripped away from them. Their bodies were hurting. Yet they were wholeheartedly praising the Lord. God can heal your broken heart if you give Him all the pieces. He'll put it back together again and give you wholehearted praise.

Don't praise God only about circumstances; praise Him for who He is. "I will be glad and rejoice in You" (v.2). Maybe you can't rejoice in your circumstances or in the way you feel. Maybe you can't even rejoice in the plans that are made for today, but you always can rejoice in the Lord (Phil.4:4). You can rejoice in the Lord today because He is worthy of your praise. "I will be glad and rejoice in You; I will sing praise to Your name, O Most High" (v.2).

The thrust of this psalm is simply this: If your cause is right, God is on your side. He is on His throne, and He is administering His world the way He wants to. David didn't quite understand all that God was doing, but he knew that God knew what He was doing. So when your cause is right, you can praise the Lord, even in the midst of apparent defeat. When God is on the throne, everything turns out all right.

If your life is broken right now, be encouraged that God knows what is going on in your life and will restore you. Until He does, rejoice in Him and praise His name.

DAY 18

Read Psalm 9:7-12

Safest Protection
IN THE WORLD

This passage teaches a great truth: The safest and strongest protection we have is the name of the Lord. "And those who know Your name will put their trust in You; for You, Lord, have not forsaken those who seek You" (v.10). As I read those words, I'm reminded that God forsook His Son for us. Jesus said from the cross, "My God, My God, why have You forsaken Me?" (Matt.27:46). Has it ever occurred to you that the only person God ever really forsook was His own Son? "He who did not spare His own Son, but delivered Him up for us all" (Rom.8:32). Because He did this, we can be sure He will never forsake us for the sake of His Son. The Father loves His Son and says to Him, "You have died for these people. I will never forsake them." God's promise to us is "I will never leave you nor forsake you" (Heb.13:5). "Lo, I am with you always" was our Lord's last statement in the Gospel of Matthew (28:20).

The safest place in all the world is in the will of God, and the safest protection in all the world is the name of God. When you know His name, you know His nature. His names and titles reveal His nature. They tell us who He is and what He can do. For example, He is Jehovah, the God who makes covenants. He is the Lord, the sovereign king. He is Jesus, the Savior. Each name He bears is a blessing He bestows on us.

Are you getting to know God? "And those who know Your name [who know God's nature] will put their trust in You" (v.10). The better you know God, the more you will trust Him. The more you trust Him, the better you will get to know Him—an exciting and enriching experience.

One of the great experiences of the Christian life is the personal relationship we enjoy with our God. To trust God is to seek Him (Isa.55:6). Today, seek Him with a desire to know Him better.

Read Psalm 9:13-16

IN HIS TIME

DAY 19

Have you ever looked at a beautiful rose and watched it slowly blossom day after day? Have you ever tried to help it open? If you try, you might kill it. God makes everything beautiful in His time. He causes everything to straighten out and line up according to His schedule. If you have a problem in your life with a person or a circumstance, rely on God to resolve it. "Vengeance is Mine, I will repay," says the Lord (Rom.12:19). One of the worst things we can do is to take judgment into our own hands.

The psalmist tells us in these verses, "Let God be the judge, the jury and the prosecuting attorney. He knows more about this than you do." The psalmist assures us that, in His time, God will catch those who are doing wrong. The nations will fall into the pit they have made. Sinners who have laid nets in the pathway will get caught in those nets. "The wicked is snared in the work of his own hands" (v.16).

It encourages me to know that I don't have to devote my time or energy, even my inward concern, to wondering what's going to happen to all the evil in the world. God is going to take care of it. Of course, we as Christians should do our part to make this a better world. We are the salt of the earth; we are the light of the world. But we've been called to do something even more wonderful—to tell these wicked people that they don't have to go to hell. We have the privilege of witnessing to them and letting them know that they can be saved. Yes, let God be the Judge. Your job today is to be a witness.

Has someone wronged you recently? Resist the urge to judge that person. Instead, pray that God might use you to reach the offender.

DAY

20

Read Psalm 9:17-20

WHO'S RULING THE WORLD?

The humanist sings, "Glory to man in the highest." And sometimes it looks as if man is prevailing and God is a failure. You recall the slogan that was popular a few years ago that proclaimed "God is dead." Then the philosophers decided God was not really dead; He was simply sick and infirm and couldn't do much about what was going on in the world.

This mindset began in Genesis 3, when Satan said to Adam and Eve, "Look, why should you be a man? You can be like God." That's the same lie that runs the world today. Man is saying, "I will be like God."

But the psalmist tells us that man is not going to prevail. "The wicked shall be turned into hell, and all the nations that forget God" (v.17). Today it looks as though man is succeeding—truth forever on the scaffold, wrong forever on the throne. But notice what David prayed: "Arise, O Lord, do not let man prevail, . . . that the nations may know themselves to be but men" (vv.19,20).

If we take the scepter out of God's hand, we make a mess of things. God runs this universe, and He has ordained us to be under His authority. The word David used for man in verse 19 means "frail man, weak man." The problem today is that men don't know they are mere mortals; they think they're the Creator. And they worship and serve the creature rather than the Creator. But the sad thing is this: When men try to be God, they don't become God—they become animals. They sink lower than men and start acting like animals. That's why our world is in such a mess today.

I rejoice that I'm just a frail person. I need God. I can come to Him and say, "O Lord, give me the strength I need to glorify Your name today."

We know that God is sovereign in His universe. His purposes will prevail. We may confidently submit to His authority and rest in His love, wisdom and strength. Though we are frail, God is our strength. Let God be King of your life and glorify His name in all you do.

HOW NEAR IS GOD?

As we read the Book of Psalms, we find that David was constantly in and out of trouble. Some people say that Christians who really love the Lord will never be in difficult places. But that wasn't true of Moses; it wasn't true of David; and it certainly wasn't true of our Lord Jesus Christ! Our Lord ended up in the most difficult place of all—crucified on a Roman cross.

Listen to David: "Why do You stand afar off, O Lord? Why do You hide Yourself in times of trouble?" (v.1). Here are those questions once again: "Why, Lord? Where are You?" Why do we think God is far away from us? What makes us think God has deserted us? First, we know that God is everywhere. Second, He has promised not to forsake us (Heb.13:5). David only felt as if God were far away.

That's a good lesson for us to learn. Don't base your judgments only on your feelings. Build your life on faith. Faith says, "I'm going to trust God no matter what I see, no matter what I think and no matter how I feel." Faith does not mean we are ignorant. It means we are walking in the will of God because we know the Word of God.

Yes, David was in trouble. The proud and self-sufficient were after him. They were persecuting and taunting him, "I shall not be moved." They were also saying, "God won't see it" and "God will not judge." But David came to the Lord and said, "Lord, You know all about this, and You are going to take care of it."

When it seems as if God is far away, remind yourself that He is near. Nearness is not a matter of geography. God is everywhere. Nearness is likeness. The more we become like the Lord, the nearer He is to us.

Do you desire to be nearer to God today? Fill your mind with the truth of the Word and your heart with prayer and trust God to take care of you.

DAY 22

Read Psalm 10:12-18

The Heart OF THE PROBLEM

David cried out and said, "God, You've got to take care of the situation." For several years Saul had been pursuing him. At one point David compared himself to a flea that was being chased. Saul's problem was that he was listening to liars in his court. Those who wanted Saul's favor were saying, "David wants your crown. He wants your throne. David said this, and David did that." They lied about him, and he could do nothing about it.

We have little control over the circumstances of life. We can't control the weather or the economy, and we can't control what other people say about or do to us. There is only one area where we have control—we can rule the kingdom inside. The heart of every problem is the problem in the heart. Once we get to that throne room inside us and let God take over, we don't have to worry about others.

David prayed in verse 12, "Arise, O Lord! O God, lift up Your hand! Do not forget the humble." The word *humble* is a key word. What is humility? Is it thinking poorly of ourselves? No, humility is simply not thinking of ourselves at all. Humility means admitting that I cannot handle my problem by myself. God is going to have to handle it by working *in* me and *through* me and *for* me. But before God can work for me or through me He has to work in me.

If you want to get on top of your circumstances, get beneath the feet of the Lord. Humble yourself, and He'll lift you up.

We cannot control the circumstances of life, nor can we avoid them. But we can take a humble attitude toward God. He takes a special interest in us and will help us handle our circumstances. Have you examined the throne room inside lately? Are you willing to let God work in you and through you to accomplish His purposes?

THE QUESTION "WHY?"

PART - 1

DAY 23

"Why?" is the easiest question to ask but the hardest to answer. David asks why three times in this psalm. The atheist's answer to this question is that there is no God; the rationalist says God is unable to act or doesn't care; and the legalist says this is punishment for personal sin. The truthful answer comes from David. There are three stages in this experience of asking why.

The first stage is *concern—God is hiding*. People have asked for centuries, "Why doesn't God do something?" (Job 13:24; Jer.14:8,9). The wicked seem to be triumphing, and in doing so, they make four false statements. First, they say, "There is no God" (vv.1-4; Ps.14:1). The fool worships the creature, not the Creator. The greatest judgment God can send is to let us have our way. He is the source of life. When we leave out God, we die. Do you consider Him when you make plans?

Then the wicked say, "I shall not be moved" (vv.5-7). They curse the God they do not believe in. They enjoy the taste of sin. Third, the wicked say, "God does not see me." They picture Him as a ferocious beast, catching the innocent unawares. They are characterized by hypocrisy, deception, intimidation, threats and selfishness. This graphically pictures many into today's business world.

Finally, the wicked say that "God does not care." But He does care, and sin will catch up with them.

Most of us at some time find ourselves asking God "Why?" Although the world offers several answers to this question; the Bible gives us insight into how to deal properly with the question. Don't be like the wicked, who make false statements about God and defy His judgment. Rest in the promises of the Word of God.

DAY

24

Read Psalm 10:14-18

THE QUESTION "WHY?"

PART - 2

In Part 1 we dealt with *concern*—the first stage of asking the question "Why?" In this segment we will cover the last two stages.

The second stage involves *commitment—God is helping.* Man's sinful condition leaves him helpless, so David turns his attention from the wicked to God. We can be encouraged by knowing that God *sees* our trouble and *knows* our grief (v.14). Objectively, He knows what we face; subjectively, He feels what we feel. Phillips Brooks said, "The purpose of life is the building of character through truth." Character is built in the storms and battles of life; it is tested in the easy times of life. The most discouraging feeling is that nobody understands. Christ endured all His earthly experiences so God could prepare Him to be a merciful and faithful High Priest. We may also be encouraged by knowing that God *investigates* (v.15). He sees and cares, and He will repay (v.14).

The third stage in asking "Why?" deals with *confidence. God is hearing* (vv: 16-18). "Man of the earth" is the wicked, living for and because of the earth. David reminds us that we're just mortal men (Ps.9:20). God hears when we call and remembers; in His time, He accomplishes His purposes. And we can be confident of that.

A day of reckoning will come when the wicked will suffer for their unrepented sin. God has appointed His Son to be the judge. If you don't know Christ as Savior, if you think you're getting away with sin, or if you wonder why God doesn't do something, be thankful that He has not judged you yet (II Pet.3:9). Jesus died for you and will save you if you will trust Him.

God does not turn a deaf ear to our questions. Nor is He inactive regarding sin. He is interested in helping us build character, and He will accomplish His purposes in due time. If you're a Christian and wondering why God doesn't act, commit yourself to the Lord and place your confidence in Him (Ps.37:5).

Want to
RUN AWAY?

Have you ever felt like running away? "In the Lord I put my trust; how can you say to my soul, 'Flee as a bird to your mountain'?" (v.1). All of us have days when we feel like quitting. We throw up our hands and say, "That's it. I've had it, and I'm leaving."

At times we do need to get away to rest and regain our perspective. Our Lord Jesus said to His disciples, "Let's just depart and rest a while." Vance Havner once remarked, "If you don't come apart and rest, you'll just come apart." But the psalmist was not talking about a vacation. "The wicked bend their bow" (v.2). He was saying, "The wicked are doing this and that. Let's get out of here and go to some mountaintop and have a good Bible conference."

When you feel like running or flying away, remember, God's throne is secure. The Lord is in His holy temple. In a difficult time Isaiah looked up and saw the Lord on His throne, high and lifted up. In the Book of Revelation, John saw the Lord on His throne, and it gave him new courage.

Don't flee to a mountain; flee to the throne of grace. When you feel like quitting or running away, remember that you can't run away from your troubles and you can't run away from yourself. The solution is not running *away;* it's running to. It's running to the throne of grace and finding grace to help in time of need.

Those times when you feel like quitting can be times of great opportunity, for God uses your troubles to help you grow. When you feel like running away, claim your privilege as a child of God and approach the throne of grace. There you will find the personal and tailored help you need.

DAY 26

Read Psalm 12:1-8

THE ELIJAH COMPLEX

Whenever you get the idea that you are the only one left who is godly, beware. That's how David was praying in Psalm 12. He said, "The godly man ceases! For the faithful disappear from among the sons of men" (v.1). I call this the Elijah complex. You will remember that Elijah had this problem (I Kings 19). He left his place of ministry, went out into the wilderness and sat down pouting. God asked, "What are you doing here?" Elijah replied, "I'm the only godly one left, and they are trying to kill me." God said, "I have 7000 people waiting in line. I can pick anyone of them to get My work done."

When you begin to think you're the only godly person, it quickly leads to pride. In this passage David refers to the sin of flattery (v.2). Our world is filled with flattery. Sometimes it's called advertising or promotion, but it's still flattery. God doesn't flatter people. He tells the truth. Flattery is manipulation, not communication. It comes from a double heart, from mixed motives. David said, "Unite my heart to fear Your name" (Ps.86:11). Don't fall for flattery or flatter yourself into thinking you are the only godly one left.

Verse 6 tells us where to turn: "The words of the Lord are pure." Listening to your own words may lead to discouragement or pride. And the words of others may be flattery, lying or vanity. So listen to the Word of God and test everything you hear by it.

The godly person has not completely vanished from the earth. We'd be surprised to find where God has His people, waiting to accomplish His will. Others are waiting to stand with you and help you. Lay hold of God's Word. It has been tested and proved. You can trust it.

The remedy for discouragement is the Word of God. When you feed your heart and mind with its truth, you regain your perspective and find renewed strength. Feeling discouraged? Encourage yourself with the Word of God.

Read Psalm 12:1-8

DAY 27

PURE WORDS

When you feel deserted, alone in standing for what's right, read Psalm 12. The emphasis in this psalm is on words, on speaking. First, *David speaks in prayer* (vv.1-3). Where are the godly? People today don't want to take a stand for the truth, but David stood for what is right.

Sometimes we feel the faithful have disappeared—those who believe in prayer, giving and commitment. Today's generation doesn't believe in commitment, especially with our words. We hear so much empty talk, lies and flattery. Flattery is manipulative, not communicative, like our advertising and some of our preaching.

Second, *the wicked speak in pride* (v.4). Never underestimate the power of speech. Jesus told the truth; His enemies argued. He gave words of life; they rejected Him. He came in love; they crucified Him. One of the evidences that a person is giving the truth of God's Word is that he is rejected. People don't want to hear truth unless they belong to truth (John 10:4).

Third, *God speaks in promise* (vv.5,7). His words are pure, not empty lying (v.6). But the words of the wicked will burn in the furnace. God's Word is precious, because it cost Jesus' life. It is proved (v.6) and permanent (v.7). He keeps His promises. God knows where His people are, and He helps them. "I will arise"; "I will protect"; "I can be trusted" (vv.5-7).

So much that is spoken in this world is untrue and empty talk. Be encouraged that God speaks in promise. His Word is pure and true. When you are surrounded by lies, rest on the promises of the Bible.

DAY 28

Read Psalm 13:1-6

HOW LONG CAN YOU WAIT?

Have you ever been impatient with God? Impatience is one of my big problems. I always get into the wrong lane on a toll road. Someone's in front of me with foreign currency, trying to buy his way through the tollbooth. I get into the wrong line at the airport, thinking, *This line is a good line; it's going to move.* But it doesn't because somebody in the line has lost his passport. And I get irritated.

It's one thing for us to be impatient with ourselves or with others. But when we become impatient with God, we should watch out! "How long, O Lord? Will You forget me forever? How long will You hide Your face from me? How long shall I take counsel in my soul?" (vv.1,2). Four times David asked, "How long?" We're so time conscious today. We have watches that show us split seconds. But what do we do with those split seconds? If we save three minutes by taking a shortcut, what significant thing will we accomplish with the three minutes we save?

We expect God to do what we want Him to do—and right now! But He doesn't always act immediately. Abraham had to wait for 25 years after God's promise before Isaac was born. Isaac had to wait 20 years for his children. Joseph had to wait 13 years before he was set free and put on the throne. Moses had a wait of 80 years. You see, God's schedule is not the same as ours. Sometimes He waits so that He can do more for us than we expect. When He heard that Lazarus was dying, our Lord waited until his friend's death before He came. But when He came, He brought a greater miracle and received greater glory. The hardest thing to do is to wait on the Lord. But we can if we will trust Him and rest on His Word.

Some of your greatest blessings come with patience. When you must wait for God to act, you can be confident that He knows what is best for you and what will best glorify Him. Are you waiting for God to act on your behalf? Align with His timing and rest on the promises of His Word.

Read Psalm 14:1-7

WHO'S A FOOL?

DAY 29

The word *fool* in Psalms or Proverbs does not refer to an unintelligent person. It refers to a person who is morally perverse. Why is he a fool? Because the fool has said in his heart, "There is no God" (v.1). And what is the result of this? "They are corrupt, they have done abominable works, there is none who does good" (v.1). God looks down and says, "Does anybody have a clean heart?" The answer is no.

The fear of the Lord is the beginning of wisdom (Prov.9:10). When people don't fear God, they have no wisdom, spiritually or otherwise. The fool says, "There is no God," which is practical atheism. Most of the world today lives by the philosophy that says, "There may be a God, but I'm not going to think about Him." God is not in their thoughts, and consequently, He is not in their lives.

The two words "there is" in verse 1 are in italics, which means they were added by the translators to help complete the meaning of the verse. We can read this: "The fool has said in his heart, 'No God.'" The fool not only says that there is no God; he also says no to God. When we say no to God, we are telling Him that we know more about life than He does and that we have more authority than He has. We cut off ourselves from the blessing He wants to give us.

Rejecting God involves a man's whole being. "The fool has said in his heart" (v.1). There we have the heart. In verse 2 God looks down to see if any understand. That involves the mind. "They have all turned aside, . . . there is none who does good, no, not one" (v.3). There we have the will. Verses 1-3 show the heart, mind and will possessed by sin, because somebody has said, "No God!" If you want peace, say yes to God. All of His promises are yes in Jesus Christ (II Cor.1:20).

The most foolish thing you can do is leave God out of your life. If you do, you cut off your source of life and blessing. Don't make the mistake of the fool. Turn to the Lord and submit to His authority.

DAY **30**

Read Psalm 15:1-5

ARE YOU WORTHY?

Imagine what would happen if I walked up to the main gate at Buckingham Palace in London and said to one of the tall, handsome, well-dressed guards, "Sir, I want to live with the royal family." He would look at me and say, "Begone, before I arrest you!"

Who is worthy to live with God? Only through Jesus Christ can we "dwell in God's holy hill." David always was a little bit envious of the priests. When we read the Psalms, we find David saying such things as, "Oh, those priests, They are able to walk in the temple of God, I can't do that. I can't go into the Holy Place." Spiritually he could, but physically he couldn't. Because we are in the Lord Jesus Christ, we can come boldly into the presence of God, not just to visit Him but to live with Him.

David describes the kind of person who is able to live with God. He must have the right kind of feet ("walks uprightly") and hands ("works righteousness"), lips ("speaks the truth") and heart. What we say with our lips always has to come from our heart. Verse 3 also talks about the tongue: "He who does not backbite with his tongue, nor does evil to his neighbor, nor does he take up a reproach against his friend." This is the person God welcomes at His front door and says, "You come and live with Me." That person has clean feet, clean hands and a clean heart that produce clean words and clean motives, one in whose eyes a vile person is despised. His eyes look upon only what is right and good.

Here is a beautiful picture of the kind of person God chooses to live with Him, And the beauty of it is this: Such a person will never get an eviction notice. "He who does these things shall never be moved" (v.5). How can we be this kind of person? Through faith in the Lord Jesus Christ.

God welcomes those with clean feet, clean hands and a clean heart. Remember, your worth is founded in Jesus Christ. It is through faith in Him that you are acceptable in the sight of God. Are your feet, hands and heart clean!

A DAY OF DELIGHTING

This is a psalm of delight. We find no trials or tribulations in this song. David is simply delighting, first of all, *in the Lord.* "You are my Lord, my goodness is nothing apart from You" (v.2). In other words, he is saying, "I have no good beyond God."

Then David delights *in the Lord's people.* "And to the saints who are on the earth, 'They are the excellent ones, in whom is all my delight'" (v.3). Do you delight in God's people? "To live above with saints we love will certainly be glory. To live below with saints we know, that's another story." Are some of God's people becoming abrasive to you? Start delighting in the Lord, and you'll start delighting in His people.

David also delights *in God's providence.* "You, O Lord, are the portion of my inheritance and my cup; you maintain my lot. The lines have fallen to me in pleasant places" (vv, 5,6). God, in His providence, knows where to draw the line. Problems arise when people don't know where His lines are. They want to keep moving the line. Let God give you your inheritance. When Israel went into the Promised Land, He gave each tribe its inheritance. It wasn't done by a real estate agent or by a lottery. God said, "Here are the lines. Maintain those lines." Do you want to delight in God and in His people? Then delight in His providence.

David also finds delight *in God's pleasures,* Verse 11 has been my life verse for many years, "You will show me the path of life; in Your presence is fullness of joy; at Your right hand are pleasures forever-more." Do you want life and joy? Here's the secret: Live on God's path, live in His presence and live for His pleasures.

You have much to delight in—God's people, His providence and His pleasures. The key to delighting in the things of God is to delight in God Himself. Sometime today take a moment to simply delight in the Lord and praise Him for who He is.

DAY

32

Read Psalm 17:1-15

HEAR ME, HOLD ME, HIDE ME

Three words summarize David's cry in Psalm 17. The first word is *hear.* "Hear a just cause, O Lord, attend to my cry" (v.1). David was saying, "I want the Lord to hear me, because my heart is right." "You have tested my heart" (v.3). When did God do that? "You have visited me in the night" (v.3). The dark times of life are when God proves us. He also proves Himself to us—if we let Him. When you're going through the darkness, when the night has come, when you can't see any light, remember, He is proving you and proving Himself to you. God knew that David's heart was right. "Hear a just cause, O Lord" (v.1). Remember, when you're in the darkness, when you're in danger, when you're facing difficulties, God will hear you.

The second key word is *hold.* Uphold my steps in Your paths, that my footsteps may not slip" (v.5). David wasn't simply standing still, doing nothing. He was on the move. When we're in the darkness, we move one step at a time as the Lord directs us. We don't just sit still and wonder what is going to happen next. David was saying, "God, I'm going to get moving. You've got to hold me up. Direct me; I don't want to slip and fall." Jude must have known this verse. He wrote, "Now to Him who is able to keep you from stumbling, and to present you faultless before the presence of His glory with exceeding joy" (Jude 1 :24).

The third word is *hide.* "Keep me as the apple of Your eye; hide me under the shadow of Your wings" (Ps.17:8). A shadow is not good protection. But if it's the shadow of God's wings, we can depend on it. What wings did David refer to? The wings of the cherubim in the Holy of Holies. David was saying, "I'm coming to the very throne of God. Please hide me and hold me and hear me." God replied, "David I'll do it. I'm going to carry you through your dark time."

Everyone must face dark times. God allows times of testing because He uses them to accomplish His purposes. Are you facing a difficulty today? Remember, God is faithful. He will hear you and direct you through the darkness. Let Him prove you, and give Him opportunity to prove Himself to you.

Read Psalm 17:1-15

FIGHTING A SPIRITUAL BATTLE

DAY **33**

Prayer is essential to the Christian life. God commands us to pray (Luke 11:2; 18:1; I Thess.5:17), and He uses people of prayer. What are the elements of an effective prayer life? First, *we need God's ear—"hear me."* David was praying for "a just cause"; he was concerned about God's will. But God won't hear us if we harbor deliberate sin in our lives, if we pray with "deceitful lips." He loves us too much to pamper us in our sins. To get God's ear, we must pray honestly, fervently and submissively. We must prepare our hearts for prayer.

Second, *we need God's eye—"examine me."* David could have killed Saul on two occasions, but by faith he left his vindication with the Lord. God knew David's heart. He probes our hearts when we pray. Often we are like Jacob; we pray and then meddle and scheme. We must not pray and then gossip. God's Word and prayer go together. If we live by the Word of God, it keeps us in the will of God.

Third, *we need God's hand—"deliver me."* The word *save* (vv.7,13) means "deliver." Notice that David's response is one of submission, and God's response is one of service. King David asks the King of kings for help, and He responds to David's faith. His enemies think they have David, but God's power goes to work for him.

Finally, *we need God's face—"satisfy me."* If our praying doesn't make us more like our Lord, our praying is in vain (Josh.24:15). God's goal is that we be conformed to the image of His Son (Rom.8:29). But we don't have to wait for the resurrection; we can be changed daily through God's Word and through prayer.

The purpose of prayer is to accomplish the will of God, for us to become like Jesus.

God uses your prayers to accomplish His will, both in your life and in the lives of others. To be effective, your prayers need God's help. Make your prayer time an alignment to His Word and His will.

DAY
34

Read Psalm 18:1-6

A SONG OF DELIVERANCE

Psalm 18 celebrates David's victory over his enemies. Notice the inscription at the beginning. This is the song David sang "on the day that the Lord delivered him from the hand of all his enemies and from the hand of Saul." David did not classify Saul as one of his enemies. Isn't that interesting? David was an enemy to Saul, but Saul was not an enemy to him.

We may not be able to prevent other people from being our enemies, but we can prevent ourselves from being enemies toward others. Our job is not to create problems and make enemies. Our job is to pray, to live for the Lord and to represent Him in all we do.

The Lord delivered David from all his enemies. The Hebrew language contains 23 different words for *deliverance*. The Jewish people knew something about deliverance. Throughout their history God had delivered them.

Who delivered David? God did. When did He do it? When David called upon Him. "I will love You, O Lord, my strength" (v.1). As we look at verses 1-6, we find nine different titles for God: my God, my Rock, my Fortress, my Deliverer, my Strength, my Shield, the Horn of my Salvation, my Stronghold, the Lord. Don't let that little word *my* upset you. You must lay hold of God personally and say, "He is my God. He is my Deliverer. He is my Salvation." Who delivers you? The Lord. When will He deliver you? When you call upon Him. "I will call upon the Lord, who is worthy to be praised; so shall I be saved from my enemies" (v.3).

David learned how to trust God for deliverance. Although his circumstances were often difficult, God was his Stronghold, and David called on Him for help. Do you need deliverance? Is God your Deliverer? If so, you may call on Him for help.

Read Psalm 18:7-15

NOT ALL STORMS ARE BAD

DAY 35

These verses present one of the greatest descriptions of a storm found in the Bible. It is a graphic picture of the way God works when He comes to the aid of His children. David was saying in these verses that God the Creator, God the Deliverer, used everything in nature to come to his aid. The earth shook, down to its foundations. Smoke came up, and fire came out. Coals were kindled. The heavens bowed down. The wind began to blow, for God was coming on the wings of the wind. We see darkness, dark waters, thick clouds, even hailstones and coals of fire. Thunder, lightning—the very breath of God was blowing across the fields.

When the child of God is in His will, all of nature works for him. When the child of God is out of His will, everything works against him. Remember Jonah? He ran away from God in disobedience, and what happened? A storm appeared. The wind and waves were violent. That little boat went up and down on the ocean like a cork. Even the mariners were worried. Jonah disobeyed God, and everything in nature worked against him. David obeyed God, and everything in nature worked for him.

God can use the storms of life to fulfill His will. Is the wind blowing? He is flying on the wings of the wind. Are the clouds thick? He will bring showers of blessing out of them. Don't be afraid of the storm. Storms can come from the hand of God and be the means of blessing.

DAY 36

Read Psalm 18:16-19

COME OUT OF CONFINEMENT

For several years David had been forced to live in confined places while he fled from Saul. More than once he fled to a cave to save his life. Then God brought him out of the caves and out of confinement and into a large place. "He also brought me out into a broad place; He delivered me because He delighted in me" (v.19). David was a man after God's own heart, and God delighted in him, just as He delighted in our Lord Jesus. God said of Him, "This is My beloved Son, in whom I am well pleased" (Matt.3:17).

We often talk about our delighting in the Lord. "Delight yourself also in the Lord, and He shall give you the desires of your heart" (Ps.37:4). That's important to do. But what about God's delighting in us? As parents and grandparents, we enjoy delighting in our children and grandchildren. In a similar way God wants to delight in us.

Because God delights in us, He delivers us. And He uses the difficult experiences of life to make us bigger. "He also brought me out into a broad place" (v.19). Verse 36 of this chapter says, "You enlarged my path under me." When God puts us into a large place, He has to give us larger feet. But don't stop there. In Psalm 4:1 David said, "You have relieved me." God delivers us so that He can put us into a larger place, so that He can enable us to take giant steps of faith for His glory. David had gone through several years of confinement, difficulty, persecution and sorrow. But when it was over he was a bigger man.

Let the trials of life make you a giant, not a midget. Let God put you into a large place, where you can take giant steps of faith for His glory.

Life's trials are not easy. But in God's will, each has a purpose. Often He uses them to enlarge you. Are you feeling confined? Be encouraged that God delights in delivering you from confinement. Difficult times build your faith, if you let Him use them for His glory.

Read Psalm 18:20-29

HOW CLEAN ARE YOUR HANDS?

DAY 37

No matter how difficult our trials are, if we have clean hands, God will fill them with blessing. "The Lord rewarded me according to my righteousness; according to the cleanness of my hands He has recompensed me" (v.20). "Therefore the Lord has recompensed me according to my righteousness, according to the cleanness of my hands in His sight" (v.24). David's hands were clean. His enemies were lying about him—those people in Saul's court who wanted Saul's attention and affection. They lied about David. They said, "Saul, David said this," but he never said it. "David is doing this to you," but he never did that. David's hands were clean. When our hands are clean and we are keeping the ways of the Lord, God will work for us. He will give us what we need, protect us and see us through.

God responds to us as we respond to Him. "With the merciful You will show Yourself merciful; with a blameless man You will show Yourself blameless; with the pure You will show Yourself pure; and with the devious You will show Yourself shrewd [opposed]" (vv.25,26). We decide how close God will be, how much affection He will be able to show us. "He delivered me because He delighted in me" (v.19). The Lord delights in children with clean hands and a pure heart. *Integrity* is the key word. David was a man of integrity. Saul was a man of duplicity. He was double-minded, looking in two directions at once. But David kept his eyes on the Lord.

When our hands are clean, no matter how difficult life may be, God will see us through. He will take us through any trial and enable us to bring glory to His name when it's all over.

God rewards us according to our righteousness. Are you keeping the ways of the Lord? If so, you may depend on His protection and strength. When your hands are clean, He sees you through your difficult trials and circumstances.

DELIGHTING IN GOD

God wants to have a personal relationship with each of us. He is the God of the individual believer through Jesus Christ, and He delights in us just as we delight in those we love. The highest and holiest experience we can have is the worshipful delight of the Lord.

This passage gives us insight into how we can delight in God and how He delights in us. First, *how does one delight God?* By one's character. David had integrity (v.20). He was not free from sin, but his heart was devoted to God. *Righteous* means "obedient." David was obedient (vv.21,22). He had the Word of God in his heart. God delights in us when we do what He wants us to do the way He wants us to do it (Matt.3:17). What counts is that He delights in what we do, not what our neighbors think about us.

Second, *how does God deal with those in whom He delights?* He treats us the way we treat Him (vv.25-27). We are as close to God as we want to be. David was wholly devoted to Him, so God was able to bless him. David was merciful to those who wronged him; God was merciful to him (v.25). David was loyal; God was loyal to him (v.25). David was pure, submissive and humble.

In contrast, Saul was devious. *Shrewd* means "to wrestle." God wrestles with us (as He did with Jacob) when we are perverse and devious. Parents often wrestle with their children when it comes to discipline. God wrestles with us to bring us where He wants us to be; then He can delight in us.

Third, *how can we increase our delight in God and His delight in us?* Believe that He wants you to be happy; happiness and holiness go together. Submit to and enjoy God's will, but not grudgingly. He will give us the best. When we delight in Him and He delights in us, life becomes delightful, and we bring glory to our Father's name.

Delighting in God is an expression of your personal relationship with Him. His delight in you is an expression of His love for you. Be the kind of person who delights God. Walk with integrity and obey His Word. He will bless you and use you to bring glory to Himself.

Read Psalm 18:30-36

GIVING US HIND'S FEET

DAY 39

Life is 10 percent how you take it and 90 percent what you make it. Notice the repetition of the word *make* in verses 30-36: "It is God who arms me with strength, and makes my way perfect" (v.32). I like verse 35: "You have also given me the shield of Your salvation; Your right hand has held me up, Your gentleness has made me great." Why does God permit difficulties to come to our lives? Sometimes He has to break us before He can make us. Sometimes He has to reveal to us what we're really like before He can make us into what He wants us to be.

David went through some difficulties. As a young man he was anointed by God as His chosen servant. He won great victories and was destined to be God's next king on the throne. And what happens to him? He becomes a fugitive. He's chased from place to place by a godless man. He's persecuted by people who lie about him. What in the world is God doing? God is making him. He is taking David's life and making him all he ought to be.

Verse 33 says, "He makes my feet like the feet of deer, and sets me on my high places." God wants to make our feet ready for His way and make us more like Jesus Christ. God wanted David to go higher. He wanted David to have feet like hind's feet that could bound over the mountains and rocks. He didn't want David to sit still, complain and pout as Elijah did later.

God gently deals with us (v.35). It didn't look like gentleness at the time, but when David later reflected over all those years of persecution, he said, "I see the gentle hand of God in all of this." God wants you to go higher and farther. Let Him make you.

The path of your walk with God is lined with both trials and blessings. When the way becomes rough and difficult, He promises sure footing to get over the obstacles. Are you traveling a rough path today? Perhaps God is using this time to make you more like Jesus Christ. Let His gentle hand make you.

DAY 40

Read Psalm 18:37-45

REVEALING WHAT'S INSIDE

We must remember that David's enemies were God's enemies and that he was fighting the Lord's battles. As Christians, we are taught to pray for our enemies and to do good to those who despitefully use us (Matt.5:44). David did that. He prayed for Saul, and on at least two occasions, he could have killed him but didn't. David had the right attitude toward Saul, but Saul did not have the right attitude toward David. As we read verses 37-45, we need to remember that David was not carrying out a personal vendetta. When he talked about his enemies, he was talking about God's enemies. He was the instrument God used to accomplish His purposes against those who opposed Him.

We find an interesting point in verse 42: "Then I beat them as fine as the dust before the wind." David had grown spiritually (Ps.19,36). When God enlarged him, his perspective changed. His enemies became as small as the dust. You see, circumstances reveal character. People say, "A man is made by a crisis." No, a crisis does not make a person. It reveals what that person is made of. When the crisis came, Saul and his crowd grew smaller and smaller as their true nature was revealed. But David grew bigger and bigger. He was also established (v.36), while his enemies became like the dust that the wind blows away.

Are your circumstances making you smaller or bigger? Are they enabling you to overcome, or are they overcoming you? David rejoiced that God had given him victory in spite of his enemies and circumstances. The victory is the Lord's. Let your circumstances make you bigger and greater for Him.

DAVID'S DOXOLOGY

David closed this long psalm of triumph and victory with a doxology. "The Lord lives! Blessed be my Rock! Let the God of my salvation be exalted" (v.46). David had been a fugitive. He had been waiting for the day when he could ascend the throne. Now the day had come. How did he respond? He glorified God.

I suppose some of us would have said, "Well, my enemies are gone. Now I can do what I please. My battles are over. I've been put into a large place. Therefore, watch out everybody, here I come!" But David didn't have that attitude at all. He gave glory to God. He ended his song with a hymn of praise to the One who had delivered him. "Therefore I will give thanks to You, O Lord, among the Gentiles, and sing praises to Your name" (v.49). Here was David, a Jew, saying, "I want these Gentiles to know how great my God is." Are you concerned about letting the nations know how great God is? Are you burdened to tell the Gospel to other people? If the Lord has saved you and delivered you, then you should be telling others what He has done for you.

David closed his song of victory by blessing the Lord. "The Lord lives!" (v.46). Isn't it good to know that we trust in the living God? Some people may worship a dead god, but we don't. We are the children of the living God. David said, "God is alive, and He is my rock and my salvation. I want Him to be exalted." And he concluded, "Great deliverance He gives to His king" (v.50).

How do you respond after a victory? So often Christians fail to exalt the Lord. You trust in a living God, who protects you and delivers you. He deserves your worship and praise. Have you given God the glory for your victories?

DAY
42

Read Psalm 19:1-14

SEEING GOD

Psalm 19 is so familiar to us. The first six verses talk about the glory of God seen in creation. Verses 7-11 talk about the glory and grace of God revealed in the Word, and verses 12-14 talk about God speaking to our hearts. He is revealed in the skies, in the Scriptures and in our own hearts and souls.

Even though creation is in travail because of sin (Rom.8:22), God's glory is revealed there. Someone has said that if the stars came out only once every thousand years, we'd stay up all night and look at them in awe and wonder.

David gives us two pictures of facing each day. The first is like a bridegroom coming out to meet his bride with wonderful hope and love and joy. The second is like a strong man running a race. David tells us to live a day at a time and to start each day with glory and grace and a goal to be reached.

Unfortunately, some people know only the God of creation. They admire the God of wisdom, power and providence, who made everything. But it's not enough to know only the Creator. We must know God as the Savior. This is why Psalm 19 talks about His revelation in the Word. The Bible is flawless. We can trust it, test it and taste it (vv.9,10). We need to have this Word in our hearts, and then we can have God living in our hearts as our Savior.

This reminds me of the Wise Men who came to see Jesus. They saw the message up in the heavens. Then they followed the star, and that led them to the Scriptures. The priests told them from the prophetical books where the Messiah would be born. Then they went and worshiped Him.

God reveals His glory in several ways. It's easy to admire God the Creator. But have you trusted His Word? Have you tested and proved it in the furnaces of life? Have you tasted it to find out how sweet it really is? Don't worship only the God of creation or the God of revelation. Let Him be the God of salvation in your heart.

Read Psalm 19:7-14

DAY 43

THE PERFECT WORD

The revelation of God in nature prepares us for His revelation in the Scriptures. Ultimately, Jesus Christ reveals Himself as Savior. This was the experience of the Magi (Matt.2). The light of nature led them to the light of the Word, which led them to the Light of the World.

The Bible meets the needs of the human heart. No other book is like it. It is God's testimony. Its name is the *Law of the Lord.* The sun is to creation what the Law is to God's people, bringing light, warmth, life and growth.

The Bible's nature is *perfect and pure.* The Bible is called the fear of the Lord because we need a reverential, holy, awesome fear of God (v.9). We teach God's Word because it enlightens (v.8). We trust it because it is true and righteous (v.9). We treasure it because it is more desired than gold (v.10). We may even "taste" the Word and test it.

The Bible *satisfies every need.* It converts the soul. It warns us. There is great reward in keeping the Law. It's a wonder that with God's revelation in nature and Scripture so many people are blind.

The Bible is the *book of our heart.* Every time we read a book, watch TV or listen to a speaker, something is being written on our hearts. Let God write His Word on your heart. The heart sees what it loves. When we love the Lord with our hearts, we see Him in creation and in the Scriptures.

If God is your Redeemer, He can be your Strength. Live acceptably in His sight, allowing the meditation of your heart to please Him. Then your life will be what He wants it to be.

God is more than the God of creation and the Scriptures; He is the God of redemption. If your heart is filled with Him and yielded to Him, you can have victory over sin. Don't simply worship the God of nature. Get into the Word of God and let God get into you.

Read Psalm 20:1-9

What Are You TRUSTING?

David wrote, "Some trust in chariots, and some in horses; but we will remember the name of the Lord our God" (v.7). The big question is, What are you trusting today? Everybody trusts in or believes in something. Some people trust in their money or credit cards. Some trust in their strength or expertise or experience. Verses 1 and 2 say, "May the Lord answer you in the day of trouble; may the name of the God of Jacob defend you; may He send you help from the sanctuary, and strengthen you out of Zion." The Christian trusts in the Lord, and he exemplifies this trust by praying.

When we are in trouble, what we do to solve our problems and turn our trouble into triumph is evidence of what or whom we're trusting. When the day of trouble arrives, some people reach for their checkbooks. They think money will solve their problems. Others reach for the telephone. They look to friends to solve their problems. While "some trust in chariots, and some in horses," Christians remember the name of the Lord (v.7). Our faith is in Jesus Christ, and we should not be afraid to let people know about it. "We will rejoice in your salvation, and in the name of our God we will set up our banners!" (v.5). In other words, we do not hesitate to wave the banner of faith because He will not fail us.

God's name is good. "The name of the God of Jacob defend you" (v.1). Take time to trust the Lord. Roll your burden on Him. Get your strength from Him. Wave your banner in the name of the Lord, and He will turn your burden into a blessing.

Where do you place your trust? Whereas wealth and others fail you, Jesus never fails. Take whatever burden you are carrying today and give it to the Lord. Trust Him, and He will work on your behalf.

Read Psalm 20:1-9

From Trouble

TO THANKSGIVING

DAY 45

D.L. Moody did not want soloist Ira Sanky to sing the hymn "Onward Christian Soldiers" because he felt the Church was anything but a victorious army marching off to war. Yet the Bible pictures God's people as soldiers in His army. As soldiers, we must be familiar with Psalms 20 and 21. The first deals with prayer and winning the victory, and the second deals with praise and holding the victory. If we trust the Lord, we will move from trouble to thanksgiving.

Several factors lead us to triumph in battle. The first is *prayer.* This is an essential element in fighting the battles of the Lord because it releases His power. There are no battles like those of the Christian life. We struggle against the enemies of the Lord: the world (I John 2:15), the flesh and the devil (Eph.6). We must pray according to the will of God. The Word of God and prayer go together (Heb.4:12; Eph.6:17,18).

Next, we need to *surrender*. Before David and his army fought, they worshiped God. That affected his battle plan and his victory. David's "burnt offering" indicated total surrender to God. If we're not walking with the Lord today, we'll not be ready when the battle comes.

Another factor is *unity.* David and his army had one goal—God's victory. And they had one joy—to serve Him and do His will. The tribes of Israel were a picture of unity. They had one army assembled from 12 tribes.

The fourth factor is *faith*. Verse 6 says the Lord "saves" His anointed. The Hebrew word used here means He "has saved." That is, God already has given David the victory (I John 5:4). The Church today often trusts in all kinds of horses and chariots but not in the Lord.

The final factor is *obedience*. David and his army obeyed God's will. The day of trouble can become a day of triumph and thanksgiving if we have trust, which is expressed by prayer, surrender, unity, faith and obedience.

Although you cannot avoid battles, you call be ready for them and, with God's help, be victorious. Are you prepared to do battle? If not, trust the Lord to help you.

DAY 46

Read Psalm 21:1-7

WHAT DO KINGS NEED?

Kings have everything. If you were a king, what would you rejoice in the most? In what did David rejoice? Psalm 21 tells us what it means to be a king—not just for a day but for a lifetime.

We are kings because we are God's children. Jesus Christ has made us kings and priests because He loves us and washed away our sins in His blood. Today, God wants us to reign in life. We are on the throne with the Lord Jesus. "The king shall have joy in Your strength, O Lord" (v.1). David is rejoicing in the *strength* that God gave him—strength to walk and strength to war; strength to build and strength to battle; strength to carry the burdens of life. Are you rejoicing today as God's king because He gives you strength?

David continues, "And in Your salvation how greatly shall he rejoice!" (v.1). He rejoices in God's *salvation*. We need to do the same. One day Jesus told His disciples, "Don't rejoice because the demons are subject to you. Rejoice because your names are written down in heaven" (Luke 10:20).

David also rejoices in *satisfaction*. "You have given him his heart's desire, and have not withheld the request of his lips. For You meet him with the blessings of goodness" (vv.2,3). If we look back, we will find goodness and mercy following us (23:6), and if we look ahead, God is meeting us with His goodness (v.3). Don't be afraid of today, and don't be afraid of the future. God will meet you with His goodness.

In verse 7 David rejoices in *stability*: "For the king trusts in the Lord, and through the mercy of the Most High he shall not be moved." I like these blessings we can rejoice in—God's strength, salvation, satisfaction and stability. All of this is for God's glory. "His glory is great in Your salvation" (v.5).

Many Christians fail to see themselves as kings. But God wants us to reign in life and has provided several blessings that enable us to live as kings. Are you enjoying the blessings of kingship? If not, claim His blessings and start living a life of victory.

Read Psalm 21:8-13

DEALING WITH ENEMIES

DAY 47

We don't like them or want them, but sometimes we can't help having enemies. A person is not only known by the friends he makes; sometimes he's better known by the enemies he makes. No, we can't help having enemies, but we can help how we deal with them. This is what David is talking about in this passage. How do you deal with your enemies? Paul said, "All who desire to live godly in Christ Jesus will suffer persecution" (II Tim.3:12). Some people are enemies of the cross of Christ. So if we take our stand at the cross, they will take their stand against us.

David gives us insight for dealing with life's enemies. First, *let God's hand work*. Keep your hands off. "Your hand will find all Your enemies; Your right hand will find those who hate You" (v.8). Then, let God's anger burn instead of yours. "You shall make them as a fiery oven in the time of Your anger" (v.9). There is a righteous anger, a righteous indignation. Paul wrote, "Be angry, and do not sin" (Eph.4:26). Our Lord was angry when He cleansed the temple on two occasions. Let God's anger blaze, not yours.

Second, *let God shoot His arrows*. "You will make ready Your arrows on Your string toward their [the enemies') faces" (v.12). God's hand will work for you. His anger will blaze for you. His arrows will be shot for you. And He will use all of this for His glory. "Be exalted, O Lord, in Your own strength! We will sing and praise Your power" (v.13). We can't praise our power, our scheming or our vengeance. But we can praise God's glory and power. When we try to take care of our enemies in our way, we only make things worse. But when we turn the situation over to the Lord, He makes things better. Let God take care of your enemies today, because then He will be glorified, you will be satisfied, and Jesus Christ will have His way.

Are you facing an enemy today? Take your hands off the problem and let God deal with those involved. He will remedy the problem in the best possible way, and Jesus Christ will be glorified.

DAY 48

Read Psalm 22:1-11

WHAT GOD WON'T DO

"My God, My God, why have You forsaken Me?" (v.1). Those are familiar words. Jesus spoke them from the cross (Matt.27:46), but they were first spoken by David when he was going through a severe trial.

Jesus Christ was forsaken that we might not be forsaken. God the Father forsook His Son on the cross when He was made sin for us (II Cor.5:21).

But David says in this psalm, "Our fathers trusted You, and You took care of them; now I'm trusting You, and nothing seems to happen" (vv.4-6). We can envision David saying, "I am a worm, and no man; a reproach of men, and despised of the people" (v.6). He did go through that. But our Lord went through it to an even greater degree. Can you imagine the Lord Jesus, who said, "I am the Good Shepherd," saying, "I am a worm"? But He became a worm for us so that we might become the children of God.

We cannot be forsaken because the Savior was forsaken *in our place.* We can't be forsaken because of His *promise* to never leave or forsake us (Heb.13:5). We cannot be forsaken because of His abiding and eternal presence with us (Matt.28:20). We cannot be forsaken because of His purpose to work all things together for good to those who love Him (Rom.8:28). And what is His purpose? That we might be conformed to the image of His Son (Rom.8:29). David became a beautiful picture of the Lord Jesus Christ. And he had to suffer to do it. In spite of your circumstances and feelings, remember: *God will not forsake you.*

When you go through trials, your circumstances and feelings can deceive you into thinking God has forsaken you. But the Bible promises us that He will never forsake you. Next time you feel forsaken, remember that God is always true to His Word and will accomplish His purpose of conforming you to the image of His Son.

Read Psalm 22:12-21

THE DEVIL'S ZOO

DAY 49

Are you an animal lover? I must confess that, apart from a certain sympathy with cats and a liking for friendly dogs, I don't really care much for animals. My wife enjoys going to the zoo, and I dutifully go along, but I would much rather be in the library.

Do you know that God uses animals to teach us about sin? Today's passage talks about the Devil's entire zoo. "Many bulls have surrounded Me; strong bulls of Bashan have encircled Me" (v.12). Our Lord was on the cross, and people were acting like animals. That's what is wrong with the world. When we leave God out of our lives, we descend to the level of animals. Here was Jesus on the cross, and the bulls had surrounded Him. Then the lions showed up. "They gape at Me with their mouths, as a raging and roaring lion" (v.13). "Dogs have surrounded Me" (v.16). "Save Me from the lion's mouth and from the horns of the wild oxen!" (v.21). That is quite a zoo! When men put Jesus on the cross, they acted like animals. And He replied, "I am a worm" (Ps.22:6). Can you imagine bulls and lions and dogs and oxen chasing a worm? Oh, how our Lord humbled Himself for us!

Don't act like a wild animal. You were made in the image of God. Let the Holy Spirit turn you into one of His gentle sheep. The Lord, our Shepherd, is glorified and honored when we don't act like vicious animals but rather like the children of God.

God made you in His image and has placed His Holy Spirit within you. You were made to glorify Him. Are you harboring sin in any area of your life? Keep clean of sin so God can work in you and through you.

DAY 50

Read Psalm 22:22-31

RESURRECTION GROUND

The last half of Psalm 22 is an expression of praise. In verse 22 we see a change: The psalmist goes from prayer to praise, from suffering to glory. "I will declare Your name to My brethren; in the midst of the congregation I will praise You."

In this passage we find the Lord singing in the midst of the congregation. Have you ever thought of Jesus singing? We think of Him preaching and doing miracles and teaching and counseling, but singing? "My praise shall be of You in the great congregation" (v.25). The meek shall praise the Lord (v.26). All this praise is starting to spread. Praising the Lord is contagious, and if Christians praise him, other people will praise Him, too.

We also find fellowship with other believers. "I will declare Your name to My brethren" (v.22). And we find a witness to the whole world. "All the ends of the world shall remember and turn to the Lord" (v.27). I hope you're not living between Good Friday and Easter Sunday. That's a miserable place to live. I hope you're living from Easter Sunday on. How can you tell if you're on Resurrection ground? Are you worshiping and praising the Lord? Are you fellowshipping with God's people? Are you witnessing to others? Are you serving others? "A posterity shall serve Him" (v.30). We are on Resurrection ground. Let's live like it.

Praise is a natural expression for the believer, especially when considering the implications of our Lord's Resurrection. Are you praising and worshiping our Lord for the redemption He has provided you? Do you fellowship with other believers? Are you reaching out to others who don't know the Lord? Take time to praise God for His great salvation.

EXPECT CHANGES

"The Lord is my shepherd; I shall not want" (v.1). That must be one of the most familiar quotations from the Old Testament. Everybody has some kind of shepherd. Jeremiah said, "It is not in man who walks to direct his own steps" (Jer.10:23). We are like lost sheep, not able to guide our own lives. We need a shepherd. Who is your shepherd?

When the Lord is your Shepherd, what will happen in your life? First, *you will live a day at a time.* "Surely goodness and mercy shall follow me all the days of my life" (v.6). Psalm 23 talks about all the days of our lives, and they are lived one day at a time when the Lord is our Shepherd. Someone has said that the average person is being crucified between two thieves—the regrets of yesterday and the worries of tomorrow. Consequently, he can't enjoy today.

Second, when the Lord is your Shepherd, *you listen for His voice.* In John 10:27 the Lord Jesus said, "My sheep hear My voice." The Shepherd does not drive his sheep from behind. Rather, He calls them from ahead. How do we listen to the Lord's voice? Through the Word of God.

Third, when the Lord is your Shepherd, *you must expect changes.* You may have green pastures and still waters. Then you go through the valley of the shadow of death. You have a table in the presence of your enemies. Then you live in the house of the Lord (heaven) forever. You will experience changes in life. Expect them; don't be afraid of them.

When you follow the Shepherd, the future is your friend, because the Lord is going before you. Live one day at a time, following the Shepherd, and you won't have to be afraid.

Some people fail to adapt to life's inevitable changes. As a believer, you need never fear the future. Trust the Shepherd, who goes before you, and listen to His Word. Commit this day to the Lord and thank Him for His guidance.

DAY
52

Read Psalm 23:1-6

THE SHEPHERD PROVIDES

Psalm 23 depicts Jesus Christ as the Great Shepherd living for His sheep. It also gives us two assurances. First, *Jesus shepherds us throughout each day.* Dr. Harry Ironside used to say that goodness and mercy are the two sheepdogs that help keep the sheep where they belong. We live our lives one day at a time, because God built the universe to run one day at a time. There must be a time for labor and a time for rest. When we try to live two or three days at a time, we cannot enjoy today. Eventually, this catches up with us physically, emotionally and spiritually. We need to remember that "as thy days, so shall thy strength be" (Deut.33:25).

As His sheep, we can begin each day with confidence. John 10 tells us that Jesus goes before His sheep. We cannot walk into any experience where Jesus has not first been. Though we may not know or understand what is taking place around us, we will fear no evil because we are close to the Shepherd. His rod takes care of the enemies; His staff takes care of the sheep (discipline and guidance). We can stay close to the Shepherd through His Word.

Our second assurance is that *Jesus shepherds us all the days of our lives.* This psalm is a summary of the Christian life. Verses 1 and 2 speak of childhood. Children need protection and provision. God loves and watches over them. Verse 3 speaks of youth. Teenagers need direction and discipline. The Great Shepherd finds these wandering youth and brings them back. Verses 4 and 5 talk about the middle years. These are not easy years, when the children are growing up and there are bills to pay. Verse 6 speaks of the mature years.

We don't understand why some things happen. But one day we'll realize that everything is under God's goodness and mercy. Then we'll look ahead and see His house.

What are your needs today? Stay close to the Shepherd by reading the Word. Resolve to follow His leading.

Read Psalm 24:1-10

NO BRAGGING RIGHTS

DAY 53

It can make a real difference in your life if you'll remember Psalm 24:1: "The earth is the Lord's, and all its fullness, the world and those who dwell therein." Because the earth is the Lord's, we can turn it over to Him. What difference will that make?

First, *it will remind us that we are stewards and not owners.* No matter what we have, we are only stewards of it. God owns everything. He doesn't own just the cattle on a thousand hills; He owns the Cadillacs in a thousand garages! God owns what you possess, and if He doesn't want you to have it, you'd better get rid of it. That brings humility, not pride. You can't brag about what you have if God gave it to you. John the Baptist said, "A man can receive nothing unless it has been given to him from heaven" (John3:27).

Second, *it makes us victors and not victims.* The world doesn't belong to the Devil. God has given him a certain amount of authority and freedom, but the earth is the Lord's. Jesus, not Satan, is on the throne of heaven.

Third, *it causes us to praise and not to complain.* I like the repetition at the end of this psalm: "Lift up your heads, O you gates! And be lifted up, you everlasting doors!" (v.7). "Lift up your heads, O you gates! And lift them up, you everlasting doors! And the King of glory shall come in" (v.9). Nothing will lift up one's head like realizing that God is in control. He's the King of glory. Wherever He rules, there will be grace and glory. If you want that kind of blessing, just remember that the earth and all its fullness is the Lord's. It doesn't belong to you; it belongs to Him, and He is in control.

Good stewardship is one of the great responsibilities of the Christian. You need to maintain a humble attitude toward what God has given you. Make sure you submit to His control: His generosity and grace are great blessings that make you a victor.

DAY 54

Read Psalm 25:1-7

DON'T BE ASHAMED

Have you ever been so ashamed that you wanted to go somewhere and hide forever? Did you want to dig a hole, crawl into it and then pull the hole in after you? Read verses 1-3: "To You, O Lord, I lift up my soul. O my God, I trust in You; let me not be ashamed; let not my enemies triumph over me. Indeed, let no one who waits on You be ashamed; let those be ashamed who deal treacherously without cause." David was concerned that he would bring disgrace upon the name of the Lord.

When we are anxious not to be ashamed, we want to live a life that is true to the Lord. We don't want anyone to use us as an excuse for sin or to single us out as "one of those Christians." So one of our first considerations must be *the glory of God.* This is what David talks about in verses 1-3. He is saying, "God, I don't want anybody to do anything that will rob You of glory." Why don't we do certain things? Because God won't be glorified. Some things might not hurt us, and some places might not defile us, but they might hurt the glory of God. They might harm an immature believer. When my wife and I started to have a family, we discovered we couldn't leave certain things on the table. When she and I were the only ones in the apartment, I could leave a knife on the table or a pair a scissors on the floor—but not when the children came along.

Our second consideration must be *the will of God.* "Show me Your ways, O Lord; teach me Your paths. Lead me in Your truth and teach me" (vv.4,5). To bring glory to God and obey His will, we must depend *on the grace of God.* "Remember, O Lord, Your tender mercies and Your loving kindnesses" (v.6). When these three elements are in your life, you will never be ashamed or bring disgrace to the name of the Lord. Instead, you will live a life that pleases Him.

Being true to the Lord involves consideration of His glory, will and grace. Do your actions and words bring glory to God? Are you living in His will? Are you depending on His grace? Take care to honor God with your life.

Read Psalm 25:8-15

FOLLOW YOUR LEADER

DAY 55

I have little sense of direction. Fortunately, my wife has built-in radar. If she didn't travel with me, I'm afraid I often would be lost. David talks about the guidance of God in these verses. So much has been said about God's guidance. Does He still guide us? Does He have a specific plan for each of our lives? How does He guide us? David gives us some simple advice on receiving God's guidance.

We must start with *meekness*. "The humble He guides in justice, and the humble He teaches His way" (v.9). Meekness means that we are not telling God what to do; we are not counseling Him. Who could possibly be His counselor? The meek person receives the Word of God and is submissive to His will. "All the paths of the Lord are mercy and truth, to such as keep His covenant and His testimonies" (v.10). God does not reveal His will to those who are curious. He reveals His will to those who are *obedient*.

God guides those who are concerned about *His glory*. "For Your name's sake, O Lord, pardon my iniquity, for it is great" (v.11). Surely goodness and mercy follow us, but they won't unless we are walking in the will of God for His glory, for His name's sake. "He restores my soul; He leads me in the paths of righteousness, for His name's sake" (Ps.23:3). That leads us to the *fear of the Lord*. Who is the man that fears the Lord? Him shall He teach in the way He chooses" (v.12). "The fear of the Lord is the beginning of wisdom" (Ps.111:10). Finally, we must be alert to God's guidance. "My eyes are ever toward the Lord" (v.15). We must watch and pray. We must keep our eyes open if we want our Shepherd to lead us.

God desires to lead His sheep and use them for His glory. Is your life characterized by meekness, obedience, a desire for God's glory and the fear of the Lord? As you remain alert to His leading, you may be assured of His guidance in the decisions and steps of your life.

DAY 56

Read Psalm 25:16-22

I WANT OUT!

"The troubles of my heart have enlarged; bring me out of my distresses!" (v.17). Have you ever prayed like that? David did. What kind of answer did God give him? Ultimately, David was brought out of his distresses and put on the throne, and his enemies were defeated. But he had to go through some difficult years before God finally brought him to that place of glory and victory.

If you have ever prayed this way, stop and ask yourself, *Is this the most important prayer I can pray?* Our first inclination in times of difficulty is to pray, "Bring me out!" But we should be praying, "Build me up." God enlarges us by enlarging our troubles. And when He sees that we are growing, He is able to give us larger places of service and ministry. It's sort of a weaning process. When a child is being weaned from his mother, he's fretful and unhappy. He thinks, *Mother doesn't love me anymore.* But why is she weaning him? Because she wants him to grow up and mature. He cannot go through life depending on his mother. That's what David discovered.

When we are in times of difficulty and distress, the important thing is not *that* we get out of it but *what* we get out of it. "Count it all joy when you fall into various trials, knowing that the testing of your faith produces patience. But let patience have its perfect work" (James 1:2-4). If you find yourself going through a time of trouble today, if the troubles of your heart are enlarged, remember that God wants to enlarge you and give you a larger place of ministry.

Growth is often a painful process. It is through difficulty and distress that God enlarges us. Are your troubles enlarged? It is important that you not waste your trials by simply enduring them or wanting to be delivered from them. Allow trials to have their "perfect work" of enlarging you for a greater ministry.

Read Psalm 25:1-22

THE GUIDANCE OF GOD

DAY 57

In Psalm 25 David points out that we can experience God's guidance if we meet certain spiritual conditions. The first is *confidence.* We give evidence of our confidence in God through worship. We need to pray so that we might have our hearts right with Him. Waiting is another evidence (vv.3, 5, 21). Every time I've rushed ahead, I've gotten into trouble. In verses 4 and 5 David talks about his willingness to follow. God won't show us His will unless we're willing to do it. Another evidence of our confidence is the witness of the Word (v.5). When we have big decisions to make, we must spend time in the Scriptures.

Penitence also is a condition for receiving God's guidance. David is sorry for his sins. He wants God to remember His tender mercies, not David's transgressions. When God remembers someone, He goes to work for that person. He never forgets His children. David asks God for mercy (vv.10,16) because he is concerned about his past sins, and he doesn't want those sins to get him off target.

Obedience is another condition. We are all sinners. We don't have to be perfect for God to guide us, just obedient. The word *humble* means "yielded to God." If we obey what God already has told us, then He will show us the next step. His guidance is not a spotlight; it's a lamp that illumines each step.

We also must exhibit *reverence.* God will guide us in our choices if we fear Him. The word *secret* (v.14) means "friendship." Godly fear doesn't mean we are slaves; it means we have loving reverence and respect for a gracious and kind God.

Finally, we must show *perseverance.* It's not always easy to know and do the will of God. Sometimes when we're seeking the Lord, circumstances get worse, and we become lonely. David was lonely and afflicted, but he remembered that God was with him. Because of that, he maintained his integrity and obedience.

Do you need God's guidance today? Make verses 1-5 your prayer for His guidance in your life. Place your confidence in Him and yield to Him in spite of circumstances. You will please God and help accomplish His purposes in your life and in the lives of others.

DAY 58

Read Psalm 26:1-12

ON THE LEVEL

Integrity means that your life is whole, that your heart is not divided. Jesus said, "No one can serve two masters" (Matt.6:24). That's integrity. *Duplicity* means trying to serve two masters. Our Lord also said that nobody can look in two directions at the same time. If your eye is single, then your body is full of light. But if your eye is double, watch out. The darkness is coming in (Matt.6:22,23). If you look at the darkness and the light simultaneously, the darkness crowds out the light.

In Psalm 25:21 David prayed: "Let integrity and uprightness preserve me, for I wait for You"; and in verse one of today's passage, "Vindicate me, O Lord, for I have walked in my integrity." When we do business with or are ministering to someone, we want that person to have integrity.

When we have integrity, David tells us, we don't have to be afraid of sliding. "I have walked in my integrity. I have also trusted in the Lord; I shall not slip" (v.1). He also says, "My foot stands in an even place" (v.12). The word *even* means "a level place." David says, "I'm on the level because I have integrity. I have nothing in my heart against the Lord. I am not disobeying Him."

We also need not be afraid of testing. David writes, "Examine me, O Lord, and prove me; try my mind and my heart" (v.2). He says, in other words, "Lord, I can go through the furnace. I can go through the X ray. Go ahead and test me. I'm not afraid." When your life is whole before God and others, when you're practicing integrity, when you have a good conscience, you don't have to be afraid of the battle or the furnace or the X ray or the testing. God will see you through.

When you walk with integrity, you walk on solid ground. Never try to serve two masters. Always keep your heart undivided before the Lord.

Read Psalm 26:1-12

A CHRISTIAN'S DEFENSE

DAY 59

Have you ever been blamed for something you didn't do? Leaders often are blamed falsely. The Israelites blamed Moses for lack of water, bitter water, enemies' attacks and lack of food. In this psalm, David is falsely accused, so he takes four steps to deal with his slanderers.

Step 1: An honest examination (vv.1-3). Human nature does not want to admit it's wrong, but we need to examine ourselves. David walked in integrity. *Integrity* means "wholeness of character." He also walked in faith, without wavering. We find David open before God, walking in the light and letting God examine him. We would save ourselves a lot of trouble if we would let Him examine us. He wants to teach us what we are really like. If we are right before God, it makes no difference what people say.

Step 2: A holy separation (vv.4,5). People accused David of being a hypocrite, even though he did not worship false gods. We must obey the biblical doctrine of holy separation (II Cor.6:14-18).

Step 3: A happy celebration (vv.6-8). David washed his hands in innocence. He was cleansed by water and blood. He was concerned about praising, loving and glorifying God. Just as Jesus sang before His crucifixion, David sang songs of praise around the altar, the place of sacrifice. Do we sing songs of praise when we have to make sacrifices?

Step 4: A humble determination (vv.9-12). David said, "As for me, I will walk in my integrity." When a person has integrity, he has a great defense, a great shield. Character is a marvelous shield against the accusations of men. A good conscience gives us courage in times of difficulty.

The Christian's defense is the grace of God, His Word and His truth. Because of this, we're able to walk. David's foot stood in an even place. He was not standing alone—he was in the congregation. Let's take the same steps David took the next time someone slanders us.

People can hurt you with false accusations, but you need not let slanderers defeat you. If you walk with integrity, your character will shield you. Keep yourself pure and avoid compromising situations. When someone slanders you, God's grace, His Word and His truth will protect you.

Read Psalm 27:1-6

I'M NOT SCARED

"The Lord is my light and my salvation; whom shall I fear? The Lord is the strength of my life; of whom shall I be afraid?" (v.1). Those are good questions. Why should we be afraid? What does God do to us and for us when we face an enemy? This psalm tells us that when we fear Him, we need not fear anyone else.

David talks about an enemy coming in. "When the wicked came against me to eat up my flesh, my enemies and foes, they stumbled and fell" (v.2). Here we have a sudden coming of the enemy. But sometimes it's not a sudden invasion. In verse 3 we read, "Though an army should encamp against me." Here the enemy has settled in. I don't know which of these two is the more difficult. I think I'd prefer to have my enemies suddenly show up than to have them camped on my doorstep. You may have an enemy camped in your home or your office or your church. Somewhere in your life an enemy has probably settled.

But David says, "My heart shall not fear; though war should rise against me" (v.3). This is not a sudden invasion or a settled battle. It's a sustained war, day after day. "Though war should rise against me in this I will be confident" (v.3). We can be confident in the Lord, because He is our Light; we don't have to be afraid of the darkness. And because He is our Salvation, we don't have to be afraid of danger."

How can we have the protection the Lord offers? By abiding in Christ. Verse 4 tells us, "One thing I have desired of the Lord, that will I seek: that I may dwell in the house of the Lord all the days of my life, to behold the beauty of the Lord, and to inquire in His temple." Don't be afraid of your disabilities and your deficiencies. God is your Light, your Salvation and your Strength. He is all you need.

The grip of fear can debilitate one's heart, mind and will. But Christians have a Strength greater than any fear we can face. Are you struggling with fear? Whatever battle you may be fighting, rest confidently in God's protection. He is your Strength, and He will deliver you.

Read Psalm 27:7-14

DAY 61

BELIEVING OR SEEING?

Have you ever fainted? The psalmist discovered a way to keep from fainting. "I would have lost heart [fainted], unless I had believed that I would see the goodness of the Lord in the land of the living" (v.13). David felt somewhat forsaken. His enemies were attacking him, and the circumstances were unbearable.

We have to walk by faith just as David did. "I would have lost heart, unless I had believed." Jesus taught in Luke 18 that men ought always to pray and not to faint. When you pray, it's an evidence of faith. The world says that seeing is believing. If the world had written verse 13 of this passage, it would read: "I would have fainted unless I had seen, and then I believed." That was Martha's problem. Lazarus, her brother, had been dead and in the grave for four days. But Jesus said to her, "Didn't I tell you that if you would believe, you would see?" (John 11:40). Thomas said, "Seeing is believing," but Jesus says, "Believing is seeing" (see Ps.20:24-29).

The evidences of faith are rather obvious. First, *we seek the Lord.* "When You said, 'Seek My face,' my heart said to You, 'Your face, Lord, I will seek'" (v.8). Do you want to build your faith and be able to walk by faith and war by faith? Then seek the Lord. Second, *call on the Lord.* "Teach me Your way, O Lord, and lead me in a smooth path, because of my enemies" (v.11). That's prayer. Third, do the hardest thing of all—*wait on the Lord.* "Wait on the Lord; be of good courage, and He shall strengthen your heart" (v.14). Believing is seeing. Trust the Lord today.

One of the most difficult aspects of the Christian life is waiting on God. It is especially difficult in the midst of trials. But that is when He builds your faith. Don't faint under your circumstances. Wait on the Lord, and He will strengthen you.

DAY

62

Read Psalm 28:1-9

CHECKING HANDS

When I was in grade school, each day the teacher would walk up and down the aisles and make us hold out our hands: first, with the palms up to make sure our hands were clean and then with the palms down to make sure our fingernails were clean. Of course, none of us liked this, because little kids would much rather have dirty hands.

Psalm 28 talks a great deal about hands. The psalmist lifted up his hands. The enemies were doing evil work with their hands. But God had His hand at work as well. "Give to them [the enemies] according to their deeds, and according to the wickedness of their endeavors; give to them according to the work of their hands" (v.4). There are wicked people in this world, and they have dirty hands. Some people defile everything they touch. This grieves us, especially when they want to touch our lives and defile us.

What did David do? He saw his enemies' evil hands, and he lifted up his hands. "Hear the voice of my supplications when I cry to You, when I lift up my hands toward Your holy sanctuary" (v.2). When an Old Testament Jew prayed, he didn't fold his hands. He lifted them up to God in praise and in expectancy that He was going to do something. When you see the evil hands of Satan's crowd doing their defiling work, don't put your hands on their hands. You'll be defiled. Instead, lift your holy hands to the Lord and trust Him to work. "Because they [the enemies] do not regard the works of the Lord, nor the operation of His hands, He shall destroy them and not build them up" (v.5).

God's hand is at work today, and the result of this is praise (v.7). Do you need help today? Lift up your hands to the Lord in supplication and in expectation, and soon you will lift up your hands in jubilation and celebration.

Unfortunately, many people fail to keep their hands clean. Their evil hands sometimes do dirty work that hurts you. When that happens, you can trust God to take care of evil hands. Keep your hands clean. Look to God, lift your hands to Him and let His hand work for you.

THE VOICE IN THE STORM

I don't know how my psychologist friends will analyze this, but for some reason I enjoy a rainy day. I especially enjoy it during a day off at home. I find it soothing to stand at the window and see the clouds and the rain and even hear the thunder.

Psalm 29 is a description of a storm. I suppose David was out in the fields or in a cave when this storm came. He saw the power of God in the turbulence. Before it started, he said, "Give unto the Lord, O you mighty ones, give unto the Lord glory and strength. Give unto the Lord the glory due to His name; worship the Lord in the beauty of holiness" (vv.1,2). He was concerned about God's glory. Perhaps he saw the clouds gathering. When you see clouds gathering and know that a storm is about to come into your life, do you think about the glory of God? David did. So often we don't. We think of escape rather than the glory of God.

In verses 3-9 David describe the storm. "The voice of the Lord is over the waters; the God of glory thunders; . . . the voice of the Lord is powerful" (vv.3,4). He saw the lightning and heard the thunder. A sequence here is rather interesting. "The voice of the Lord breaks the cedars, . . . the voice of the Lord shakes the wilderness; . . . the voice of the Lord makes the deer give birth" (vv.5,8,9). God's voice can *break* and *shake* and *make*. David ends the psalm by acknowledging God's sovereignty. He is King forever. "The Lord sat enthroned at the Flood, and the Lord sits as King forever" (v.10). God is sovereign today. Don't be afraid of the storm. Just look for His glory and His power.

God often speaks to you in the storm. The next time you find yourself in a storm, listen for His voice. Look for His glory and power and be reminded that He is in control.

DAY 64

Read Psalm 30:1-12

NEVER BE MOVED?

Two words are repeated seven times in Psalm 30—"you have." David is praising God for what He had done for him. Are you doing that today? Perhaps you've seen the plaque that says, "Prayer changes things," and that's true. I've also seen a plaque that says, "Praise changes things," and that also is true. It's amazing how our whole attitude and whole outlook can be transformed by praising God.

In verse 6 David gives a testimony: "Now in my prosperity I said, 'I shall never be moved.'" When we have *prosperity* without *humility*, it leads to *adversity*. Why? Because we start to be more concerned with things than we are with God. David said in his prosperity, "I shall never be moved." But then he found out that he could be moved. He found out that his prosperity did not guarantee security. So instead of saying "I shall" or "I shall not," he began saying "You have." He submitted his will to God's will. "You have" defeated the enemy. "For You have lifted me up, and have not let my foes rejoice over me" (v.1). "You have" given me victory. "You have" answered prayer. "You have healed me" (v.2). "You have brought my soul up from the grave; You have kept me alive" (v.3).

God did some marvelous things for David. He defeated his enemy, answered his prayer, saved his life and established him (v.7). And then He gave him joy. "You have turned for me my mourning into dancing; You have put off my sackcloth and clothed me with gladness" (v.11). Do you want your life to be transformed today? Move from "I shall" to "You have" and, in humility, praise God for what He has done.

Submitting to God is an exercise in humility. Until you humble yourself before Him and concern yourself with the things of God, you will not become established. For God to work in your life, your will must be aligned with His. Are you submitted to Him? If not, humble yourself before Him and allow Him to transform your life.

Read Psalm 31:1-8

DAY 65

WHOSE HANDS?

Psalm 31 is one of David's exile psalms. He wrote it when Saul was chasing him through the rough hill country of Judah. David was going from cave to cave and from hill to hill.

During his exile, David discovered that *God's hand was adequate for every need of every day.* Have you noticed in the Psalms how often David talked about hands? As a shepherd he knew the importance of his hands. He had to carry the shepherd's crook, the staff. He also used a slingshot and later exchanged it for a sword. Occasionally he would exchange his sword for a harp. The hands that had been in battle produced beautiful music for the glory of God.

David also talked about the hand of the enemy. "And [You] have not shut me up into the hand of the enemy" (v.8). "My times are in Your hand; deliver me from the hand of my enemies" (v.15). We do have enemies. "Be sober, be vigilant; because your adversary the devil walks about like a roaring lion, seeking whom he may devour" (I Pet.5:8). Our enemies would like to destroy us, but God's hand protects us.

"Into Your hand I commit my spirit; You have redeemed me, O Lord God of truth" (v.5). This is the prayer of Jewish boys and girls in the Old Testament times. Whenever he went to bed, the little child would say, "Into Your hand I commit my spirit." When our Lord Jesus Christ gave His life for us on the cross, He said, "It is finished! Into Your hands I commend My spirit" (John 19:30; Luke 23:46). When you commit your life into God's hand, you don't have to worry about any other hand, because His hand protects you, provides for you and guides you.

It is good for us to depend on God's hand, the hand of provision, protection and guidance. What are your needs today? Have you asked God to provide for them? Depend on the hand of God; you will find Him faithful.

Read Psalm 31:9-13

LIKE A LEPER

We can't help what others do and say. We can help only what we do. When others start talking about us or fighting against us, we may not be able to control that. It's difficult when people start to slander the righteous. But this is what David had to endure. In verse 11 we read, "I am a reproach among all my enemies." We expect that. "But especially among my neighbors." Now that hurts. "And am repulsive to my acquaintances." That hurts even more. "Those who see me outside flee from me." Can you imagine your neighbors and your acquaintances running away from you as if you were a leper?

What was causing all of this for David? Saul was lying about him. He was telling his assistants and officers, "David said this. David did that." And this gossip, this awful slander, was spreading through the nation, and David was suffering. "I am forgotten like a dead man, out of mind; I am like a broken vessel" (v.12). David wanted to be a vessel filled to overflowing, but now he was broken.

What should you do when people start slandering you? First, *be sure your life is right.* "For my life is spent with grief, and my years with sighing; my strength fails because of my iniquity, and my bones waste away" (v.10). David is saying, "Lord, if I've sinned, I'll confess it." Second, *trust in the Lord.* "But as for me, I trust in You, O Lord; I say, 'You are my God'"(v.14). Third, *remember that others have gone through this.* You're not experiencing something unique. Everyone who has done anything for the Lord has been slandered, ridiculed, criticized—including the perfect Son of God. Don't listen to the slander of the enemy; listen to the Word of God. Get close to His *heart*, and you'll have His *help* when you suffer misunderstanding.

When someone falsely accuses you, take comfort in knowing that others have gone through the difficulty of slander. Then look to the Lord, for He is your Strength and Salvation. Use this difficult experience to examine your own heart and draw closer to Him.

AVAILABLE TIME

David often talked about God's hand and the hand of the enemy. "My times are in Your hand; deliver me from the hand of my enemies, and from those who persecute me" (v.15). That's a marvelous declaration of faith. And David didn't write it from a hotel suite somewhere. He was out in the Judean wilderness, where it was dark and dirty and dry. And he was being chased by Saul.

In writing "my times are in Your hand," David teaches us several lessons. First, *time* is important. If you waste time, you're wasting *eternity*. If you waste time, you're wasting *opportunity*. All I can give to God is my body, my ability and my time. And if I don't give Him my time, He can't use my body or my ability. Time is valuable—don't waste it. Invest it.

Second, David reminds us how important *surrender* is. Who controls the available time we have when we're not working or doing the things that must be done to maintain life—that unregistered, undirected time? If we surrender to the Lord, He can control that time. I learned many years ago to turn my entire day over to Him at the beginning of every day. If I have interruptions, He's in control. If my plans are changed, He's in control.

Third, this leads to God's *blessings* for us. When our times are in His hand, we can trust Him; He has blessings especially prepared for us. "Oh, how great is Your goodness, which You have laid up for those who fear You" (v.19). God has some wonderful blessings prepared for you today. But you are not going to enjoy them unless you truly say, "Lord, my times are in Your hand."

Time is perhaps your most basic resource. How you use God's gift of time has a profound effect not only on your life but on the lives of others. It's important that you surrender your time to His care. When you give God your time, you surrender it to His control. He will bless you for it.

DAY

68

Read Psalm 32:1-7

CONFESSING SIN

Psalm 32 is the record of David's experience after he sinned with Bathsheba and then confessed his sin to the Lord. He feels *the heavy hand of God's discipline*. "For day and night Your hand was heavy upon me; my vitality was turned into the drought of summer" (v.4). In other words, David says, "God, Your hand was so heavy on me that it was like squeezing a sponge. You have just squeezed all of the energy out of me." It's difficult to have the heavy hand of God's discipline on us, but it shows that God loves us. "Whom the Lord loves He chastens, and scourges every son whom He receives" (Heb.12:6).

Discipline leads to *the forgiving hand of God's mercy*. "Blessed is he whose transgression is forgiven, whose sin is covered. Blessed is the man to whom the Lord does not impute iniquity, and in whose spirit there is no guile" (vv.1,2). While David was silent and would not confess his sin, he felt God's hand of discipline draining him. But when he confessed his sin, that heavy hand was lifted. Then God went to the record book and graciously wiped the record clean. That's the meaning of that word *impute*. It means "to put on the account." First John 1:9 tells us that "if we confess our sins, He is faithful and just to forgive us our sins and to cleanse us from all unrighteousness."

Confession leads to *the protecting hand of God's grace*. "You are my hiding place; You shall preserve me from trouble; You shall surround me with songs of deliverance" (v.7). David went from silence to confession to singing. When your soul is clean, you have a song in your heart.

It's good to know that God forgives sin. Let's confess our sin and sing His praises.

Unconfessed sin is a terrible burden. God loves His children too much to allow unconfessed sin in their lives. The hand that disciplines is the same hand that forgives and protects. Are you harboring unconfessed sin? Confess it now and thank God for His forgiveness and protecting hand of grace.

Read Psalm 32:8-11

THREE LEVELS

DAY 69

Did you know there are three levels on which God can deal with you? You must decide whether you want Him to treat you as a thing, an animal or one of His own children. God had to treat David as a thing (a sponge), and His hand was heavy on him (vv.3,4). David was rebelling. He was not acting like God's child. Instead of *confessing* his sin, he was *covering* it. But the Bible says, "He who covers his sins will not prosper" (Prov.28:13). So God had to treat David like a thing. He put His hand on David and began to squeeze all the life out of him. David finally woke up and confessed his sin.

God also had to treat David like an animal. He warns us, "Do not be like the horse or like the mule, which have no understanding, which must be harnessed with bit and bridle, else they will not come near you" (v.9). David had acted like a horse—impulsively, he rushed ahead and sinned. And then he became stubborn like a mule and would not confess his sin. So God dealt with him as He would an animal.

But God wants to deal with us as children. "I will instruct you and teach you in the way you should go; I will guide you with My eye [on you]" (v.8). He doesn't want to control us with bits and bridles, although sometimes He has to do that. Sometimes He has to send us sickness or a handicap or an accident to break our wills. He says, "I'd much rather guide you with My eye on you. I'd much rather instruct you." You can instruct a horse or a mule to a certain extent—but not the way you can a child. Decide today: Is God going to treat you as a thing because you are rebelling or as an animal because you are stubborn? Or will you let Him guide you as His own child? Oh, how much He loves you! He wants to work *in* you and *through* you and *for* you to bring about His best in your life.

God loves you and wants to guide you as His child. The way you live decides whether or not He can. Rebellion and unconfessed sin in your life will change the way He works in you. Are you living as a child of God? Decide now on which level He will treat you.

DAY 70

Read Psalm 33:1-5

A NEW SONG

"Sing to Him a new song; play skillfully with a shout of joy" (v.3). Have you sung a new song to the Lord lately? Where do you find this new song, and how can you best express it? The psalmist is talking about worshiping the Lord. Worship should have a freshness to it. Sometimes in our worship we sing the old songs in the old way, and we lose some of our skill. David was a harpist. He said, "Praise the Lord with the harp; make melody to Him with an instrument of ten strings [a psaltery]. Sing to Him a new song" (vv.2,3).

We get a new song from several sources. First, we get a new song from *God's Word*. "For the word of the Lord is right" (v.4). When I read my Bible, I ask God to show me new things. Psalm 119:18 is a good prayer: "Open my eyes, that I may see wondrous things from Your law." He gives me new insights from His Word, and that gives me a new song.

Next, we get a new song from *God's works*. "For the word of the Lord is right, and all His work is done in truth. He loves righteousness and justice; the earth is full of the goodness of the Lord" (vv.4,5). When we look around, we may see sadness, but the psalmist saw goodness. We may see unrighteousness and injustice, but the psalmist saw God's righteousness and justice. Open your eyes and look around you. See the wonderful new things God is doing.

Finally, we get a new song from *our walk with the Lord*. When we go through new experiences and new challenges, God gives us new victories. Then we have a new song to sing. I want to have freshness in my worship. I want fervor and freshness in my witness for the Lord. I want Him to do something new in my life. I want to sing a new song. Do you?

God wants you to walk closely with Him so He may lead you into new experiences and challenges. If you're singing an old song, it could mean that you need to renew your walk with the Lord. Feed on the Word of God and look at what He is doing in your life. Ask Him to give you a new song.

Read Psalm 33:6-11

NO CARBON COPY

DAY **71**

Are you depending on the counsel of the Lord? The Word of God, His counsel, runs this whole universe. How did God create it? "And God said, 'Let there be . . .'" (Gen.1). He spoke, and it was done, which shows the power of His Word. Did you know that the same Word that created the universe holds the universe together and is guiding the universe and human history for you? When we are in tune with the Word of God, we're in tune with the whole universe and with what He is doing in this world.

Let no one rob you of the beautiful truth that God has His counsel for you. He has an individual plan for your life, just as He did for Moses, Joshua, David, the apostles and the great men and women of Church history.

Notice that the Lord's counsel comes from His heart. "The counsel of the Lord stands forever, the plans of His heart to all generations" (v.11). The will of God doesn't come from a machine. He doesn't photocopy one plan for everyone's life and fax it to all believers. No, God's will comes from His heart, completely tailor-made for your life. And His will lasts forever, unlike human plans.

The will of God is His expression of love for you. Don't be afraid of it. Build your life on the counsel of the Lord.

Because God's tailor-made plans for you come from His heart, they are an expression of His love. Stay in tune with the Word of God, and He will guide you according to His will.

DAY

72

Read Psalm 33:12-19

THE BEST CITIZEN

So often the psalmist says, "Blessed is the man" or "Blessed is the family," But in verse 12 he says, "Blessed is the nation." Does God bless nations? Yes. He blessed the nation of Israel. He endowed the Israelites with some special blessings and gave them special tasks. They failed, however, in some of the things He gave them to do. But eventually God brought His Word and His Son through the people of Israel. Christ was born of the tribe of Judah in the family of David.

Are you the kind of person God can use to be a blessing to your nation? Believers were chosen by God, in Christ, before, the foundation of the world. We are His own inheritance, God looks down on us with favor and grace. And the Bible tells us that God wants us to be the right kind of citizens.

God is watching us. "The Lord looks from heaven; He sees all the sons of men" (v.13), And He made us, "He fashions their hearts individually; He considers all their works" (v.15). Here we are, the people of God in a wicked and dark nation. What should we do? Remember, He is watching us. He made us and He's protecting us. "Behold, the eye of the Lord is on those who fear Him" (v.18). We don't have to be afraid.

Be the best citizen you can be. Do so by obeying the Lord, by letting your light shine for Him, by praying for your nation, by sharing His Word with others and by exercising the privileges you have as a citizen of your nation.

God uses people to bless nations, Christians are to be good citizens, the kind of people He can use to strengthen a nation. Pray for your country and its leaders, Do your part to exercise the freedom you have to share the Word of God and be a witness for Him.

Read Psalm 33:20-22

DAY 73

CAN YOU WAIT?

Waiting is one of the hardest things for me to do. I would rather work than wait. Somehow I always end up in the wrong lane or the wrong line, and I'm forced to wait. My impatience is probably why the Lord reminds me of verse 20: "Our soul waits for the Lord; He is our help and our shield." Why does God delay in answering prayer? He wants to give us a better blessing. Why does God delay in bringing deliverance or healing? He has something better in store for us. Our times are in His hands.

We must remember that when we wait on the Lord, we are not being idle or careless. Waiting prepares us. God works *in* us so that He can work *for* us. He knows what He is doing and has His own schedule. "The Lord is not slack concerning His promise, as some [people] count slackness, but is longsuffering toward us, not willing that any should perish" (II Pet.3:9).

"Our heart shall rejoice in Him" (v.21). Waiting ultimately leads to worship. The day will come when you will rejoice in the Lord because you have trusted in His holy name. "Let Your mercy, O Lord, be upon us, just as we hope in You" (v.22). We have hope and faith in waiting on the Lord. If you find it hard to wait, remember that God's delays are not His denials. He has a greater blessing in store for you. You can be sure that one day the waiting will end, and you will start worshiping and praising Him.

Are you waiting for God to answer a specific prayer? Keep trusting Him to work on your behalf. Your waiting will turn into worship and praise.

DAY

74

Read Psalm 34:1-3

CONTINUAL PRAISE

"I will bless the Lord at all times; His praise shall continually be in my mouth" (v.1). That verse is much easier to read than it is to practice. How can we praise the Lord at all times? Sometimes it's difficult to praise Him. Sometimes we are weak, and our bodies hurt or circumstances are difficult. Sometimes we must helplessly watch people we love go through hard times.

If we are to praise the Lord at all times, then praise must be important. Notice the results that come when we truly praise the Lord continually. Praise *sanctifies our lives* at all times. It sanctifies us when we're in the dentist's chair or when we are standing by an open grave. The Lord Jesus sang before He went to Calvary. "And when they [Jesus and His disciples] had sung a hymn, they went out" (Matt.26:30). Paul and Silas praised the Lord in prison when their bodies hurt (Acts 16:25).

Praise also *unifies God's people.* One thing we can all do together is praise the Lord. We may not always agree on the sermon, but we can agree on the hymnbook. That's why there will be so much singing and praising in heaven.

Finally, praise *magnifies the Lord.* That's why we should do it at all times. Anybody can praise the Lord when things are going well. But it's during the "furnace experiences" that praise really magnifies the Lord.

Let praise sanctify your life, unify your fellowship and magnify the Lord.

Is praising God part of your Christian experience? Praise Him always, for praise is a necessary part of the life of faith.

Read Psalm 34:4-10

A BIBLICAL TESTIMONY

DAY **75**

When I was a young Christian, the church I attended held testimony meetings. I would hear people say, "I thank the Lord that He saves, keeps and satisfies." So I asked myself, *That sounds good, but is it in the Bible?*

Yes, it is. We find it in Psalm 34:6-8. "This poor man cried out, and the Lord heard him, and saved him out of all his troubles" (v.6). The Lord *saves.* It's interesting to notice that we aren't saved *from* trouble. Sometimes when we trust the Lord and pray He saves us from troubles. But here David says, "He saved me *out* of troubles."

He also *keeps.* "The angel of the Lord encamps all around those who fear Him, and delivers them" (v.7). The word *angel* conveys the idea of many angels, not just one. David is talking about an encampment of angels surrounding us for protection. So the Lord does save and keep. I'm glad for His keeping power. He's able to save and keep us because of His work on the cross and His present ministry in heaven.

Verse 8 says that the Lord also *satisfies:* "Oh, taste and see that the Lord is good; blessed is the man who trusts in Him!" Some of the experiences of life taste sour. Sometimes the cup that is handed to us is not one of sweetness but of bitterness. Our Lord had to drink a bitter cup. Do you know what makes the bitter cup satisfying and sweet? It's "tasting" the Lord in it. When you taste the Lord in the experiences of life, they become sweet in Him. Therefore, that testimony is biblical: He saves, He keeps, He satisfies.

What problem are you facing today? Perhaps you are struggling with physical or financial difficulties. Whatever your problems, God promises to help you through them. Are you trusting Jesus to save you and keep you? Have you "tasted" the Lord and found that He satisfies?

DAY 76

Read Psalm 34:11-16

HOW TO HAVE A GOOD DAY

How often has someone said to you, "Have a good day"? That's a nice statement, but what does it mean? When you review the day's activities before you go to bed, how do you know whether the day was good or bad? When Joseph's brothers sold him into slavery, that was a bad day. But God turned it into good for him. When Potiphar's wife lied about Joseph and had him put into prison, it was a bad day. But God turned that into good for him also. You see, we don't always know what a good day is. However, we can make our days good if we follow the instructions given in today's passage.

First, *control your tongue.* David asks, "Who is the man who desires life, and loves many days, that he may see good?" (v.12). Of course, everybody wants long life and good days. So you must "keep your tongue from evil, and your lips from speaking deceit" (v.13). When you say the wrong thing, you will have a bad day. So keep your tongue under control.

Second, *"depart from evil and do good"* (v.14). If you want to have a good day, do good. If you sow the seeds of goodness, you'll reap the harvest of goodness.

Third, *"seek peace and pursue it"* (v.14). Don't go around with a revolver in your hand. Don't be bothered by every little slight or by everything that people say. If somebody cuts in front of you in a line, don't let it bother you. Be a peacemaker, not a troublemaker.

Finally, *trust the Lord because He's watching you.* "The eyes of the Lord are on the righteous, and His ears are open to their cry" (v.15). The word open means "attentive to." You don't have to worry about what other people do. God is watching you, and He's listening to you. You can have a good day if you'll just follow these instructions. So, have a good day!

"Have a good day!" may be a trite expression, but you can have a good day if you follow certain instructions from Scripture. Try following the guidelines of this psalm. Not only will you have a good day, but those with whom you come in contact will be blessed.

Read Psalm 34:17,18

DAY 77

SMASHED RAINBOWS

A little girl and her mother were walking down a sidewalk after a rainstorm. Someone had spilled some automobile oil on the pavement. Seeing that, the little girl said, "Mommy, look at all of the smashed rainbows!"

Maybe your rainbows have been smashed, and you have a broken heart. Perhaps you don't feel close to God because of your heartache. What can you do to be near to Him? First, *keep in mind that nearness is likeness.* 'The Lord is near to those who have a broken heart" (v.18). The more we are *like* God, the nearer we are to Him. How close can you get to God? You can get as close to Him as *you* want. Draw near to Him, and He will draw near to you. Remember that God knows the meaning of a broken heart. Jesus Christ literally experienced one. He was "a man of sorrows and acquainted with grief" (Isa.53:3). Let your experiences make you more like Jesus, and He will draw near to you.

Second, *remember that God gives grace to the humble.* "God resists the proud, but gives grace to the humble" (James 4:6). David also said, "A broken and a contrite heart—these, O God, You will not despise" (Ps.51:17).

Our Lord came "to heal the brokenhearted" (Luke 4:18). Do you have a broken heart that needs healed? Here's the simple secret: Give the Lord all the pieces, and He will heal you.

Everyone has experienced dashed hopes and smashed plans. Take comfort in knowing that your Lord heals the broken heart. Are you getting over a crushing experience? The Lord understands what you are going through. Draw near to Him with a humble spirit and give Him the broken pieces of your heart.

DAY 78

Read Psalm 34:19-22

GOD'S TOOLS

"Many are the afflictions of the righteous, but the Lord delivers him out of them all" (v.19). The psalmist does not say, "I thought the Lord kept us *out of* afflictions. I thought that if I read my Bible every day and prayed and tried to obey His will, I would never have any afflictions." Instead, he says that we will face *many* afflictions.

Why do we have afflictions in our lives? We have some afflictions simply *because we are human*. They are just a part of human life. We get older, and our bodies begin to run down. Not every sickness, every accident or every problem we face comes because God is angry at us or is disciplining us. They may just be a part of life.

We also have afflictions *because Satan is against* us. He'd love to destroy us. Or, afflictions may come because we have disobeyed the Lord. I'm glad for those; I'm glad that God loves me enough to "spank" me when I've disobeyed Him.

But often, *afflictions are God's tools for helping us grow.* We don't really grow until we've been through the furnace, through the storm or through the battle. God is not raising hothouse plants that shrivel when the hot wind blows on them. No, He wants to raise mature sons and daughters, and that's why we have afflictions. "Many are the afflictions of the righteous, but the Lord delivers him out of them all" (v.19). He doesn't keep us *out of* them. He delivers us *from* them. Sometimes He changes the circumstances. Sometimes He changes us. The real secret of deliverance is not the *circumstance around you* but the *faith within you.* Expect affliction, but trust God for deliverance.

Perhaps God's greatest use of affliction is as a tool for helping you grow into a mature Christian. The good news is that you may trust Him to deliver you from your afflictions. The next time you face affliction, trust the Lord for your deliverance.

Read Psalm 34:17-22

TRUSTING THE LORD

Christians must entrust five burdens to the Lord to receive blessings from Him. First, *trust the Lord with your frustrations* (v.17). The word *trouble* means "to be in a bind" or "frustrated." Sometimes we bring trouble on ourselves, as did David. The only safe place is in the will of God. Sometimes other people cause our troubles, as Saul often did for David. And sometimes we have troubles because God knows we need them. When we have troubles, we need to pray for His help. Trust the Lord with your frustrations.

Second, *trust the Lord with your feelings* (v.18). David was repenting because of his sin, and his heart was broken. God respects that attitude; He is always near those who have a broken heart.

Third, *trust the Lord with your future* (v.20). The word *guard* means "to exercise great care over, to protect." When Jesus was on the cross, the Devil was doing his worst, yet he could do only what God permitted. God was guarding His own Son, and He will guard us, for He is concerned with our future.

Fourth, *trust the Lord with your foes* (v.21). Their own sin will slay them. "Evil shall slay the wicked." Give your enemies to the Lord. Let Him be the Judge (Rom.12:17-21).

Finally, *trust the Lord with your failures* (v.22). The word *condemned* means "to be held guilty." David sinned against the Lord (the cause of his broken heart), but God rescued and forgave him.

If you want to have a good day, trust the Lord with these five burdens.

When you became a Christian, you trusted Jesus as your Savior, and He saved you from the penalty of your sin. But don't stop there. You need to entrust your life to God daily. Entrust these burdens to Him and receive the blessings He has for you.

DAY **80**

Read Psalm 35:1-10

WHAT TO DO FIRST

"And soul shall be joyful in the Lord; it shall rejoice in His salvation" (v.9). This is David's glad response to God's gracious deliverance from his enemies. David was in trouble; his enemies were accusing him and lying about him. What did he do? He prayed.

Our first reaction to false accusations is to fight. We want to fight back and defend our name and protect our reputation. But David was far more concerned about his character than his reputation. He knew that if he was right with God, it made no difference what people did to him or said about him. So he started with prayer. "Plead my cause, O Lord, with those who strive with me; fight against those who fight against me" (v.1). When the Enemy fights against you, he's really fighting against the Lord. That's a good principle to remember. When the child of God is in the will of God, he can claim the help and the protection of the Father.

David started with prayer, and he admitted his own helplessness. "All my bones shall say, 'Lord, who is like You, delivering the poor from him who is too strong for him?'" (v.10). Our enemies are too strong for us. We have to turn them over to the Lord. David trusted God to work on his behalf, and He did.

God will work for you today, too. In His time and in His way, He will accomplish what needs to be done. And when that day comes to an end, or whenever the opportunity might arise, you will say, "And my soul shall be joyful in the Lord; it shall rejoice in His salvation." It's not *your* salvation—it's not based on what you have done for yourself but on what God has done for you. I trust that today you'll have the joy of His victory in your life.

When dealing with your enemies, your first response might be to react instead of to act positively. Your best response is to pray. As God's child, you can turn your enemies over to Him and claim His help and protection. Is the Enemy attacking you? Give your burden to the Lord, and He will work on your behalf.

Read Psalm 35:11-21

THE DIVINE LEVEL

On which level of life are you living—on the human level, the demonic level or the divine level? On the *human level* we return good for good and evil for evil. That's the way most people live. But when we live on this level, we really don't grow. In fact, we become like other people. The human level turns life into a war, into a selfish competition. And that's not the Christian way to live. Only God knows when something is truly evil. What someone does to you today might ultimately turn out to be the best thing that's ever happened to you. On the surface it may look like evil, but God can turn it into good.

Nor do we want to live on the *demonic level.* In Psalm 35 we read about those who return evil for good. David says, "They reward me evil for good, to the sorrow of my soul" (v.12). That's the level the Devil lives on. He always returns evil for good.

But David lived on the *divine level.* He returned good for evil (vv.13,14). He expressed love toward his enemies. He didn't simply return good for good and evil for evil. And he certainly didn't return evil for good. No, David returned good for evil. He anticipated the words of our Lord Jesus Christ: "Love your enemies, bless those who curse you, do good to those who hate you, and pray for those who spitefully use you and persecute you" (Matt.5:44).

Let's live on the divine level—that dynamic level of love where we live like the Lord Jesus Christ.

It's often difficult to do good toward those who have wronged you. But God wants you to live on the divine level and return good for evil. How do you treat others? The next time you are wronged by someone, choose to treat that person with kindness. God will use your actions to bring glory to Himself.

DAY 82

Read Psalm 35:22-28

BEING A LENS

Each of us is a lens that magnifies what we live for. People can look at and through our lives and see what is really important to us. The athlete magnifies his sport, his team and his winning record. The musician magnifies the instrument he plays. The scholar magnifies his discipline. As God's people, we should magnify the Lord.

The sinner, however, wants to magnify only himself. David said, "Let them be ashamed and brought to mutual confusion who rejoice at my hurt; let them be clothed with shame and dishonor who magnify themselves against me" (v.26). Notice the phrase "who magnify themselves against me." Whenever you live to magnify yourself, you are always against someone else. This means competition. And God doesn't want us to live competitively.

Our great desire should be to magnify the Lord, not ourselves. David said, "Let them shout for joy and be glad, who favor my righteous cause; and let them say continually, 'Let the Lord be magnified'" (v.27). The Apostle Paul said, "Christ will be magnified in my body, whether by life or by death" (Phil.1:20). Are you magnifying the Lord today? Can people listen to your words, look at your life, measure your actions and say, "She belongs to the Lord. He belongs to the Lord"? It's important that people see the Lord, not us.

The most important quality of a lens is cleanliness. When the lenses of my glasses get dirty, I see the dirt. So I have to clean them. When we are dirty, people see us rather than the Lord. Let's keep our lives clean today. Let's magnify the Lord together; He is worthy of all praise.

Christians are on display before the world. What an opportunity and responsibility you have to impact others for Christ! If you love the Lord, you will want to magnify Him. Watch your words and actions. Are you living for Jesus? Keep the lens of your life clean so that He may be magnified through you.

Read Psalm 36:1-12

DAY 83

PROTECTED BY A SHADOW

When we trust Jesus Christ and live in fellowship with Him, we have all we need for life and for service. When you were saved, you were born again, complete in Christ. When the Holy Spirit came into your life, He came to give you fullness of life in Jesus Christ.

Psalm 36 indicates that when we walk in the Lord and seek to serve Him, we have His *protection.* "How precious is Your lovingkindness, O God! Therefore the children of men put their trust under the shadow of Your wings" (v.7). David is talking about the tabernacle, about the wings of the cherubim in the Holy of Holies. How strange that the safest place in the world is under a shadow! When we live in the Holy of Holies, in fellowship with God and under His wings, we have His protection.

In verse 8 David changes the picture. He says we have God's *satisfaction:* "They are abundantly satisfied with the fullness of Your house, and You give them drink from the river of Your pleasures." Our Lord not only protects us but also provides for and satisfies us. A river constantly flows, yet it's always the same. God is always the same, yet He constantly wants to bring new blessings to us. A river is known for its power and abundance. So is God. "For with You is the fountain of life" (v.9). We don't drink at the river and get thirsty again. We always have that Fountain of Living Water within us.

We also have His *guidance.* "In Your light we see light" (v.9). What more can you want? In Jesus Christ you have all that you need. Be sure to live under the shadow of His wings.

God's lovingkindness addresses your human weaknesses. Where they might betray you or leave you vulnerable, He divinely provides. You have the promise of His care. He protects, satisfies and guides. Is your life holy and acceptable before Him? Trust yourself to God's care and rest under the shadow of His wing. "The Lord takes pleasure in those who fear him, in those who put their hope in his mercy" (Ps.147:11).

Read Psalm 36:7-12

BLESSEDNESS OF BELIEVERS

In this psalm David ponders the fourfold blessedness of believers. First, *we are under God's wings* (v.7). His mercy is possible because of the blood of Jesus Christ. David refers to the Holy of Holies in the tabernacle, where the Ark of the Covenant held the tables of the Law, with a golden mercy seat over the box. Because he has trusted God, David is in the Holy of Holies and protected by Him (Ps.61:4; 90:1). Christians today are living in the presence of God at the mercy seat.

Second, *we are at His table* (v.8). When the Jews brought their sacrifices, they ate a sacrificial meal. As believers, we share all that God has for us in His house. Are you satisfied with the things of God (Ps.63:1-5)? In the tabernacle were 12 loaves of bread representing the 12 tribes. Today believers are God's priests in His tabernacle and the only ones allowed to eat the bread.

Third, *we are by His river* (v.8). God wants us to live in paradise and drink from His pleasures. Why would the people of God want to imitate the world and try to get their delight from it? Jerusalem was one of the few ancient cities not built beside a river. But God is the River of His people (v.4; John 4:13,14). We shall always have satisfaction for our spiritual thirst.

Fourth, *we are in His light* (v.9). God's light is different from what the world has to offer. If we want to see the lights in this world we need the Light of the World, the Lord Jesus (John 8:12; Ps.119:105). We who have eternal life need not be afraid of the wicked. The wicked keep affirming that they don't fear God and keep flattering themselves. They will fall because of their own sin. Are you living in the wickedness of sinners or in the blessedness of believers?

The believer never should settle for what the world has to offer. Are you living in the presence of God and enjoying His blessings? Remember His mercy is always available to you.

Read Psalm 37:1-4

MEASURE YOURSELF

DAY 85

Psalm 37 begins with a personal and practical admonition: Do not fret. How do we calm a fretful spirit and bring peace to a troubled heart? "Do not fret because of evildoers, nor be envious of the workers of iniquity" (v.1). Why do we envy the wicked? They seem to be prospering; they seem to be so happy. But what do they have that we need? In God we have everything we need. Whenever we find ourselves fretting, it's probably because we are measuring ourselves against others. That's the wrong thing to do. Instead, measure yourself against yourself. You're not competing with others; you're competing with yourself. Also measure yourself against the Lord Jesus Christ, because He is the One you are to be like: "The measure of the stature of the fullness of Christ" (Eph.4:13).

David reminds us: "For they [the wicked] shall soon be cut down like the grass, and wither as the green herb. Trust in the Lord, and do good" (vv.2,3). When you fix your eyes on the Lord and trust and obey Him, that fretful spirit quiets down, and peace comes to your heart. Whenever I stop trusting the Lord for my needs and for His help, my heart becomes heavy and burdened, and then I become fretful and worried. So "trust in the Lord, and do good; dwell in the land, and feed on His faithfulness" (v.3). God takes care of His own.

We find a third admonition. "Delight yourself also in the Lord, and He shall give you the desires of your heart" (v.4). When we delight in the Lord, we learn to appreciate the delights of the Lord. Our desires become His desires, and we pray and live in His will.

Don't fret today. Look to the Lord in faith, trust in Him and delight in Him.

Competing with others and comparing yourself to them can lead to fretting. Measure yourself only against yourself and against Jesus Christ. Consider your needs. Are there any the Lord cannot provide? Place your trust in His provision. He is faithful.

DAY
86

Read Psalm 37:5-7

HE WILL DO IT

"Commit your way to the Lord, trust also in Him, and He shall bring it to pass" (v.5). Bring what to pass? God will bring to pass the thing that does you the most good and that brings Him the most glory. This is a good verse to memorize. No doubt there is something in your life you would like God to do. You've been thinking about it, dreaming about it and praying about it. If God is going to accomplish things *for* us and *in* us and *through* us, we must follow certain instructions.

First, *we must commit our way to the Lord.* This is a definite act of our will. We don't commit it to the Lord and then take it back, anymore than a farmer plants his seed and then keeps digging it up to see if it's growing! Committing our way to the Lord is an act of the will, an act of faith. We make our way His way, and we make His way our way.

Second, *we must trust God.* What does it mean to trust God? It means to believe His promises and to know that He is such a wonderful God that He always can be trusted. We trust people because of their good character or performance. God's character is perfect, and His record is perfect.

Third, *we must wait on the Lord.* When will He act? When He wants to. This is why David adds, "Rest in the Lord, and wait patiently for Him (v.7). Martin Luther translated this, "Be silent to God, and let Him hold thee." I like that. Just rest in the Lord. Wait for Him. He's working in you and on you while He's working for you. Commit trust and wait, and He will bring it to pass.

What would you like to see God do in your life? Start by aligning your will with His. Commit your way to Him, trust Him and wait on Him. God is working for you. In His time He will accomplish His work.

ARE YOU MEEK?

"But the meek shall inherit the earth, and shall delight themselves in the abundance of peace" (v.11). Our Lord echoed this same idea when He said, "Blessed are the meek, for they shall inherit the earth" (Matt.5:5). Meekness is not weakness. Moses was called the meekest man on the face of the earth, yet he boldly stood before Pharaoh and led the children of Israel. At times he had to execute judgment. In the same way, our Lord Jesus said, "I am gentle [meek] and lowly in heart" (Matt.11:29). And Jesus certainly was not weak! One day He took a whip and went through the temple and cleaned house. He was not weak, but He was meek.

Meekness means "power under control." Moses had the power and authority to crush people, but he didn't. He used that power only as God guided him and worked in him. The meek are those who know they have authority and power but keep that power under control. In the New Testament the word translated "meek" also was used in that day to describe a colt that had been broken, its power brought under control.

God can afford to give an inheritance to those who are under control. It's not the proud or arrogant who inherit but the meek—those who say, "Oh, Lord, we want Your will." Too often our fists are clenched. When your fist is clenched, your hand is not open to receive what God wants to give you. What do the meek inherit? The delightful things of the Lord. All God is and has made belongs to the meek.

Meekness indicates strength of character, not weakness. God uses people who exhibit power under control. Are you able to claim the inheritance He promises to those who are meek? Submit to His will and enjoy the spiritual riches you have in Christ Jesus.

DAY

88

Read Psalm 37:16-20

HE KNOWS

When you look at the wicked and see their prosperity, don't fret or do anything foolish. The Lord is on your side, and "If God is for us, who can be against us?" (Rom.8:31). In this passage God gives us all the assurance we need to have peace in our hearts. "A little that a righteous man has is better than the riches of many wicked" (v.16). Here is your first assurance: *God knows how much we need,* and all of His wealth is available to us. What good is it to have a million-dollar house if it's not a home? What good is it to have a huge bank account if our values are not right? David is telling us that it's better to have a little and have God (because then we have everything) than to have much and not have God.

Our second assurance is that *God knows how much we can take.* "For the arms of the wicked shall be broken, but the Lord upholds the righteous" (v.17). He knows how great a burden we can bear, how fierce a battle we can fight. When God puts us in the furnace, He always keeps His eye on the clock and His hand on the thermostat.

Third, *God knows the days that we will live.* "The Lord knows the days of the upright, and their inheritance shall be forever" (v.18). He has a plan for your life. That sounds like a Christian cliche, but it's true. Whenever we've gone on trips, I am assured to know that the tour guide knows where he's going and what he's doing. I can just sit back and let him do the driving and the worrying. That's how God wants us to live. He wants us to leave everything with Him, because He knows how much we need, how much we can take and what will happen each day. Don't worry; live a day at a time. God's Word is clear, "As your days, so shall your strength be" (Deut.33:25).

Take comfort in knowing that God is intimately aware of your needs. He knows what you need and what your limits are. Do you have pressing needs? Leave them with Him. Trust Him to provide them and resist the urge to look ahead and worry. Concentrate on what God is doing for you today.

Read Psalm 37:21,22

BORROWING OR INHERITING?

DAY 89

Someone has said that when your outgo exceeds your income, then your upkeep is your downfall. David may have had that idea in mind when he wrote this passage. He is talking about two different attitudes toward life: *How much can I give?* and *How much can I get?*

Nothing is wrong with an honest debt or a loan. In fact, the Lord Jesus, in the parable of the pounds and the parable of the talents, talks about putting money in the bank and investing money and receiving interest. These verses say, however, that the wicked go through life depending on others by borrowing from them. They borrow their joy and their strength. But believers go through life inheriting. "For those blessed by Him shall inherit the earth" (v.22). Because we are children of God, we are in His will. He's written our names into His last will and testament. Jesus Christ died on the cross to probate His own will. Now we are living on that inheritance.

Are you going through life borrowing? Do you have to borrow happiness, wisdom and joy? Or are you going through life inheriting—drawing from that marvelous spiritual account in the Lord Jesus Christ? The wicked go through life thinking only of getting, but God's people go through life thinking of giving, of sharing with others and of showing mercy.

God has blessed us. We have inherited everything through His Son. No matter what you're facing today, don't be afraid or alarmed. He has everything you need to live a happy, holy and victorious life. Don't go through life borrowing. Draw on His inheritance.

In Christ Jesus you have everything you need. God has given you a spiritual inheritance you can draw from. You need not depend on others for your spiritual resources. Instead, confidently depend on God for your strength and resources.

DAY

90

Read Psalm 37:23, 24

STEPS AND STOPS

I like these verses because they give us three exciting assurances as we go through each day with the Lord. First, *God directs us in the best way.* The steps of a good man or a good woman are ordered by the Lord. David isn't talking about fate or chance. He isn't saying that life is a rigid machine. But he does say, "Your Father in heaven is watching you. He has planned a wonderful day for you. You may not understand all that He has planned, but everything is in His hands." Romans 8:28 tells us that "all things work together for good to those who love God."

Second, *God delights in us as we obey Him.* Just as human fathers experience delight when their children obey them, so our Father in heaven enjoys delight when we obey Him. "This is My beloved Son, in whom I am well pleased" (Matt.3:17). That's what God the Father said about God the Son, and I want Him to say the same about me. At the close of the day, I want to be able to come to my Father and hear Him say, "Today you've been a good son. You have delighted My heart."

Third, *God delivers us when we stumble.* "He restores my soul" (Ps.23:3). He upholds and lifts us up, so we don't have to be afraid of stumbling. Sometimes we do stumble on the path of life, but our steps are ordered by the Lord, and He observes our stops. He knows when you've stumbled, and He's right there to pick you up and get you started again. Stay close to Him, for He guides and guards your path.

God promises to guide you through life, and He gives assurances that you may depend on daily. Be encouraged that your life is not left to chance. Does God delight in you as an obedient son or daughter? Remember, your Father is ready to guide and protect you.

Read Psalm 37:25-29

CAN YOU BELIEVE IT?

DAY 91

We see and hear all kinds of testimonials from famous people in advertising today. Quite frankly, I don't put much faith in what these celebrities say. What do football players really know about automobile tires? What do actors or actresses know about computers? We know they are used in ads to lend the authority of their name to the product. When we hear a testimonial, we'd better find out who said it, what was said and if we can really believe it.

We find a testimonial in verse 25: "I have been young, and now am old; yet I have not seen the righteous forsaken, nor his, descendants begging bread." Let's ask three questions. First, *who said it?* David did. Think of him as a young shepherd taking care of his sheep, God gave him strength to overcome the lion, strength to defeat the bear and strength to overcome the giant, Goliath; As a shepherd, David saw God take care of His own. Think of David the soldier, David the king or even David the sweet singer of Israel. Oh, David knew that he was talking about. God took care of him at each stage in His life. Even David the sinner saw God provide for him.

Second, *what did David say?* "I have been young, and now I'm old; but I've never seen God forsake His own." He didn't say, "I've never seen the righteous go through trouble. I've never seen God's people suffer sorrow or affliction." David knew a great deal about sorrow, affliction, tears and trials. What he did say was this: "I have never seen one of God's children left alone." God has been faithful through the years. We don't have to be afraid of being young or getting old, because He remains with us.

Third, *can we claim this for ourselves?* Yes, we can. Jesus said, "I will never leave you nor forsake you" (Heb.13:5). He also said, "Lo, I am with you always, even to the end of the age" (Matt.28:20). You can trust His Word.

God always is faithful to His people. The history of Israel confirms His faithfulness. That He will never leave you nor forsake you is a great promise. And you can expect Him to keep His promises. Have you claimed the promises of God's Word and experienced His faithfulness?

Read Psalm 37:30-34

SAY "AH"

Visiting the doctor for an annual checkup is necessary. God, too, is concerned about us and wants to give us a spiritual checkup once in a while. My doctor says, "Open your mouth. Stick out your tongue." Then he wants to listen to my heart. He even looks at my feet. David refers to a similar examination in these verses.

God is concerned about your *mouth.* "The mouth of the righteous speaks wisdom, and his tongue talks of justice" (v.30). What do you talk about? If God were to say to you, "Open your mouth and stick out your tongue," what would He find out about you? I hope He wouldn't discover that you are being deceitful or are speaking defiling words. It's amazing what a doctor can discover by examining the tongue. It's also amazing what God can discover about us—and what we can discover about ourselves! The Word of God needs to be on our lips.

God also is concerned about your *heart.* "The law of his God is in his heart" (v.31). When God listens to your heart, does He hear His Word? When God's Law is in your heart, He can do something through you and in you and for you. "But his delight is in the law of the Lord, and in His law he meditates day and night" (Ps.1:2). What's in your heart will determine what's on your lips. If the truth of God is in your heart, then the Word of God will be on your lips.

God also is concerned about your *feet.* "None of his steps shall slide" (v.31). The righteous person doesn't backslide; his feet are walking on the right path because his heart is filled with God's truth. He's also not ashamed to tell that truth through his lips. He has a testimony and a witness for the Lord.

Taking care of the heart is the most important thing we can do. "Keep your heart with all diligence, for out of it spring the issues of life" (Prov.4:23). If our heart is right with God, our lips and our feet will be what He wants them to be.

Have you had a spiritual checkup lately? You can remain healthy by keeping the Word of God in your heart. That truth will spread to the other parts of your body. Do you glorify God with your mouth, feet and heart?

Read Psalm 37:35-40

YOUR ROOTS

DAY **93**

As David finished Psalm 37, he described two different kinds of people and what would happen to them. First, he described the *powerful.* "I have seen the wicked in great power, and spreading himself like a native green tree. Yet he passed away, and behold, he was no more; indeed I sought him, but he could not be found" (vv.35,36). The powerful are rooted in this world. They are like a tree that looks strong and stable. One day a storm comes and blows the tree over. It is then cut up for kindling and is gone. The most important part of a tree is its root system.

If you are rooted in this world, you have no security, for everything here is temporary. But if you are rooted in the Lord Jesus Christ, you have the permanence of eternity upon your life. Don't envy the powerful or those whose names are blazoned abroad. Don't worry about what happens to this crowd. God tells us what happens: They could not be found; they're gone. But "he who does the will of God abides forever" (I John 2:17). That's why it's important to live for the Lord today.

Second, David described the *perfect man* or *woman.* "Mark the blameless man, and observe the upright; for the future of that man is peace" (Ps.37:37). The future of the powerful person is destruction; the future of the perfect person is peace. The word *perfect* doesn't mean "sinless." Nobody is sinless. Instead, David meant the sincere person, the wholehearted person, the person who practices Matthew 6:33: "But seek first the kingdom of God and His righteousness, and all these things shall be added to you."

When we are perfect in Christ, accepted in the Beloved One, we have peace, we have strength, and we have God's salvation. "And the Lord shall help them and deliver them; He shall deliver them from the wicked, and save them, because they trust in Him" (Ps.37:40). Today, don't walk by sight, looking at the native green tree. Walk by faith. Be perfect in the Lord, and He'll bless you.

Our spiritual root system is important to our spiritual well-being. Where we send our roots will determine which resources we will draw from. Are you rooted in the world or in Jesus Christ? Are you living by faith or sight? Trust in the resources you have in Christ and grow in His grace.

DAY

94

Read Psalm 38:1-8

SAYING NO

Nobody can deny there is pleasure in sin. If there were no pleasure in sin, nobody would fall into temptation. The Bible speaks about the pleasures of sin for a season. What season? The season of sowing. The pleasure of sin comes when we sow, but the pain comes when we reap. This is why David gave such a vivid description in Psalm 38 of what we suffer when we sin. "O Lord, do not rebuke me in Your wrath, nor chasten me in Your hot displeasure!" (v.1). He went on to say that God's arrows were piercing him and His hand was pressing down on him. All of his bones hurt. His iniquities had gone over his head as if he were drowning in a sea of sin. "My wounds are foul and festering," David said. "I am troubled, I am bowed down greatly; I go mourning all the day long" (vv.5, 6).

Why did God put this description in the Bible? Why does David compare the consequences of sin to being pierced by arrows, being pressed by His hand, sickness, a heavy burden, drowning, smothering and no peace? Because God wants us to hate sin. If for no other reason, the consequences of sin ought to warn us against sinning. The next time you're tempted, look past the pleasure to the pain and learn to say no. Remember what David says in this Psalm. You say, "I'm a Christian. I can sin." No, you can't, because you'll reap the same consequences. God chastens His own, for He wants us to walk in holiness.

Let's encourage other people to say no. Let's live in such a way that we don't encourage other people to sin. Also, let's have sympathy for those who have fallen. It's sad to reap the consequences of sin—even forgiven sin. David knew that. So let's encourage others and try to restore them. Let's also love the Lord more. Why? Because He went through all of these consequences on the cross for us. He felt the burden. He felt the arrows. And He did it so that we could be forgiven.

David greatly suffered for his sin. Those who sin reap its consequences. God wants us to hate sin for what it can do to us and for what it did to His Son. If you are harboring unconfessed sin in your life, confess it and ask for God's forgiveness. Next time you're tempted to sin, remember David's description of the consequences.

DON'T GIVE UP

Christians are not supposed to sin. But if we do sin, we are not to give up. David had sinned, and now he was paying for his sin! He had sown the seeds of sin, and now he was reaping the terrible harvest. But he didn't give up.

Let's remember that though our friends may forsake us, and though the Enemy may attack us, God never gives up on His children. David said, "My loved ones and my friends stand aloof from my plague, and my relatives stand afar off" (v.11). Sometimes when we've disobeyed the Lord, even our closest friends and our nearest and dearest relatives are of no help to us. Sometimes we're ashamed to tell them what's happened. But even when they do know, they often avoid us.

And when we sin, the Enemy wants to fight us. He is always waiting for an opportunity. "Those also who seek my life lay snares for me" (v.12). You would think that after we've succumbed to temptation, the Devil would leave us alone. No, he knows that we're weak and discouraged, so he lays even more snares for us.

But God sees the heart. "Lord, all my desire is before You; and my sighing is not hidden from You" (v.9). He also hears your cry. "For in You, O Lord, I hope; You will hear, O Lord my God" (v.15). What will God hear? He will hear our prayer of confession and repentance. "If we confess our sins, He is faithful and just to forgive us our sins and to cleanse us from all unrighteousness" (I John 1:9). God in His government must allow us to reap what we sow. But in His grace He forgives us and cleanses us. Reaping the consequences of sin is one thing; experiencing His judgment for sin is quite something else. Don't give up if you've stumbled and fallen. God sees your heart and hears your cry. He will forgive and restore you.

Although God requires that we reap the consequences of our sin, He loves us and wants to restore us to fellowship. Don't allow Satan to rob you of God's grace. He forgives, cleanses and restores. Have you stumbled? Confess your sin and repent. He is faithful to forgive.

DAY
96

Read Psalm 38:17-22

PLAYING INTO SATAN'S HANDS

"For I am ready to fall, and my sorrow is continually before me" (v.17). David was ready to quit. David, the great conqueror and disciplined soldier, the one who killed Goliath, was ready to quit. He had sinned against the Lord, and he was suffering for it. Even his friends were against him. Let's learn some lessons from David to avoid his experience.

Don't give up. Satan is so subtle and mean. When his tempting you, he whispers in your ear, "You can get away with this." Then after you've sinned, he sneers, "You'll never get away with this. You're done for." Satan wants us to give up, but if we do, we're playing right into his hands. We're denying that God can help us and forgetting that we belong to Him. What earthly father would forsake his child when he stumbles? Instead, that father reaches down in love, picks up his child, comforts him, cleanses his wounds and helps him walk again. If you sin, don't give in to your feelings, don't watch people around you and don't listen to the Devil.

Confess your sin. "For I will declare my iniquity; I will be in anguish over my sin" (v.18). David didn't say, "I will be sorry that I'm suffering for my sin" or, "I will be sorry for the consequences." He said, "I'm sorry I have sinned."

Trust in the Lord. "Do not forsake me, O Lord; O my God, be not far from me! Make haste to help me, O Lord, my salvation!" (vv.21, 22). God is not going to forsake you. He cannot forsake you—He owns you, He purchased you, He made you, and He lives in you. Let Him draw near and restore you again.

After you've stumbled into sin, you are vulnerable—both to your feelings and to the Devil. You must claim the truth of God's Word and not give in to your feelings or listen to the Devil. Instead, confess your sin to a loving Father and trust Him to restore you to fellowship.

Read Psalm 39:1-6

NO EXCUSES

DAY **97**

"I was mute with silence, I held my peace" (v.2). Usually David was singing a song or giving an order or rejoicing in the Lord, but now he is silent. Why? Because God had rebuked him for a sin he had committed, and he knew better than to argue with God. Sometimes when we sin, we want to argue. We make excuses instead of confessions. We give reasons for not escaping the temptation. But David didn't do that. He was silent.

But as he meditated, something stirred within his heart. "My heart was hot within me; while I was musing, the fire burned. Then I spoke with my tongue: 'Lord, make me to know my end, and what is the measure of my days, that I may know how frail I am. Indeed, You have made my days as handbreadths, and my age is as nothing before You; certainly every man at his best state is but vapor'" (vv.3-5). As David mused and meditated, he learned two lessons.

First, he learned about the *brevity of life.* Verse 6 reads, "Surely every man walks about like a shadow; surely they busy themselves in vain." This means that they are disquieted in vain; they're merely walking in a performance. David says, "I don't know how long this performance is going to last. My life is a handbreadth." Life's brevity ought to warn us not to waste our lives sinning.

Second, David learned about the *frailty of man.* "Help me to know how frail I am" (v.4). He is telling us, "It's not the length of life that counts—it's the depth of life." It's not important how strong we are in ourselves but how strong we are in God. What counts is that we are investing our lives in eternal things.

Don't argue with God. Don't come with excuses. Rather, come and say, "Lord, make my life count."

Life is short, so why devote precious time to sin and its destructive power? Invest your life in the eternal things of God. Draw your daily strength from Him. When you sin, confess it right away and get back to investing your life for God's glory.

Read Psalm 39:7-13

A LIVING HOPE

David asked, "And now, Lord, what do I wait for? My hope is in You" (v.7). That's a good question. What are you waiting for? And how can you be sure that what you're waiting for is going to come?

David said his hope was in the Lord. Biblical *hope* means confidence in the future. It's a confidence born of faith. Faith, hope and love go together (I Cor.13). When we have faith in God, we claim His promises, and they give us hope for the future. Hope for the Christian is not a feeling of "I hope it's going to happen." It's exciting expectancy because God controls the future. When Jesus Christ is your Savior and your Lord, the future is your friend. You don't have to worry.

Why is this hope so important? When we lose hope, we lose joy in the present because we have no confidence for the future. I have been in hospital rooms when the surgeon has walked in and said to a patient's loved ones, "I'm sorry. We did the best we could. There is no hope." The faces of the loved ones fall. Sadness fills the room. We live on hope; it springs eternal in the human breast. But it's more than a feeling down inside; it's a confidence that God is in control, and we have nothing to fear.

What is the basis for our hope? It is the character of God. We've been born again unto a living hope (I Pet.1:3). It's not a dead hope that rots and falls apart but a living hope whose roots go deeper and whose fruits grow more wonderful. You can have joy, confidence, encouragement and excitement today if you will remember that you have a living hope.

Your hope for the future is founded in the promises of God's Word. Do you have confidence in the future? Make a mental list of His provision on your behalf during the past year—answered prayers, met needs and other blessings. God's faithfulness in keeping His promises in the past gives you confident hope for the future.

Read Psalm 40:1-3

DAY 99

FROM MIRE TO CHOIR

When we wait *for* the Lord and wait *on* Him, we aren't being idle. In this psalm David cries out to the Lord and asks for help. "He also brought me up out of a horrible pit, out of the miry clay, and set my feet upon a rock, and established my steps" (v.2). Waiting on the Lord is worthwhile because of what He is going to do for us. It is not idleness, nor is it carelessness. And it certainly isn't complacency. Instead, waiting is that divine activity of expecting God to work. And He never disappoints us.

Figuratively, David had been down in a horrible pit. He was sinking in the mire. But he waited on the Lord. And God not only pulled him out of the pit, but He put him on a rock and established his footing. He said, "David, I'm going to take you out of the mire and put you in the choir." "He has put a new song in my mouth—praise to our God" (v.3).

Are you waiting on the Lord? Are you praying about something and asking, "O God, when are You going to do this? When are you going to work?" Remember, one of these days your praying will turn to singing. Your sinking will turn to standing. Your fear will turn to security as He puts you on the rock. Just wait on the Lord. He's patient with you. Why not be patient with Him and let Him work in His time?

Waiting for the Lord's help sometimes forces you to your limits. But take comfort in knowing that while you wait on Him, God is working out His purposes in your life. Are you in a difficult situation, waiting for God to do something? Leave your burden with the Lord and trust Him to act. He never disappoints you when you wait on Him.

DAY 100

Read Psalm 40:4, 5

A NEW PERSPECTIVE

What are the blessings that come to us when we make the Lord our trust? First, we start seeing life through His eyes. Look at verse 4: "Blessed is that man who . . . does not respect the proud, nor such as turn aside to lies." When we walk by faith, we have God's discernment. We see the world more clearly. But that's not all.

We also start appreciating God's works. "Many, O Lord my God, are Your wonderful works which You have done" (v.5). He is always at work for us. Romans 8:28 is true: "All things work together for good to those who love God, to those who are the called according to His purpose."

Verse 5 continues, "And Your thoughts toward us cannot be recounted to You in order; if I would declare and speak of them, they are more than can be numbered." Not only do we start seeing and admiring God's works, but also we start enjoying His Word and contemplating His thoughts. When we trust the Lord, His Word becomes precious to us, because "faith comes by hearing, and hearing by the word of God" (Rom.10:17).

Don't trust yourself or your circumstances; trust the Lord. When you roll all your burdens onto Him, you gain a new perspective. You see life through His eyes, you appreciate His works, and you enjoy His Word. Is the Lord your Trust today?

Read Psalm 40:6-8

THE HEART OF THE MATTER

DAY 101

"I delight to do Your will, O my God, and Your law is within my heart" (v.8). Ponder that statement. The will of God is not something we do; it's something we *enjoy and delight* in. His will is the expression of His love. He doesn't declare things and do things because He hates us but because He loves us. We may not always understand His ways. Sometimes we may even think that God has forsaken us. But we should love His will. If our hearts are delighting in His will, then we are close to His heart.

God's Word reveals His will. When the Word of God is in our hearts, then the will of God is in our hearts, and we obey Him wholeheartedly. Paul wrote about this in Ephesians 6:6: "Doing the will of God from the heart." It's possible to follow God from the will only: we can be drudges or obedient slaves, performing a duty. Or we can be children who obey out of love for our Father.

The result is that we delight in God's will. Indeed, the heart of the matter is our heart.

Because God's will originates in His heart, we can respond to it emotionally—we can love it. Are you in touch with His will? Do you delight in it? Place the Law in your heart so you may know the will of God and obey it.

DAY 102

Read Psalm 40:9-17

Who's Thinking ABOUT YOU?

A little boy asked his father, "Dad, what does God think about?" Now that is a profound question. After all, if God knows everything—past, present and future—what does He have to think about? According, to verse 17, He thinks about you and me. "But I am poor and needy," David said, "yet the Lord thinks upon me."

God thinks about us *personally*. He doesn't have to be told about us. He doesn't have to send a committee of angels to investigate our feelings, problems, frustrations or needs. God knows us personally and He knows our names. It always encourages me to read in the Bible that God calls His people by name. He knows us better than our closest friends or loved ones do. He knows our needs and what's bothering us today.

God thinks about us *lovingly*. He doesn't think thoughts of evil about us. He is not a policeman looking to arrest us. No, our Father in heaven thinks about us lovingly, the way a father and a mother think about their children.

God thinks about us *wisely*. He has a perfect plan for our lives. David said, "The Lord will perfect that which concerns me" (Ps.138:8). He'll do that today. We don't see all the pieces and how they fit together, but our Father does, and that's all that matters.

Nothing is hidden from the eyes of God. Being out of His will can be a great source of conviction and fear. He knows where your sin will lead you. So walk with the Lord. Say, "Thank You, Father, for thinking about me. I'm going to think about You."

God knows you intimately. He knows not only your name but your every need. He knows what is best for you and always does what is right. You are always on God's mind. Is He on your mind? Determine to know Him more intimately.

Read Psalm 41:1-13

DAY 103

How Is
YOUR CHARACTER?

When was the last time you heard a preacher or Sunday school teacher talk about integrity? I hope it's been recently, because integrity is an important part of the Christian life. To have integrity means to have character. Integrity is the opposite of duplicity. A person who practices duplicity is a hypocrite, a pretender. Integrity means to have one heart and one mind and to serve one master. It means not being divided, not always changing.

David wrote, "As for me, You uphold me in my integrity, and set me before Your face forever" (v.12). God knows us by our character, whereas people judge us by our conduct. When we become more worried about conduct than about character, our conduct starts to go down the wrong road. Conduct and reputation are closely related, but neither one guarantees good character. For example, the Pharisees had a great reputation, but their character was evil. God sees us. He knows all about us, and He says, "Put Me first in your life."

Not only does God see us, we also see Him. "Set me before Your face forever" (v.12). That is what gives us integrity: knowing that we're walking, living, thinking and speaking before the face of God. When we fear Him, we don't have to fear anything else. And when we walk in integrity and honesty, when we flee duplicity and hypocrisy, we can face anything. David was able to face all his foes because he had integrity. He prayed, "Unite my heart to fear Your name" (Ps.86:11). Integrity unites, so it helps us put our lives together.

Today, let's walk in integrity before the face of God.

Don't be so concerned with your reputation and conduct that you fail to look after your character, because you cannot hide that from God. How is your character? Are you unified—do you have one heart and one mind to serve one Master?

DAY

104

Read Psalm 42:1-11

ARE YOU DOWN?

Twice in Psalm 42 the writer asks: "Why are you cast down, O my soul? And why are you disquieted within me?" (vv.5, 11). Perhaps you have asked the same thing. Why do we have hours, sometimes days, perhaps weeks of depression and discouragement? There may be times when we are not at our best physically. I think of Elijah, who had that difficult experience on Mount Carmel when he battled the prophets of Baal and God sent fire from heaven. When it was over, he was tired. His nerves had been stretched to the breaking point, and he got discouraged and ran away. He needed food and sleep, so God sent an angel to feed him and give him rest.

Sometimes our depression is satanic. The Enemy is throwing darts at us. And instead of holding up the shield of faith, we fail to trust God. Those darts then start fires of depression and discouragement in our lives. Sometimes our depression comes from guilt because of unconfessed sin. Sometimes it's just sorrow because of circumstances. We may have lost a loved one or a friend. Sometimes we feel that we have failed and that everything has come to an end.

What's the cure for all of this? "Hope in God, for I shall yet praise Him for the help of His countenance" (v.5). You have a secure future in Jesus Christ. The best is yet to come. Hope in God and start praising Him. The psalmist said, "I shall yet praise Him." But don't wait! Start praising Him now. I've discovered that when I get discouraged, the best thing to do is praise the Lord immediately. Praise is the greatest medicine for a broken heart. The psalmist praised God for "the help of His countenance." No matter how you feel or whatever your circumstances, if you'll look to the face of God, you'll discover that He's smiling on you.

How do you cope with discouragement? Certainly, if it is caused by guilt from unconfessed sin, you need to repent and ask forgiveness. Generally, the cure for being down is to hope in God and praise Him. Your hope in Him is well founded, for He is ever faithful to His Word. Are you discouraged? You may not be able to change your circumstances, but you can praise God.

Read Psalm 43:1-5

GUIDE AND GUARD

DAY **105**

We all have days when we feel as though God has forsaken us, when it seems as if the Enemy is winning and we are losing. On such a day the psalmist prayed, "Oh, send out Your light and Your truth!" (v.3). These words represent the deep desire of the psalmist to know and do the will of God. He was not having an easy time.

I like the words *light* and *truth.* We live in a world smothered in moral and spiritual darkness. "Everyone practicing evil hates the light and does not come to the light" (John 3:20). Not only is our world dark, but it's also deceived. People love and believe lies. Mark Twain used to say that a lie runs around the world while truth is putting on her boots! But we have God's light and truth to guide and guard us. We must pray, "oh, send out Your light and Your truth!"

Where do we find God's light and truth? In His Word. "Your word is a lamp to my feet and a light to my path" (Ps.119:105). God's Word is truth. "Sanctify them by Your truth. Your word is truth," Jesus said (John 17:17). The Word of God guides His children on the path He has chosen. And that path ultimately leads to Him. "Let them [light and truth] bring me to Your holy hill and to Your tabernacle" (v.3). The psalmist is talking about the location of the tabernacle, the house of God. When we are in the will of God, it's as though we are dwelling in His house.

You live in a dark and deceived world. But God has promised to guide and guard you through His Word. The Bible is a spiritual treasure, and without it, you soon lose your way and become vulnerable. Do you feed daily on the truth of His Word? If not, begin a program of daily meditation in Scripture.

DAY

106

Read Psalm 42-43

OUT FROM THE DEPTHS

The next time you feel like quitting, read these chapters. The psalmist presents contrasts that depict the ups and downs of life. First, he contrasts *the desert and the temple* (42:1-4). He is thirsting for God. In fact, he is so thirsty he is using his tears as food. We, too, have spiritual senses: taste, hearing and sight. When your soul is thirsting for the living God, you won't be satisfied with substitutes. Don't feed on your feelings, because you will poison yourself.

The psalmist then reminisces about the temple. There's nothing wrong with memories as long as you don't live in the past. They can either encourage or discourage. Let them be a rudder to guide you and not an anchor to hold you back. We find the answer to the psalmist's grief in 42:5. So often we mourn because we want to, but this verse tells us to hope in God.

Second, he contrasts *the heights and the depths* (42:6,7). The psalmist goes through a range of emotions—from the mountaintop to the valley. And then the waves roll over him. Have you ever felt as if you were drowning? Jesus went through a similar experience (Matt.20:22). When you pray, be honest with God and tell Him how you really feel. Remember that Jesus knows exactly how you feel, and He understands every experience of life.

Third, the psalmist contrasts *day and night* (42:8). This is the central verse of Psalms 42 and 43. Sometimes we're in the darkness because of sin, but this psalmist is in darkness because he's going through a difficult time. We all have those times. God commands the daytime and nighttime (Job 35:10) and gives songs in the night (Acts 16:25). Remember to look not at yourself but to God. Hope in Him, and He will help you.

The contrasts of this passage show that life has its range of experiences. You can expect to have dark days and, at times, to find yourself in the depths. Be encouraged that Jesus understands how you feel. Are you going through a dark time? Remember God's help in the past. He will be just as faithful in helping you now. Tune your spiritual senses to Him and hope in Him.

WHAT A HISTORY!

The older we get, the more we are inclined to start talking about "the good old days." The writer of this psalm must have been listening to such a discussion, because he writes, "We have heard with our ears, O God, our fathers have told us, the deeds You did in their days, in days of old" (v.1).

Then he describes how God had driven out other nations and planted the nation of Israel. When Jewish people reviewed their history, they reviewed one miracle after another: the deliverance from Egypt, the opening of the Red Sea, the path through the wilderness, victories over great armies, the opening of the Jordan River and the conquering of the Holy Land. What a history!

Good days are not only *old*. We can have good *new* days as well. Yes, God did do some great things for Israel. We must always remember His mighty works. That includes the great things He has done for His Church, such as in the Book of Acts. And He is still doing great things for His people today. When you have a discouraging day and everything seems to be going wrong, just sit and meditate on what God has already done for you. It will lift your heart in praise and adoration.

The psalmist said, "You are my King, O God" (v.4). When God is our King, the same power to perform miracles that was available to Moses and Joshua and David is available to us. "You are my King, O God; command victories for Jacob. Through You we will push down our enemies; . . . You have saved us from our enemies" (vv.4,5,7). Don't live only on the memories of the good old days. God's promises are still valid. Trust Him today and make Him your King.

Israel's history is a track record of God's faithfulness. The same God who worked miracles for Israel is still doing great things for His people today. Are you longing for the good old days? Don't live on nostalgia; trust God to do new works in your life.

Read Psalm 44:9-16

WHERE'S THE VICTORY?

Israel in its early days recorded one victory after another. God delivered Israel from Egypt. He then took the Israelites through the terrible wilderness and brought them victoriously into the Promised Land. And there they defeated nation after nation.

But the writer of this psalm is concerned that the people of God are no longer experiencing victories. "But You have cast us off and put us to shame, and You do not go out with our armies. You make us turn back from the enemy, and those who hate us have taken spoil for themselves" (vv.9,10). The psalmist is confused. Why isn't God doing for them now what He had done for His people centuries ago? The author describes the people as sheep being slaughtered, and those that aren't slaughtered are scattered. The people are being sold like commodities on the market. "You make us a reproach to our neighbors, a scorn and a derision to those all around us" (v.13).

Why did this happen? Because God's people had rebelled against Him. They would not listen to His Word nor heed the message of the prophets. For 40 years Jeremiah had pleaded with the people to repent. Oh, they had religion. The temple was filled with activity: more people were attending services, and more sacrifices were being offered. It was tremendously successful, but it was not genuine worship. The Israelites turned the house of God into a den of thieves when it should have been a temple of prayer. And because they rebelled, God had to chasten them. But He also restored them.

When we rebel against God, He will forgive, but He must chasten us. We must reap what we sow. "You have cast us off" (v.9)—but not forever. "You make us a byword among the nations" (v.14)—but not forever. God restored His people, and He can restore us.

When you fail to listen to God's Word, the Enemy tries to entice you with lies. Soon you find yourself in sin and rebelling against God, and then He must chasten you. Stay victorious in life. Feed on the truth of God's Word and stay in close fellowship with Him.

Read Psalm 44:17-26

IS GOD ASLEEP?

DAY 109

Have you ever thought that God is asleep? Maybe it seems He isn't concerned about your problems and difficulties. Or perhaps you feel He isn't listening to your prayers. The writer of Psalm 44 had a similar feeling in his difficult situation. He writes: "Awake! Why do You sleep, O Lord? Arise! Do not cast us off forever. Why do You hide Your face, and forget our affliction and our oppression? . . . Arise for our help" (vv.23,24,26).

God does not sleep! How we feel doesn't necessarily reflect what is true. Psalm 121:4 says that He who keeps Israel does not slumber or sleep. God is eternally vigilant and eternally alert. Our mothers learned how to sleep with one ear open. When we cried out, they were right there to help us. But God doesn't sleep at all, so both of His ears are open. "The eyes of the Lord are on the righteous, and His ears are open to their cry" (Ps.34:15).

God is awake, and He is mindful of our needs. Then why doesn't He do something? He always waits to do His will at a time when it will do us the most good and bring Him the most glory. The delays of God are not denials.

Because His timing is perfect, we must wait, trust and not complain. It's easy to complain, but we need to wait in silence before the Lord. And praise Him, because one day you will look back and understand why you had to wait.

God is ever mindful of your needs, and He will act when it will do the most good. His delays are preparation. Are you waiting for Him to answer your cry? Trust in Him and wait patiently. He will answer you.

Read Psalm 45:1-5

RIDING IN MAJESTY

We often think of Jesus as gentle, meek and mild. He was that, of course. "I am gentle and lowly in heart" (Matt.11:29) is what He said in His invitation to us. But the Lord is also a conqueror. The psalmist said about Him: "Gird Your sword upon Your thigh, O Mighty One, with Your glory and Your majesty. And in Your majesty ride prosperously because of truth, humility and righteousness" (vv.3,4). That doesn't sound like the meek and gentle carpenter of Nazareth!

Have you ever considered Christ as Conqueror? So often we view Jesus only through the four Gospels, where we find Him a Servant. We see Him as a humble man, the Servant of God, ministering to people. But here we read about a Conqueror with a sword who is riding in majesty. On the cross, Jesus completely defeated Satan. He also overcame the world. He said to His disciples, "Be of good cheer, I have overcome the world" (John 16:33). And He certainly overcame the flesh. Christians are identified with His victory. We have crucified the flesh (Gal.2:20). We have been raised to walk in newness of life (Rom.6:4). And Christ wants to give us victory today.

But first, *we must want victory.* Some people would rather walk on the margin of the battlefield and be a walking victim instead of a marching victor. So examine your heart and say, "Lord, I want victory today."

Second, *we must yield ourselves to Christ.* We don't fight for victory; we fight *from* victory. The simple secret of winning in the Christian life is to identify ourselves with Christ, trust Him and follow Him. We'll have battles to fight, to be sure, and sometimes we might stumble and fall. But keep in mind that Christ is riding in majesty. Why don't you ride right along with Him by faith?

Jesus has conquered life, and we may stand with Him in victory. Before we can, though, we must want victory, and we must yield ourselves to Him. Are you a conqueror? By faith identify with Christ and share His victory.

Read Psalm 45:6-12

A RIGHTEOUS THRONE

DAY 111

Whenever things are shaky around you, whenever you are afraid, just remember that God is on His righteous throne, which He deserves. It was not given to Him. He didn't purchase it. He didn't have to conquer kingdoms to get it. Our eternal God is on His eternal throne. "Your throne, O God, is forever and ever."

Many rulers in history thought their thrones would endure forever. But those thrones were toppled. In fact, we have to search through history books just to find the names of long-forgotten kings and queens. Not so with Jesus Christ. His throne is not ruined by the ravages of time. It is eternal and righteous, and it can never be over-thrown by the attacks of men. Whatever our Lord does is right. He never rules unjustly, and He never causes evil. His scepter is righteous.

To fight against the throne of God is foolish, because that is fighting against something eternal, righteous and holy. God wants to rule in our lives. That's why it's important for us to bow before Him and say, "I crown You King of my life. You shall receive the glory." Let the eternal throne of God rule in your life today.

Have you recognized God's authority and rule in your life? One day, every knee shall bow before Him (Phil.2:10). Do you know Jesus as your Lord of lords and King of kings? If not, bow before Him now and allow Him to rule in your life.

DAY

112

Read Psalm 45:13-17

BEAUTY WITHIN

Psalm 45 is a wedding psalm. It says this about the bride: "The king's daughter is all glorious within: her clothing is of wrought gold" (v.13, KJV). Often after a wedding someone will ask, "What did the bride wear?" Her gown draws everyone's attention. But notice what the bride wore at this wedding. "The king's daughter is all glorious within: her clothing is of wrought gold." It's not important what we wear on the outside, but it is important what we wear on the inside. Jesus Christ wants His Bride, His people, to be beautiful within.

We are married to Jesus Christ—not because we loved Him, but because He loved us. Before we ever thought about Him, He thought about us. In His love He purchased us and came to us. When I perform a marriage ceremony, I don't ask the bride and groom, "Do you know each other?" or "Do you think about each other?" The question is, "Will you commit your lives to each other?" In the same way, trusting Christ for salvation is an act of the will. It's not enough to think about Jesus Christ or know Him intellectually. We must say, "I will trust Him." In the Book of Revelation we read, "Whosoever desires, let him take the water of life freely" (22:17).

Yes, you belong to Jesus Christ, and your true beauty ought to be within. And, if it is within, it's going to come out through your life. The Christian life is a wedding, not a funeral. Don't wear the sorrowful clothes of a mourner, for Christ has clothed you with beauty—the gold of His righteousness. Enjoy the wedding today!

Christians are the Bride of Jesus Christ. He purchased you with His love and clothed you with righteousness. Are you committed and yielded to Jesus Christ? Do you love Him and trust Him? Renew your commitment to Him daily, so you may grow and enjoy Him.

HELP IN TIGHT PLACES

"God is our refuge and strength, a very present help in trouble" (v.1). This assurance from the Lord ought to take care of all of our fears and problems. God is our refuge—He hides us. God is our strength—He helps us. These two go together. At times in our lives we need a refuge. The storm is blowing and the battle is raging, and we have to run somewhere to hide. It's not a sin to hide, but it *is* a sin to stay hidden. God hides us so that He can help us. Then we can return to the battle and face the storm. This is not escape but rejuvenation.

The Old Testament contains 21 different Hebrew words for trouble. Here the word *trouble* means "in tight places." If you are in a tight place today, let me suggest that you run by faith to Jesus. But don't go to Him to escape. Go there and tell Him, "Lord, I want to go back to the battle. I want to go back to my work. I want to carry the burdens of life, but you have to give me the strength." Then you can claim this marvelous promise of verse 1.

Notice the conclusion: "Therefore we will not fear" (v.2). When God is available as your refuge and your strength, you have nothing to fear. Take time to run to the Lord.

Are circumstances overwhelming you? Take refuge in the Lord. He will enable you to continue with renewed strength and confidence.

DAY **114**

Read Psalm 46:4-7

DRINK—DON'T FAINT

God is our Refuge, so we need not fear. But He is also our River, so we need not faint. "There is a river whose streams shall make glad the city of God, the holy place of the tabernacle of the Most High" (v.4).

Until I visited the Holy Land, I had no idea how *critical* water is there. Without water almost nothing can exist there. Jerusalem is one of the great ancient cities that was *not* founded on a river. It wasn't until Hezekiah dug his famous tunnel that Jerusalem had a water source within the city walls. The psalmist says here that though Jerusalem is not situated beside a river, it has a River. And it comes from the Holy Place, from the throne of God. "God is in the midst of her, she shall not be moved; God shall help her, just at the break of dawn" (v.5).

Our Lord said, "If anyone thirsts, let him come to Me and drink" (John 7:37). The rivers of Living Water, the rivers of joy, flow out from His throne. In the Bible, water for washing is a picture of the Word of God. But water for drinking is a picture of the Spirit of God. We may drink from this hidden River. And because we drink at this River, we have the joy, the refreshment and the empowerment of the Lord.

The psalmist continues, "The Lord of hosts is with us; the God of Jacob is our refuge" (v.7). He is the Lord of the armies. All the armies of heaven and earth belong to the Lord Jesus Christ because He has all authority. He is with us, not against us. He is Immanuel, "God with us."

Take time to drink at the River. Let God refresh you and restore you and strengthen you for the day.

Hidden resources are as critical to spiritual well-being as they are to physical well-being. If you want to work and not faint, you must depend on God's provisions. His people have the Holy Spirit within them to refresh and strengthen them. When you drink from the rivers of water He provides, you find strength and the joy of the Lord.

Read Psalm 46:8-11

TAKE YOUR HANDS OFF

DAY **115**

"Be still, and know that I am God; I will be exalted among the nations, I will be exalted in the earth!" (v.10). The Hebrew word translated "be still" actually means, "take your hands off." God is saying to us, "Take your hands off, and let Me be God in your life." So often we want to manipulate and control. We talk about those who are "hands on" people. In the Christian life, God uses our hands. He used Noah's hands to build the ark. He used David's hands to kill a giant. He used the apostles' hands to feed 5000 people. But sometimes only God's hand can do the job. Sometimes our hands get in the way because we are manipulating, plotting or scheming.

A friend of mine used to remind me, "Faith is living without scheming." Whenever I discover myself pushing and prodding, God says to me, "Take your hands off. Be still, and know that I am God." The difference is simply this. If we play God in our lives, everything is going to fall apart. But if we let Him truly be God in our lives, He will be exalted, He will be with us, and He will get the job done.

Are you facing a problem or a challenge today? Are you wondering what you will do? Give it to the Lord. A time will come when He will say, "All right, I will use your hands." But until then, keep your hands off. Know that He is God. He does not expect us to do what only He can do. We can roll the stone away from the tomb of Lazarus, but only He can raise the dead. We can hand out the bread, but only He can multiply it. Let Him be God in your life.

To remain still seems to go against human nature. You want control. But as a believer, you need to remain yielded to God's will and give your burdens to Him. What problem are you facing? Are you keeping your hands off and allowing Him to work in your life?

DAY **116**

Read Psalm 46:1-11

HIDDEN RESOURCES

Agnostic writer H.G.Wells said, "God is an ever absentee help in times of trouble." He was wrong. Psalms 46–48 grew out of a marvelous miracle in Israel's history. Hezekiah was king of Judah when the Assyrians invaded the land. The king took this crisis to the Lord, and He protected Israel. One morning 185,000 Assyrians died by the hand of the Lord's angel. We, too, can stand strong because of the divine resources God gives us.

God is our refuge; we need not fear (vv.1-3). He is available, accessible and sufficient—an abundantly available help in trouble. God's people go through trouble. Sometimes it's because we've been disobedient; sometimes it's because we've been obedient; and sometimes He knows we need to be strengthened and helped. Have you fled to your refuge? Hide in Him to gain the strength and grace you need to go back and face your responsibilities.

God is our strength; we need not faint (vv.4-7). We go from the turbulent sea in verse 2 to a quiet river in verse 4. Jerusalem was not established beside a river. To compensate, Hezekiah built an underground water system that brought water into the city. Similarly, we must live on hidden resources. We can't depend on the world around us or other people. When you trust Jesus as Savior, God puts an artesian well of Living Water within you. While the world has only broken cisterns, the Fountain of Living Water becomes a River. It is from Jesus that we get the spiritual resources we need. Are you drinking today at that River? Get your eyes off the sinking world and remember that God is your Strength.

God is an ever-present help; we need not fret (vv.8-11). "Be still" means "to take your hands off and let God be God." So often we fret about His timing and methods. Fretting leaves us vulnerable to the Devil's attacks. We should be still, stand still and sit still.

Your life depends on hidden resources God gives you. You need not faint nor live with worry and fear. Perhaps you are feeling the attacks of the Enemy or are going through a trial today. Be sure to take your strength and nourishment from God's spiritual resources. He is your Refuge and Strength.

Read Psalm 47:1-9

OUR SONG OF PRAISE

DAY 117

"For God is the King of all the earth; sing praises with understanding" (v.7). If anything should turn our hearts to joy and praise, it is that God is the King of all the earth. "God reigns over the nations" (v.8). Circumstances may not always reflect this. What we read in the newspapers or see on the news may not give evidence that God is reigning, but He is! The Lord Jesus is enthroned in heaven today, and everything is under His sovereign control.

Someone may say, "But if He's running the whole world, He can't take much time for me." That isn't true. God sees your needs. He knows your name. He has numbered the hairs on your head. The King of all the universe *is* concerned about *you.*

Because God is King, we should sing. This psalm starts, "Oh, clap your hands, all you peoples! Shout to God with the voice of triumph. For the Lord Most High is awesome; He is a great King over all the earth" (vv.1,2). God is sovereign, gracious and loving and therefore deserves our adoration. The psalmist implores in verse 6, "Sing praises to God, sing praises! Sing praises to our king, sing praises!" The best way to prove you believe that God is King is to sing praise. When we complain, we are saying that God doesn't know what He is doing, that He is not in control. But when we sing praises to the Lord, we acknowledge that He is King over all the earth.

The world refuses to acknowledge God as King and rebels against His authority. But God's people know He reigns over all the earth. You can sing His praises, for you know that He is also a gracious and loving God. You can praise Him because, as your personal Lord, He meets your needs. Praise Him today for who He is and what He has done in your life.

DAY 118 — Read Psalm 47:1-9

TIMELESS PRAISE

Our praise of God is a timeless act of worship. We can look at this psalm from three different points in time. First, we can view it from the *historic past*. This is one of three psalms that highlights Hezekiah's great victory over Sennacherib (Ps.46-48). What did the Lord do for the people of Judah? He came down (vv.1-4), went up (v.5) and sat down (vv.8,9). This is a picture of what the Lord did for us: He came to earth to die for our sins, was resurrected and is now seated in heaven.

We also can view this psalm from the *prophetic future*. Israel has yet to go through the time of Jacob's trouble. But Jesus will come down and win the victory (Rev.19), and Israel will enter into the glorious praises of the Lord. Today all the nations rage, but in the future they will praise Him. Jesus will come and establish His kingdom and keep His promise to Abraham to multiply his descendants so that they are innumerable.

Or we can view this psalm from the *practical present*. To worship God means to render to Him all the praise and adoration of our heart—a total response of all we are for all that He is. This psalm gives us hints about worship. First, the center of our worship is God (v.1): We worship a victorious God. Second, the purpose of our worship is to exalt Him (v.9). We are to magnify His greatness. Praise is a witness as well as an experience of worship. Let's exalt the Lord, for He is worthy of our praise.

Praising God knows no time boundaries. His people always have and always will praise Him. We praise God to exalt Him and to magnify His greatness. Do you worship Him with praise?

CITIZENS OF ZION

The people of Israel always have been proud of Jerusalem. Psalm 48 describes the city this way: "Beautiful in elevation, the joy of the whole earth, is Mount Zion" (v.2). Not everyone would agree with that description today, especially in light of the serious political and racial problems connected with Jerusalem. But I think the psalmist is referring here to the heavenly Mount Zion as well. Hebrews 12 tells us that Christians are citizens of the heavenly Zion.

God dwelt in Jerusalem. The psalmist describes how armies came to capture Zion. But when they saw this great city, they went away in fear. "For behold, the kings assembled, they passed by together. They saw it, and so they marveled; they were troubled, they hastened away. Fear and pain took hold of them" (vv.4-6). What did the armies discover when they looked at Jerusalem? First, they discovered the *greatness of God*. "Great is the Lord, and greatly to be praised in the city of our God" (v.1).

Second, they realized God is a *Refuge to His people*. "God is in her palaces; He is known as her refuge" (v.3). God is not only a King; He's One to whom we can come with all of our problems and needs. As God established Mount Zion, so He will establish us. As God built this city, He is building our lives. You may wonder why you experience sorrow, disappointment, heartache, perhaps even tragedy. God is building you and protecting you. So you don't have to be afraid.

God established the city of Jerusalem, and His greatness in and around the city was evident. Likewise, you are a citizen of the heavenly Zion, and He dwells within. As your Refuge, God protects and looks after your needs. Let Him care for you and establish you.

DAY

120

Read Psalm 48:9-14

EVEN UNTO DEATH

No one has more civic pride than the Jewish people who live in Jerusalem. While talking to a tour guide in Israel, my wife asked, "Where were you born?" The guide stood tall, his face brightened, and he said, "I was born in Jerusalem." The Jews love their city, and for good reason.

The psalmist says, "Walk about Zion, and go all around her. Count her towers; mark well her bulwarks; consider her palaces; that you may tell it to the generation following" (vv.12,13). But he isn't referring to a city.

He means God, the One in whom you trust: "For this is God, our God forever and ever; He will be our guide even to death." That is a marvelous statement! *He is our God.* He owns us. He purchased us. He made us. He lives in us. He is our God forever and ever. The thought overwhelms me!

But He is more than just our God—*He is also our Guide.* He will be our guide even unto death. He guides us in this life, so we don't have to be afraid. He has a path for each of us to follow today. He wants to keep us off detours and help us reach the goal He has planned for us. Verse 14 applies to you and me today. He is our God and our Guide, so we don't have to be afraid. Whatever He starts, He finishes.

God is your God not only for this present life but for eternity. As you meditate on the Word of God, His Spirit uses its truth to guide you along the path of His will. You never have to fear death, for your Lord is with you in death and beyond it. Is Jesus Christ your Savior? If so, let Him also be your Guide throughout life.

PILGRIMAGE TO ZION

Many Jews made a pilgrimage to Jerusalem to celebrate when they heard about Hezekiah's great victory over Sennacherib (II Kings 18,19). Christians today are citizens of the heavenly Zion and are also making a pilgrimage (Heb.12:18-24).

As pilgrims, *we talk about Zion* (vv.1-3). We talk about the God who has made Zion great and about His protection. We talk about Zion's beauty. Spiritually, Zion is the joy of the whole earth (Gen.12:1-3).

As pilgrims, *we see Zion* (vv.4-8). We look to Jerusalem and are encouraged in our faith. Hezekiah had no way to fight the Assyrians, but he had the Lord. He spread a blasphemous letter from the Assyrians before the Lord and turned everything over to Him. God acted. The Assyrian army was outside, waiting to plunder the City, but they were gone as suddenly as a woman who is taken by childbirth (v.5). When we're in the will of God, we have His protection.

As pilgrims, *we enter Zion* (vv.9-11). The Jews went to the temple first. It's good to ponder history. I trust that when you are at church you think about God's lovingkindness and about taking His praise to the ends of the earth (v.10). We have a greater victory to share with the earth: our Lord Jesus died for us and has risen again.

As pilgrims, *we walk about Zion* (vv.12-14). This is a triumphant procession of praise. When Nehemiah rededicated the wall, two choirs walked around the wall and met (Neh.12:27-47). Appreciate what you have and what God has done for you, that you may tell the following generation. Unfortunately, the people of Israel did not stay faithful (Lam.2:15). Let's be careful that we don't take our blessings for granted.

You are making a pilgrimage to the heavenly Zion. Be encouraged, for you have God's protection. That you are on a pilgrimage should be evident in your daily living. Praise Him for what He has done for you.

DAY

122

Read Psalm 49:1-13

DON'T TRUST IN WEALTH

The writer of this psalm certainly had the right attitude toward wealth. He warns, "Those who trust in their wealth and boast in the multitude of their riches, none of them can by any means redeem his brother, nor give to God a ransom for him" (vv.6,7). *Money cannot take us to heaven,* "for the redemption of their souls is costly" (v.8). It cost the precious blood of the Lord Jesus Christ! In fact, Jesus warned that money keeps some people out of heaven. "It is hard for a rich man to enter the kingdom of heaven" (Matt.19:23).

Not only can money not take us to heaven, but *money cannot rescue us from death.* "Their inner thought [the thoughts of these wealthy people] is that their houses will continue forever, and their dwelling places to all generations; they call their lands after their own names" (v.11). But, the psalmist says, these wealthy people will die just as animals die.

Money cannot conquer death, and *money cannot go with us,* but we can use it wisely while we have it. "For he sees that wise men die; likewise the fool and the senseless person perish, and leave their wealth to others" (v.10).

The psalmist advises us not to trust in wealth but to trust in the Lord. It is not a sin to have the things that money *can* buy as long as you don't lose the things that money *can't* buy (eternal life). Don't have any false confidence that simply because the bank account looks good you're going to live. You can't take your money with you, but you can use it today for God's glory. When you do that, you are investing it in eternity. Make your wealth eternal by letting God direct your use of it.

Wealth can't be trusted. Although a powerful resource, its power is limited to this temporal world. It cannot get you into heaven or conquer death. Do you trust in the world's resources when you should be trusting in God?

Read Psalm 49:14-20

TWO WARNINGS

DAY 123

"Do not be afraid when one becomes rich, when the glory of his house is increased; for when he dies he shall carry nothing away" (vv.16,17). Wealth is temporary. We can't take it with us, so we must use it for the glory of God while we have it. God gives us riches because of His goodness. First Timothy 6:17 says He gives to us "richly all things to enjoy." But we are stewards of wealth, not owners. That comes as a shock to some people. A person may think he owns his house and all of the possessions he has purchased. Yet when he dies, he is separated from them forever.

The psalmist gives two warnings regarding material possessions. First, *beware of having a false security*. People buy houses and put their names on them, but one day those houses will be torn down. Or, if the house isn't torn down, someone will come by and say, "That name on that house. Who was that fellow?" And the reply will be, "I don't know. Never heard of him." People try to perpetuate their fame through their wealth, but eventually they fail.

Second, *beware of wasted opportunity*. We can invest what God has entrusted to us in His work. We can help other people. The wealth that God gives to us—if we are faithful stewards—can be transformed into ministry that brings everlasting glory to Him. Don't waste your opportunity to serve Him this way.

To many, wealth often is their security. But it is a false security because riches are temporary. God alone gives wealth, and He expects it to be shared and used for His glory. Are you a faithful steward of what God has given you?

DAY

124

Read Psalm 50:1-6

COURT SUMMONS

The psalmist is describing God's arrival at the court He is convening. "From the rising of the sun [the east] to its going down [the west]" (v.1), God calls everyone together and says, "I am going to have a judgment." We don't usually think of God as the Judge, but He is. "He shall call to the heavens from above, and to the earth, that He may judge His people" (v.4).

Why does God judge His people? Shouldn't the wicked be judged instead? Peter tells us that judgment begins at the house of the Lord (I Pet.4:17). Our *sins* were judged at Calvary. "There is therefore now no condemnation to those who are in Christ Jesus" (Rom.8:1). But our *works* will be judged at the Judgment Seat of Christ.

God does this because *He's concerned about His glory*. "Out of Zion . . . God will shine" (v.2). He wants us to glorify Him. He wants us to do His will. Also, *God wants to reward His faithful servants*. If you need a motivation for faithful service, remember that God will judge and will reward those who are faithful. If you are obeying Him today, you won't have to fear your court summons.

God will one day judge all His saints. Have you been faithful to the Lord? Have you glorified Him with your life? Make your "court appearance" a time that will glorify Him.

WHAT GOD WANTS

"Offer to God thanksgiving, and pay your vows to the Most High. Call upon Me in the day of trouble; I will deliver you, and you shall glorify Me" (vv.14,15). The people had come to God's court and said, "You can't judge us. We have been offering You sacrifices." And God replied, "I will not rebuke you for your sacrifices or your burnt offerings, which are continually before Me. I will not take a bull from your house, nor goats out of your folds" (vv.8,9). He also said, "If I were hungry, I would not tell you; for the world is Mine, and all its fullness" (v.12). He was saying, "When you bring Me these sacrifices, you are only giving to Me what I have already given to you."

Think about that. When you put your offering in the plate, are you giving God something that isn't already His? Who gives you the strength to work? God. Who protects you to and from work? God. Who gives you the skills to work? God. Therefore, when we bring material offerings to Him (and He wants us to do this), we are only bringing what He already has given us. God wants us to give Him what He has *not* given us: "Offer to God thanksgiving, and pay your vows to the Most High" (v.14).

The sacrifices God wants most from us originate in our hearts calling upon Him, thanking Him and obeying Him. Bring to Him *thanksgiving* and *praise*. God does not give us thanksgiving and then say, "Give it back to Me." No, He waits for us to praise Him. Bring to Him *obedience*: "Pay your vows to the Most High" (v.14). Bring to Him *prayer*: "Call upon Me in the day of trouble" (v.15). When we bring these sacrifices, we glorify the Lord.

God wants your sacrifices to be from the heart. So often we receive from Him without returning thanks and praise. Do you want to bring glory to God this day? Thank Him for what He is doing for you. Obey His Word. Bring your problems to Him. These are all opportunities He can use to bring glory to Himself.

DAY

126

Read Psalm 50:16-23

IS GOD SELFISH?

"Whoever offers praise glorifies Me" (v.23). Today we don't sacrifice bulls and goats and lambs. We don't have a literal altar to which we bring literal sacrifices. The sacrifices God wants from us come from our hearts. Even when we bring money—which is a literal and real sacrifice—it must be given from a heart of love, sincerity and faith. Our purpose for living is to glorify God and enjoy Him forever.

The more you glorify God, the more you delight in Him. The more you delight in Him, the more you enjoy Him. Your life becomes enriched as you glorify God.

Is God selfish when He wants us to glorify Him? If I walked up to you and said, "I want you to glorify me by praising me," it would sound terribly proud. But God is the greatest Being in the universe. None is greater. None is higher. God is sovereign. So when He asks us to praise Him, He wants us to experience the highest thing possible—the praise and worship of God.

One way we praise God is by doing good works. "Let your light so shine before men, that they may see your good works and glorify your Father in heaven" (Matt.5:16). We praise Him through worship. We praise Him through an orderly, godly lifestyle. "And to him who orders his conduct aright I will show the salvation of God" (v.23). We have something to *offer*, and we have something to *order*. We offer praise by faith. We order our lives by obedience. Verse 23 is simply saying what the well-known hymn "Trust and Obey" says:

Trust and obey,
For there's no other way
To be happy in Jesus,
But to trust and obey.

God deserves to be glorified. And He gives us the privilege of worshiping Him. Do you delight in the Lord? Live in obedience to His Word and start enjoying Him.

Read Psalm 50:1-23

A REPRIEVE FOR THE GUILTY

DAY 127

This psalm describes God's courtroom and the judgment of His people, who made a covenant with Him by sacrifice. There are three stages to this trial. First, *God convenes the court* (vv.1-6). God calls the earth and then comes. He comes shining and will not keep silent (v.3; Heb.12:29). He calls heaven and earth to witness (vv.5,6).

Second, *God presents the charges* (vv.7-21). He starts with those who bring sacrifices to Him. He doesn't rebuke their sacrifices, but He is concerned about the way they bring them. God wants spiritual sacrifices from the heart: praise, obedience and prayers (v.15).

Then he speaks to the wicked. They declare God's statutes, yet they aren't obeying them (Matt.7:21). They think His silence is His approval.

Third, *God declares the conclusion* (vv.22,23). He could declare everyone guilty. Instead, He offers a reprieve. "Whoever offers praise glorifies Me; and to him who orders his conduct aright I will show the salvation of God."

One day our lives will be judged. Let's do what God asks us to do and walk out of the courtroom free.

Someday you will be on trial at the Judgment Seat of Christ, where your works will be judged by God. Are you prepared for trial in His courtroom? Do your sacrifices come from your heart?

DAY 128

Read Psalm 51:1-19

Restored

FELLOWSHIP

All of us struggle with sin. Human nature pulls us down as gravity does, yet God has made us and saved us to lift us up (I John 1:5-2:6). There are three ways we may deal with our sins.

Cover them. We cover our sins with our words. This is lying—deceiving others and ourselves and lying to God. Lies are darkness, whereas God's truth is light. When we lie, our character erodes (Prov.28:13). When we cover sin, we lose God's light, fellowship and character.

Confess them. Admit and judge them—agree with God about your sin. This involves the heart and the will. Some people have died because they repeatedly, willfully, proudly and arrogantly defied the will of God. Admit you are a sinner, say what is wrong and then come to Him and name it. Confess your sin only in the circle of those influenced by it—individuals or family. (Don't become an exhibitionist with the public.) Confession brings release, freedom, forgiveness and a new beginning.

Conquer them. Jesus is in heaven today as our Advocate—as a Lawyer before the Father. Abide in Him, love Him, walk with Him in the light of His Word. Keep His commandments. Fellowship is a by-product of our walk with God. To love Him is to serve Him and obey His commandments.

Are you covering sin or conquering sin in your life? Confess any known sin and ask God to clean your heart. He wants to forgive you so He can restore fellowship with you.

Read Psalm 51:1, 2

The High Cost of
COMMITTING SIN

DAY
129

The most priceless thing in the universe is the human soul. We see its value at Calvary, because the most costly thing in the world—our sin—required the payment of Jesus' blood to redeem us.

We also see sin's toll on our lives. Before David sinned he was a friend of God, straight, meeting His goals. After he sinned he was a crooked rebel, missing the mark. Psalms 32 and 51 relate the spiritual change that took place when David confessed his sin of adultery and murder.

We don't have to rehearse David's sin. The story of how he committed adultery, murdered a man and tried to cover up his sin for a year is well known. The effects were disastrous. If we really understood what sin is and what sin does, it would keep us from deliberately sinning against God. But we don't see sin the way He does.

Sin is a process. David uses three different words for what he did. *Transgressions* refers to rebellion against God. *Iniquity* conveys the crookedness of the sinner. Sin means to miss the mark. David also uses three verbs to ask for forgiveness. *Blot out* refers to paying a debt. *Wash* indicates that sin defiles the entire person. *Cleanse* means the sinner is like a leper, in need of total healing.

Before you yield to temptation, remember how it damaged David. Count the high cost of committing sin, and you will be less inclined to do it.

The human soul was purchased at the highest cost possible—the death of God's Son. Do you entertain temptations? The cost of committing sin is greater than you can afford. When you find yourself beginning the process of sin, claim the promises of God's Word. God will strengthen and protect you and enable you to overcome temptation. Also, rejoice that He forgives you when you do sin.

DAY
130

Read Psalm 51:3-6

DIRTY WINDOWS

Sin is much more than a word in the dictionary. It is a powerful evil that damages our lives and our world. David describes a guilty conscience: "For I acknowledge my transgressions, and my sin is ever before me" (v.3). Conscience is a marvelous gift from God, the window that lets in the light of His truth. If we sin against Him deliberately, that window becomes dirty, and not as much truth can filter through. Eventually, the window becomes so dirty that it no longer lets in the light. The Bible calls this a defiled, seared conscience.

David covered his sin for about a year. He refused to be broken. He refused to humble himself before God. And what was his life like? "He who covers his sins will not prosper" (Prov.28:13). Did David prosper? No. Wherever he looked he saw his sin.

Before he sinned, David saw *God* wherever he looked. His heart was pure. "Blessed are the pure in heart, for they shall see God" (Matt.5:8). Your heart affects your eyes; what you love in your heart, your eyes will seek.

God wants truth in our inner being. "Behold, You desire truth in the inward parts, and in the hidden part You will make me to know wisdom" (v.6). David confessed because he wanted to see God again—in nature, in His Word and in the temple.

Do you keep a clean conscience? It is a part of your inner being that responds to God's truth. When you sin, the window of your conscience becomes dirty and filters out truth. Avoid sin in your life and live with a clean conscience. Every day feed yourself truth from the Word of God.

Read Psalm 51:7-9

WHAT DO YOU HEAR?

DAY 131

When we sin, it does terrible damage to our spiritual life. David's sin affected his eyes, but it also affected his ears. "Make me hear joy and gladness" (v.8). Keep in mind that David was not only a soldier but also a singer. He would come back from the battlefield, put down his sword and pick up his harp. He played it and sang praises to God. He listened to the choirs in God's house as they sang praises to Him. David's ears were open to the music of heaven—but not in this psalm.

David heard sorrow and sadness. The choir was off-key. Everything he heard was wrong. We, too, have days like that. When we are not right on the inside, nothing is going to be right on the outside. The good news will be bad news, and the bad news will be worse news. No wonder David prays, "Wash me, and I shall be whiter than snow" (v.7). He also asks to be purged with hyssop, the little shrub the Jews used to put blood on the doorposts at Passover. "The blood of Jesus Christ His Son cleanses us from all sin" (I John 1:7), if we confess our sins.

If your ears have not been hearing joy and gladness, perhaps the problem is not *around* you but *within* you. Perhaps your heart needs to be cleansed. When your heart is tuned to the music of God and the harmony of heaven, then everything around you will remind you of the Lord.

Unconfessed sin leaves you with a dirty heart. When your heart is not right, you don't hear joy and gladness—the music of God. Confess your sin to the Lord, and He will forgive you and restore you.

Read Psalm 51:10

GOOD FAUCET, BAD WATER

This verse was David's prayer as he confessed his sins to the Lord. *Sin defiles the heart.* You may say, "Well, no one can see that. David didn't look any different after he sinned." But when your heart is defiled, everything is defiled. Solomon wrote, "Keep your heart with all diligence, for out of it spring the issues of life" (Prov.4:23).

Suppose you turn on a faucet at home, and out comes dirty water. You go to the hardware store, buy a brand-new faucet (a more expensive one), install it and turn it on. Out comes dirty water. Obviously, the problem is not the faucet but the water source. So it is with us. Jesus said, "Out of the abundance of the heart the mouth speaks" (Matt.12:34). The heart is the center of our lives, and sin defiles it. This is why David said that everything around him was defiled: his eyes (Ps.51:3); his ears (v.8); his heart (v.10); and his spirit.

Sin also weakens the spirit. All of us want an enthusiastic, steadfast spirit. But David was vacillating. Every time he saw someone, he wondered, *What does he know about me?* Whenever people were talking together in a corner, David wondered, *Are they talking about me?* He had a dirty conscience, a vacillating spirit.

God can create a new heart and give a steadfast spirit. How? Not by our excuses but by our confession. We are so prone to excuse our sin. Instead, David confessed his sin, and God forgave him. Yes, David had to pay dearly for his sin. He suffered the discipline of God. But God cleansed his heart, strengthened his spirit and created something new within.

What is your heart condition? Is it clean or dirty? Unconfessed sin in the heart defiles the whole body. Never hold onto a sin or cover it; confess it immediately. When you do, God can cleanse and restore you.

THE GREATEST LOSS

Many sad consequences occur when a believer sins, but the worst is the loss of close fellowship with the Lord. No wonder David prayed, "Do not cast me away from Your presence, and do not take Your Holy Spirit from me" (v.11). David was remembering what had happened to his predecessor, King Saul. Saul turned against the Lord and became rebellious. So God took His Spirit from him and gave the power of His Spirit to David.

God does not remove His Holy Spirit from us today. Jesus told His disciples that the Spirit of God would abide with them forever. When the Holy Spirit comes into your life at conversion, He seals your salvation. He is the witness that you are a child of God and assures you that you belong to Christ.

But when we sin against the Lord, we lose that closeness of the Holy Spirit, the source of our blessing. Everything in the Christian life depends on our fellowship with the Lord. David constantly depended on God's presence, whether he was writing a psalm or leading an army. Therefore, he was anguished about losing the powerful presence of the Holy Spirit.

Fellowship is the New Testament word for the presence of the Lord. Sonship and fellowship are two different things. Sonship comes from our faith in Jesus Christ—we are born into the family of God. Fellowship is the result of our faithfulness to Him. We keep our lives clean. We obey Him. We talk to Him in prayer. And He talks to us in His Word. Don't lose this by sinning.

Fellowship with God is conditional. If we have sin in our lives, we cannot have fellowship with Him. Do you take care to walk with the Lord daily? If you're not careful, the Enemy will gain a foothold in your life. Avoid sin, obey the Word of God and maintain a prayer time with Him. Make walking with the Lord a priority.

LOST JOY

David did not lose his salvation when he sinned, but he did lose the joy of his salvation. It's interesting to see how much David said about joy in the Psalms. Joy is essential in the Christian life. It is the evidence that we are truly born again. Jesus said, "Do not rejoice in this, that the spirits are subject to you, but rather rejoice because your names are written in heaven" (Luke 10:20). Whatever your circumstances today, you can rejoice in the salvation of the Lord.

Nehemiah 8:10 says that the joy of the Lord is our strength. When you enjoy doing something, the enjoyment gives you sufficient strength to do the task. On the other hand, all of us have tasks to perform that we don't enjoy. We do them out of duty and because it's the right thing to do, but they don't provide the strength that comes from joy.

We need the joy of the Lord to witness for Him. Joy shows unsaved people that it is worthwhile to know Jesus. He is the Power for our service.

David lost that joy, so he prayed, "Restore to me the joy of Your salvation, and uphold me with Your generous Spirit" (v.12). Joy and willing obedience go together. When you enjoy doing something or when you enjoy the person for whom you are doing it, you serve willingly. David is saying, "I have been in bondage because I have not confessed my sin. Therefore, I lost my joy and my willing spirit. I lost that real delight that comes from obeying God."

How can you restore joy? Confess your sin. Then look to Jesus Christ, not yourself. If you look at yourself, you won't rejoice. But if you look to Him, you will rediscover the joy of His salvation.

God intends that you rejoice in your salvation. Have you lost the joy of your salvation? Do you miss the delight that comes from obeying the Lord? Make sure your life is free from sin, and then ask Him to restore your joy.

Read Psalm 51:13-15

SILENCED WITNESS

DAY 135

The sins we commit not only affect us, but they affect others—even the unsaved. David discovered this when he tried to witness for the Lord. No wonder he wrote, "Deliver me from blood-guiltiness, O God, the God of my salvation, and my tongue shall sing aloud of Your righteousness" (v.14). *His hands were bloody.* Why? He had killed Uriah, the husband of the woman with whom he had committed adultery. God saw him do it, and Joab, the general of David's army, knew what he had done.

Sin also silenced his tongue. He had no song and no witness. "O Lord, open my lips, and my mouth shall show forth Your praise" (v.15). David was accustomed to praising the Lord, but now he is silent. When we lose our song and our praise and our testimony, we affect others. David was not able to talk to people about the Lord. But when God forgave him and his sin was washed away, he was able to say, "Then I will teach transgressors Your ways, and sinners shall be converted to You" (v.13).

If you are ever tempted to say, "I can sin and get away with it," just remember David. He sinned, but he didn't get away with it. Sin affected his whole being, his family and the people to whom he should have brought the witness of the Lord.

God has called each of us to be His witness. Our task is to teach transgressors His ways. Our privilege is to lead sinners to the Lord. "You shall receive power; . . . and you shall be witnesses to Me" (Acts 1:8). Our sin affects our witness. Let's ask God to cleanse us and open our lips so we can share the good news of the Gospel with others.

Sin spreads like a disease. It not only robs your joy, but it affects your witness to others. As long as you give sin room in your life, your spiritual life will be ineffective. Don't let sin steal your witness for the Lord. Keep your heart clean before Him.

DAY

136

Read Psalm 51:16, 17

BROKEN THINGS

Have you ever studied the broken things in the Bible? A woman broke a vessel at the feet of Jesus and anointed Him. Jesus took bread and broke it as a picture of His body given for us. God uses broken things, and He starts with broken hearts. This is what repentance is all about. God doesn't listen to the lips. He doesn't measure a material sacrifice. He looks at the heart and says, "If your heart is broken, then I can cleanse it."

When David sinned, he could have brought all kinds of sacrifices. But they would not have pleased the Lord. God was waiting for the sacrifice of a broken heart. That's why David said, "The sacrifices of God are a broken spirit, a broken and a contrite heart—these, O God, You will not despise" (v.17). David's sins should have brought him condemnation and death. He committed adultery, and he murdered a man. No sacrifice could be found in God's sacrificial system for this kind of flagrant, rebellious, deliberate sin. But David did not die. Even though no sacrifice was available for his sin at the time, God looked down the corridors of time and saw a cross where Jesus Christ would die for David's sin.

God looks at the heart, not the hand. He wants sincerity from the heart, not religious routine.

A broken heart is not remorse, nor is it regret. It is repentance, a turning away from sin. It's telling God you hate sin, are judging it and claiming his forgiveness. Bring to Him the sacrifice of a contrite heart.

WHAT PLEASES GOD?

We can live to please ourselves. We can live to please others. But above all we should live to please the Lord. David closes his prayer of confession, "Then You shall be pleased with the sacrifices of righteousness" (v.19). Everything we do should please the Lord.

A. W. Tozer used to say, "God is not hard to get along with." And this is true. One day David said, "Let [me] fall into the hand of the Lord, for His mercies are great, but do not let me fall into the hand of man" (II Sam.24:14). God knows us, loves us and is patient with us. Everything He plans for us is for our good, our enjoyment and His glory. So what pleases Him the most? An obedient walk, not sacrifices. David says, "If I brought sacrifices without repentance, You wouldn't accept them. But if I repent and bring you a broken and a contrite heart, then you will accept my sacrifice and my service."

It's interesting how David ends this psalm. "Do good in Your good pleasure to Zion; build the walls of Jerusalem" (v.18). David in his sin had been tearing down, not building up. He had given opportunity to the enemies of Israel to blaspheme God. The word got out. Soon everyone knew what David had done. So he says, "O God, when I was sinning, I was tearing down. I was not pleasing You. Now I want to please You. And because I'm pleasing You, I will be building up. And the walls of Jerusalem, walls of protection, will be strong." Are you tearing down or building up?

God plans everything for your good, your enjoyment and His glory. As His child, strive to please and honor Him in all you do. Is your walk with God one of obedience? Make your life the kind that pleases Him.

Read Psalm 51:4, 6, 10.11

The High Cost of CONFESSION

What does it mean to confess sin? It does not mean to admit our sins, for we can hide nothing from God. The word *confess* means "to say the same thing." We are to see sin as God sees it. This is repentance, not penance. Jesus' blood is the only thing that can pay the cost of sin.

True repentance involves the *mind*, the *emotions* and the *will*. David had to change his mind about his affair with Bathsheba, with Nathan's help (v.4). The prophet confronted David about his sin (II Sam.12). He wisely told him a story about the ewe lamb to illustrate his sin. David replied, "I have sinned." Pharaoh also said this, but he didn't mean it. King Saul also said this when he got caught doing wrong. Saul had regret; Pharaoh had remorse. *Regret* involves only the mind—we are upset that we got into a mess or got caught. *Remorse* involves only the mind and emotions—we feel terrible.

Confessing sin means that we have David's attitude and recognize that we are sinners by nature: each of us is capable of committing *any* sin.

The high cost of confessing sin is a broken heart. When we see ourselves as God does, we will have broken hearts. He does not have to discipline us to break our hearts. Jesus only had to look at Peter, and Peter's heart was broken (Luke 22:61). If you come to God with a broken heart and confess your sin, He will forgive and restore you.

Confession of sin is not a light matter. It involves the whole inner person. When you see sin as God does, it breaks your heart. Bring your broken heart to God, and He will heal it.

Read Psalm 51:18, 19

The High Cost of
CLEANSING

DAY
139

Cleansing sin is not cheap. Keep in mind what God has to do. Sin creates debt, defilement and disease, which can be rooted out and forgiven only through the shed blood of Jesus Christ. Everyone of us deserves eternal death, but He died in our place. Mercy is God not giving us what we deserve; grace is God giving us what we don't deserve.

When we confess sin, Jesus represents us before God (I John 2). He is our Advocate. When you are tempted to sin, remember that your sin put Jesus on the cross. And when you sin, you don't simply sin against family and friends; you sin against the Savior, who died for you. He is standing in heaven, wounded, representing you before the throne. The high cost of cleansing sin is that Somebody had to die. This is a great motivation not to sin.

If you are saved, you are forgiven—your debt to sin is eliminated. Remember, God is not keeping a record of your sins, but He is keeping a record of your works, and sin hinders your ability to serve Him.

Never take for granted God's act of cleansing sin. Forgiveness was purchased at a great price—the blood of Christ. Next time you are tempted to sin, remember that it cost Jesus His life to provide redemption for you.

DAY 140

Read Psalm 51:18, 19

The High Cost of CONQUERING

One element of spiritual maturity is realizing the horror of sin. It brings great tragedy. Bishop William Culbertson used to speak of the tragic consequences of forgiven sin. For example, David was forgiven, but his baby died, and Absalom and Amnon were slain. God will forgive our sins. In His grace He forgives; in His government we face the consequences. God requires that we reap what we sow.

Temptation is not sin, but it is a sin to cultivate temptation and yield to it. Sin is usually a process, and David went through several stages that led to his sin.

First, *David laid down* his *armor* (II Sam.11). Do you put on the spiritual armor? (Eph.6). We put it on through prayer. We need to come to the Lord each morning and put on the armor. Second, *David was not looking to God.* He was looking at Bathsheba. We need to make sure our bodies belong to God. After you put on your armor, turn yourself completely over to Him (Rom.12:1). Third, *David did not watch and pray.* The flesh is weak. As we mature in the Christian life, sin becomes more subtle. We must guard against this. Fourth, *David was alone.* He was not fellowshipping with the saints. When people try to rely solely on themselves, they usually fail. Fifth, *David ignored God's Word.* The Word keeps us clean. Finally, *David did not depend upon the Spirit.* We need to yield to Him. If you do, you will conquer sin.

Commit these six stages to memory and read Ephesians 6. Don't make the same mistakes David made. Never cultivate a temptation with a view to yielding to sin. Meditate on the Word of God, obey it and guard your heart with its truth. Stay in fellowship with the Lord.

Read Psalm 52:1-9

WHEN PEOPLE HATE YOU

DAY
141

Ahimelech was a priest who assisted David. Because of that, he was considered a traitor, and Saul ordered Ahimelech and his family killed. When David heard about it, he was saddened and wrote this psalm.

Psalm 52 gives a threefold description that puts man's evil into perspective. First, *David describes the treacherous man* (vv.1-4). Doeg was a descendant of Esau, who represents the worldly person (Heb.12:16). Esau's descendants were enemies of the Jews. Doeg was probably a proselyte. Although he was a mighty and wealthy man, he didn't get his strength from God. Doeg boasted of, reveled in and loved evil. It's dangerous to love a lie (II Thess.2:11; Rev.22:15). As in Doeg's case, lying can be telling the truth with a wrong motive.

Second, *David describes the righteous Judge* (vv.2-7). God will break down this evil man and uproot him from the land of the living. Those who depend on themselves will one day be uprooted and destroyed.

Third, *David describes the victorious servant* (vv.8,9). He had seen the olive trees by the house of God. He knew God would take care of him, just as He did the trees, and he depended on Him for his strength. David was planted, productive and praising God.

When people are treacherous to us, we must focus on God's goodness, not on man's badness. Leave all judgment to the Lord. Continue to bear fruit for God, and praise Him in the midst of trouble.

You can be victorious when others target you with their hatred. The next time someone treats you with hate, focus on God; leave the matter in His hands and praise His name.

DAY

142

Read Psalm 52:1-4

LIKE A RAZOR

The tongue is one of the smallest parts of the body, yet it can do the most damage. In these verses David writes about an experience he had with Doeg, who had a wicked, boastful tongue. David cautions us about two kinds of damaging tongues.

First, beware of a *boastful tongue.* Doeg was a proud man. In his boastful pride, he told Saul about David, and it cost people's lives. We like to boast because it inflates our ego. But those who boast should boast in the Lord. If we boast in the Lord, we glorify Him.

Second, beware of a *sharp tongue.* David says of Doeg, "Your tongue devises destruction, like a sharp razor, working deceitfully" (v.2). He had a lying, sharp tongue. "You love evil more than good, and lying rather than speaking righteousness. You love all devouring words, you deceitful tongue" (vv.3,4). Have you ever been cut by someone's sharp tongue? Or worse, have you ever cut someone with your words? What really hurts is when we cut someone with lies. Lying is a terrible sin. Satan is a liar and a murderer. He wants to use our tongues to spread deceit, not righteousness.

In verse 1 David magnifies the goodness of God: "The goodness of God endures continually." When we boast of the goodness of God, our tongues are medicine that heals, not sharp razors that cut. Our tongues are used to speak righteousness, not to spread lies. They will boast about the Lord, not about ourselves. Let's yield our hearts to God so that our tongues might be used for blessing.

We need to keep our tongues under control. They are capable of causing great damage. Beware of having a boastful or sharp tongue. Be careful that your tongue does not spread lies. And when others slander you, don't reciprocate with your own tongue. Instead, use your tongue to glorify God and to speak of His goodness.

Read Psalm 52:5-7

THE LAST LAUGH

DAY 143

One of the problems with humanistic philosophy is that it causes people to think they are self-sufficient. They think they don't need any outside help, that in and of themselves they have all they need for life and for death. David describes this kind of person: "Here is the man who did not make God his strength, but trusted in the abundance of his riches, and strengthened himself in his wickedness" (v.7). That's a description of the self-sufficient person who doesn't know how dangerous his situation really is. Notice that *God was not his strength*. He trusted in his own wickedness. He was strengthened in his sin.

When life is built on sin, it has no foundation. Remember the parable Jesus told about the two men who built houses (Matt.7:24-27). The foolish man built his house on the sand; he didn't obey God. The wise man built his house on the rock; he obeyed God. And when the storm came, the house that was built on the rock remained strong and firm, whereas the house built on the sand collapsed.

God was not this self-sufficient person's strength, and *God was not his confidence*. He depended on his wealth. Most people today think that money can solve every problem. This person "trusted in the abundance of his riches," David said (v.7). And what happened to him? "God shall likewise destroy you forever; He shall take you away, and pluck you out of your dwelling place, and uproot you from the land of the living" (v.5).

We can see this person in his home, surrounded by his wealth. But God reaches in and plucks him out—the way you would reach into a den and pull out a rabbit. This person is like a beautiful tree. But God says, "I'm going to uproot you." The righteous get the last laugh. "The righteous also shall see and fear, and shall laugh at him" (v.6). Are you going to be a part of the last laugh, or is someone going to be laughing at you?

God is your strength and confidence. Don't be like the self-sufficient person, who trusts in the world's substitutes for strength and confidence. Let the Word of God permeate your mind and hide its truth in your heart. Place yourself in God's care and let Him establish you.

DAY
144

Read Psalm 52:8, 9

BE AN OLIVE BRANCH

If you compared yourself to something in nature, what would you choose? Would you say you are like a mountain, or a hill or perhaps a lake? David wrote, "But I am like a green olive tree in the house of God; I trust in the mercy of God forever and ever" (v.8). David compared himself to something *permanent*, in contrast to the wicked, who will be uprooted from the land of the living (v.5).

David's permanent position was also a *privileged* position because he was planted in the house of the Lord. The most important part of a tree is the root system, for it absorbs nourishment. In addition, it provides stability and strength in the storm. We can discern what kind of root system people have when the winds of life blow harder. Some people are like tumbleweeds; they just rootlessly blow from one place to another.

David was also *productive*. He was like a green olive tree in the house of God, bearing fruit for His glory. Fruitfulness is one of the great joys in the Christian life. Jesus used the image of a vine to tell believers that we should produce a lot of fruit (John 15:1-8).

Look at these symbols. A green tree symbolizes freshness and power. Olives contain oil, which is a symbol of the Holy Spirit. No wonder David ended this psalm by praising the Lord! "I will praise You forever, because You have done it; and in the presence of Your saints I will wait on Your name, for it is good" (Ps.52:9).

An olive tree in the house of God is an accurate picture of the believer's position. You are permanent, privileged and productive. You bear fruit for God's glory only when you are yielded to Him and allow the Holy Spirit to work in your life. Can you describe yourself as an olive tree in the house of God?

PRACTICAL ATHEISM

"The fool has said in his heart, 'There is no God'" (v.1). He doesn't say this outwardly with his lips. He simply says it in his heart. This is a description of practical atheism. Most people would not say, "I don't believe God exists." But most people live as though He doesn't exist. David reminds us that what we believe about God in our hearts determines how we live.

Most of the people in this world do not know God. Perhaps that's the fault of Christians. Perhaps we should be praying more, giving more and witnessing more. But the fact is that most people live as if God doesn't exist. They rarely think about Him unless they're facing sickness or tragedy or death, and even then they forget about Him soon after. But David tells us that *what you believe about God affects your will.* "They are corrupt, and have done abominable iniquity; there is none who does good" (v.1). To say there is no God is to say there is no good.

Verse 2 tells us that *what you believe about God also affects your mind.* God looked down from heaven upon humanity to see if there were any who understood, who sought Him. Not one was found. They do not understand, and they don't want to understand. They want to live their lives without God.

Verse 5 says that *what you believe about God affects your heart.* "There they are in great fear where no fear was." The fear of God comes upon people even though they don't believe in Him.

Do we live our lives as though God were not watching? Do we speak as though He were not listening? Do we think and ponder in our hearts as though He were not aware? Let's live as those who say, "Yes, we know God, and we want to glorify Him."

It has been said that everybody believes in someone or something. Trust involves the whole inner being; what you believe affects your heart, mind and will. God responds to your inner man and fellowships with you. He wants you to trust Him and glorify Him with your life. Are you a witness to those around you? Do you live to glorify God?

Read Psalm 53:1-6

THE FOOL'S FOLLY

This psalm describes the atheist and gives eight reasons why he is a fool. First, *he does not acknowledge God* (v.1). He lives as if there is no God. *He does not obey God* (v.1). Some people think that human nature is basically kind and good. Not so. We are abominably corrupt by nature (Rom.3:9). *He does not understand God* (v.2). If you don't have the Spirit of God, you can't understand the things of God. Atheists say they won't accept anything they can't understand. Actually, there is little in the world they *do* understand!

The fool does not seek God (v.2). No one by himself seeks God and comes to know Him. God invites us to seek Him, and He has mercy on us. *He does not follow God's way* (v.3). God has ordained the right path for us. Being a Christian is not easy, and many people do not want to pay the price. The narrow road leads to life and is tough; the broad road is the easy way until the end (Matt.7:13,14).

The fool does not call on God (v.4). Such people are mercenary and do not treat others right. *He does not fear God* (v.5). The day will come when the fool will be afraid. He lives with a false confidence and one day will face judgment. *He does not hope in God* (v.6). The person who leaves God out of his life has no future.

God's people have a future of eternal life. However, anyone who professes to be a Christian but lives like an atheist also is a fool. May Jesus help us to acknowledge the goodness, greatness and majesty of Almighty God.

The atheist lives as if there is no God. You, as God's child, eagerly await eternal life. However, if you fail to walk with the Lord, you behave as a fool. Lay hold of your spiritual resources in Christ and hope in Him.

WHO'S YOUR MAINSTAY?

"Behold, God is my helper; the Lord is with those who uphold my life" (v.4). David wrote those words when he was hiding from King Saul. We can translate this verse, "The Lord is the Mainstay of my life." Is God the Mainstay, the Main Support, of your life today?

David went through several stages waiting for God to help him. He began with *prayer.* "Save me, O God, by Your name, and vindicate me by Your strength. Hear my prayer, O God; give ear to the words of my mouth" (vv.1,2). That's a great way to pray. David was being attacked by the enemy, by those who did not believe in God. He needed help, so he cried out to Him.

We see a turning point at verse 4, where David's *faith* goes to work. "Behold, God is my helper; the Lord is with those who uphold my life [the Lord is the mainstay of my life]. He will repay my enemies for their evil. Cut them off in Your truth" (vv.4,5). David now is trusting the Lord. It's one thing to cry out to God, but it's something else to believe that He is going to hear and answer.

David ends his psalm with *praise.* "I will freely sacrifice to You; I will praise Your name, O Lord, for it is good" (v.6). Why? "For He has delivered me out of all trouble; and my eye has seen its desire upon my enemies" (v.7). This is an interesting sequence of experiences: David had *trouble.* This led him to *trust* God, which resulted in *triumph.* He had a *problem,* so he turned to *prayer,* which brought about *praise* to the Lord.

When you're in trouble and forced to wait for help, where you place your faith is all-important. Is your sequence of experiences similar to David's? (Problem to prayer to praise? Trouble to trust to triumph?) Next time you must wait for help, let your faith go to work. God will hear you and answer your prayer.

DAY
148

Read Psalm 55:1-23

SOAR ABOVE THE STORM

David wrote this psalm during the early stages of Absalom's conspiracy. He tells us that in times of trial we can take one of three approaches. One is that *we can flee* (vv.1-8). David talks about his emotions. He was in a difficult situation and wanted to fly away. But these troubles were part of God's discipline for him.

Second, *we can fight* (vv.9-15). Absalom's conspiracy had gone so far that David could not overcome his enemies. He could only try to save his own life. He saw a sinful city and his friends turn against him, but God was able to overcome them. Absalom and his followers were rebels who had to be disciplined.

Third, *we can fly above our trials* (v.16-23). The wind that blows down everything lifts up the eagle. We get that kind of power when we wait on the Lord in prayer and worship. David looked at his feelings and foes, but then he focused on his faith in the Lord.

David triumphed because he sought God: *I will call* (v.16); *I will cast* (v.22); and *I will trust* (v.23). God gives us burdens, and we are to give them back to Him. Don't ask for wings like a dove to fly away. Instead, let God give you wings like an eagle so you can soar above the storm.

Trials force you to respond. You can flee, fight or fly above them. Are you facing a trial today? God has a purpose in your trial and wants you to learn how to fly above it. Cast your burden upon Him and trust Him for the strength to fly above your difficulty.

Read Psalm 55:1-8

WANT TO FLY AWAY?

DAY 149

Have you ever felt like flying away just to get away from it all? Has life ever been such a burden that all you can think about is escaping? David felt like that one day. That's why he wrote, "And I said, 'Oh, that I had wings like a dove! For then I would fly away and be at rest. Indeed, I would wander far off, and remain in the wilderness. I would hasten my escape from the windy storm and tempest'" (vv.6-8).

Now let's be honest. This is a natural feeling. All of us have felt like getting away, just packing our bags and saying, "I've had enough! I can't take anymore! I've got to get away." It's a normal, natural reaction. But it is *not* a good solution to any problem. We usually take our problems with us. We can go on vacation and enjoy a short respite. But when we return, the battles and burdens are still there. In fact, sometimes when we try to run away, we only make the problems worse.

Why does the Lord allow us to go through windy storms and tempests? They help us grow and mature. If we keep running away, we are like children who never grow up. No, we don't need the wings of a dove to fly away. We need the wings of an eagle. Isaiah 40:31 says, "Those who wait on the Lord shall renew their strength; they shall mount up with wings like eagles." The eagle faces the storm, spreads his great wings and allows the wind to lift him above the storm.

Don't run away. Run to the Lord, and let Him lift you high above the storm.

God allows trials to make you grow and mature and become like His Son. The next time you go through a storm, resist the pressure to run from it. Let God use the storm to accomplish His purposes.

DAY

150

Read Psalm 55:9-15

NOT MY FRIEND

Perhaps the greatest trial is when someone you really love—a friend, a family member—betrays you. David wrote: "For it is not an enemy who reproaches me; then I could bear it. Nor is it one who hates me who has exalted himself against me; then I could hide from him. But it was you, a man my equal, my companion and my acquaintance" (vv.12,13). It takes a diamond to cut a diamond and sometimes our friends can hurt us deeply. And we can deeply hurt them. David said about his friend, "The words of his mouth were smoother than butter, but war was in his heart; his words were softer than oil, yet they were drawn swords" (v.21).

Jesus could have applied these words to Judas. He could have said, "Yes, my own familiar friend, the one who walked with me, the one who ate with me—he is the one who betrayed me."

"We took sweet counsel together, and walked to the house of God in the throng" (v.14). How sad it is when church members, people we fellowship with in the house of God, turn against us and hurt us. But we must do what David did. He simply said, "Lord, you are the only One who can take care of this. I don't understand it. I'm not going to return evil for evil. I'm just going to leave it with You." God met David's needs. He magnified him and healed his wounds.

We find two lessons here. First, *all of us are human*. Others will hurt you sometimes. But leave your hurt with the Lord and don't fight back. Second, be careful *not to hurt others*. Be a friend who blesses, not betrays.

Betrayed trust is one of life's most difficult pills to swallow. How you respond to those who hurt you is a true test of your faith. When someone hurts you, do you live on the divine level and return good for evil? When others do their worst, leave it with God. He will meet your needs and use you to glorify Himself.

Read Psalm 55:16-21

LEARNING FROM CHANGE

DAY 151

David was going through intense difficulty. Some of his friends, including his most familiar friend, were turning against him, and it was painful.

How did David solve this problem? First, *he called upon the Lord.* "As for me [no matter what they may do], I will call upon God, and the Lord shall save me. Evening and morning and at noon I will pray, and cry aloud, and He shall hear my voice" (vv.16,17). Apparently, David had a systematic prayer life. He called upon God and told Him his troubles.

Second, *he let God do the judging.* "God will hear, and afflict them, even He who abides from of old" (v.19). David believed God would resolve the problem. We should do the same. Let God give you the friends you need to help you in your ministry, and let Him take care of your enemies. Don't treat others the way they treat you. Instead, treat them the way you would want to be treated. Don't return evil for evil.

Third, *David was determined to learn from this experience.* "Because they do not change, therefore they do not fear God" (v.19). David was going through a change of friends, and this was helping him to fear God more. We usually don't like changes. But whenever God brings change to our lives, we can learn from it. Let's not get so comfortable, so settled, that God can't do anything new in our lives.

Determine to learn from difficult experiences. God has a purpose for allowing every difficulty and problem. Let Him teach you new truths and work in your life in new ways.

DAY 152

Read Psalm 55:22, 23

GIVE IT BACK

"Cast your burden on the Lord, and He shall sustain you; He shall never permit the righteous to be moved" (v.22). This promise tells us that *Christians do have burdens*. David is not talking about concern for others, although it's good to bear one another's burdens. Instead, he means the burdens that the Lord allows each one of us to bear. One translation reads, "Cast what he has given thee upon the Lord."

Burdens are not accidents but appointments. The burdens you have in your life today are what God has ordained for you—unless they are the result of your own rebellious sin against Him. Burdens help us grow; they help us exercise the muscles of our faith. They teach us how to trust God and live a day at a time.

This promise also tells us that *we can cast these burdens on the Lord*. Peter said, "Casting all your care upon Him, for He cares for you" (I Pet.5:7). The Lord gives us the burden, and then He says, "Now give that burden back to Me. But don't stop there; give Me yourself as well." If we try to give Him our burdens without giving Him ourselves, He really can't help us. It's like stepping onto an elevator with many heavy packages and failing to put them down on the floor until you reach your destination. Let the elevator carry both you and your packages.

Notice that the verse doesn't say He'll *keep* you from problems all the time. He's going to use problems to build your character. But he'll make sure the righteous will not be moved. Cast your burden on the Lord. Let Him sustain you today.

Giving your burden to God is an act of faith. But giving yourself to Him and letting Him use that burden to help you grow is taking an extra step of faith. He will invest that burden in building your character. Give your burden to the Lord today.

Read Psalm 56:1-9

DAY 153

BOTTLES AND BOOKS

Are you the kind of person who keeps a daily record of what you do? When I was in the pastorate, I carried a special diary with me. I wrote down where I visited and who I saw. When I got back to the office, I told my staff, "Here is what I did, and here are the needs we have to pray about."

Did you know that God is keeping a journal about you? His journal is composed of bottles and books. David said, "You number my wanderings; put my tears into Your bottle; are they not in Your book?" (v.8). God watches our traveling and notices our weeping. He has His eyes on our feet, and He has His eyes on our eyes.

God *sees where we walk*. He knows the paths we've been on. Some of these paths are rather bumpy. But that can be for our good, for as a little boy once said, "The bumps are what you climb on." God sees our wanderings, and He's marked it all in His record.

God *sees when we weep*. He sees and records our tears and files them for future reference. Among the Semitic peoples, mourners often catch their tears in a little bottle, a symbol of their sorrow. Then they place the bottle in a tomb or casket. One day God will show you the book and the bottle. He's going to say, "I knew when your heart was broken. I knew what you were going through. I've kept a record of it. Now, that sorrow shall be turned into joy." And everyone of your tears will become a jewel of beauty to the glory of God.

God knows your difficulties and sorrows. The day is coming when your sorrow will be turned to joy, and your tears will glorify Him.

DAY **154**

Read Psalm 56:10-13

DAVID'S PATTERN

Many of David's psalms contain a pattern. He starts with a problem, then he prays, and finally he praises God for solving the problem. At the end of this psalm David praises the Lord. "In God I have put my trust; I will not be afraid. What can man do to me? Vows made to You are binding upon me, O God; I will render praises to You, for You have delivered my soul from death. Have You not delivered my feet from falling, that I may walk before God in the light of the living?" (vv.11-13).

First, *he praises God for His Word.* David didn't have as much of the Bible as we have. In fact, he was writing some of it for us! But he had the Word of God, and he depended on it rather than on his feelings or his circumstances. When we love the Word and depend on it daily, ultimately we will praise God for it.

David praises God for being trustworthy. Where did this faith come from? The Word of God. "Faith comes by hearing, and hearing by the word of God" (Rom.10:17). David is saying, "I'm so grateful for the Word of God because it has taught me to trust the God of the Word. And where there is faith, there will not be fear."

David praises God for all the help He has given him. God delivered his soul from death. I wonder how many times that happened in David's life. God's past deliverance was the assurance of His future care and concern. "Have You not kept my feet from falling, that I may walk before God in the light of the living?" (v.13). God delivers us so He can delight in us and direct us that we might bring glory to His name.

Is David's pattern evident in your life? Are you able to praise God in the midst of difficult situations? Praise Him even before He answers your prayers. Praise Him for His Word, His trustworthiness and His previous help.

HANDLING FEAR

Fear can grip us when we feel life is out of control, and that's what happened to David when he was hiding from King Saul. But instead of running from his fears, with God's help he faced them. By understanding how David handled his fears, we can better handle ours.

First, David honestly admitted his fears (vv.1-7). He admitted the enemy was against him (v.2). We won't win the victory if we pretend the Enemy is not there or if we try to suppress our fears. David's enemies were chasing him like ferocious animals, and they oppressed him all day long. They were slandering him and hunting him. It was a matter of life and death. What did he do? He admitted his fears and trusted in God.

A lady once came to D. L. Moody and said, "I've found a verse to help me conquer my fear—Psalm 56:3." Moody replied, "I'll give you a better verse—Isaiah 12:2." Psalm 56:3 tells us that when we're afraid, we'll trust. Isaiah 12:2 says that we'll "trust and not be afraid." Faith overcomes everything (Ps.103:5). Let's face our fears honestly.

Second, David humbly confessed his faith (vv.8-13). He spoke about God, not his enemies. He clung to the Word of God and did not back out of his commitment to Him just because he was going through trouble. What was the result of David's ordeal? God's protection and provision brought forth David's prayer and praise (vv.12,13).

Although everything may seem stacked against you, God is on your side. He knows who you are, where you are and what you're up against. He will protect you and deliver you.

If you are facing enemies and are gripped by fear, admit your fear and then turn to the Word of God. Trust in His promises to protect and provide. God knows what you are going through, and He will deliver you. Your faith will overcome your fear and lead to praise.

DAY

156

Read Psalm 57:1-11

CONCERT IN A CAVE

I have attended concerts at concert halls, parks and churches, but I have never attended a concert in a cave. David wrote this song when he fled from Saul into a cave. It's difficult to sing even in the midst of the blessings of life, so how could David possibly turn his situation into a song? How could he turn a cave into a concert hall?

He *had God's protection.* "My soul trusts in You; and in the shadow of Your wings I will make my refuge, until these calamities have passed by" (v.1). This means David is in the Holy of Holies, protected by the presence of God. Our protection does not come from circumstances. It comes from the presence of the Lord.

He *knew that God would perform all things for him.* "I will cry out to God Most High, to God who performs all things for me" (v.2). While he was in the cave, David couldn't do very much. But God could—and did—intervene for him.

He *was concerned only about God's glory.* "Be exalted, O God, above the heavens; let Your glory be above all the earth" (v.5). No matter where you are—even in a cave—if you're concerned about the glory of God, that's all that really matters.

David had a joyful tongue because he had a fixed heart. "My heart is steadfast, O God, my heart is steadfast; I will sing and give praise" (v.7). I don't know what kind of cave you might be in today. Perhaps it's one of your own making. I can assure you of these two truths: you have God's protection, and He is working for you. So be concerned only about His glory.

Do your circumstances have you under siege? Do you find yourself in a "cave"? Be encouraged that God will protect you and intervene for you. Be concerned about His glory, not your own. Take time today to praise Him for His care.

Read Psalm 57:1-11

How to
BEGIN AND END EACH DAY

DAY 157

David wrote this psalm when he fled from Saul into a cave. He records one day's experience and gives advice on how to live our lives. First, *close each day in prayer* (vv.1-4). Take all your concerns to God. When you start trusting Him, He changes you, and you see your surroundings in a new way. By faith you enter into His presence. Storms don't last forever, but when they come, God will take care of your problems. He performs and perfects all things for you.

Second, *open each day with praise* (vv.5-8). While David was sleeping, God was working for him. When he awoke, David wanted God to have all the glory and wanted to tell the world what He had done for him. God answers prayers, and whatever He does is for your good and His glory. Calamities pass, so praise God for seeing you through them.

Lock up each day with prayer and unlock each day with praise. Praise is great medicine and will take all bitterness, envy, jealousy and unrest out of your life.

When you are in a tight place, your great concern should not be how you can get out of it but how God will be glorified because of it. Do you find yourself simply enduring difficulties instead of using them to help yourself grow? Try closing each day in prayer and opening each day with praise. Give God an opportunity to accomplish His purposes in your life.

Read Psalm 58:1-11

RIGHTEOUS INDIGNATION

Today there is a need for God's people to display righteous indignation. May we never complacently accept babies being aborted, the poor being exploited and politicians breaking the law. God does not want people in authority to use their authority for themselves. A true statesman uses his authority to build people and his country. David was righteously indignant when he wrote this psalm. He was not angry but anguished.

David denounces the leaders' sin (vv.1-5). Their speech was unrighteous, and they did not judge uprightly (Job 31:6). Their hands were tipping the scales the wrong way because their hearts were evil. David compares these leaders to snakes (v.4).

David pronounces the leaders' judgment (vv.6-9). He presents six pictures of coming judgment for the leaders: (1) a lion without teeth (v.6)—God one day will pull their teeth and they will be defenseless; (2) water soaking into the ground (v.7)—after the dry season, rain disappears and is soaked into the soil; (3) broken arrows (v.7)—God will take away all their defense; (4) a snail melting away (v.8)—the wicked will gradually destroy themselves the further they go; (5) a stillborn child (v.8)—they will experience a lot of pain and then death; and (6) a meal being cooked that is destroyed by a whirlwind (v.9)—their schemes won't last, and they will be destroyed by God's living, burning wrath.

David announces his praise of God (vv.10,11). We do not avenge ourselves, but we can rejoice at God's righteous judgment of the wicked (Rev.18,19). He will stand on His enemies (Ps.68:23).

The righteous will one day enjoy the victory of God. He is patiently waiting to judge the world. When that happens, God will be vindicated, and Jesus will be glorified.

The misuse of authority is an age-old problem. The Bible tells us what will become of those who abuse their positions of authority. God's people may confidently express their righteous indignation, for we know that He will one day judge corrupt leaders. Praise Him for His coming victory and vindication.

Read Psalm 58:10, 11

THE BEST IS YET TO COME

DAY 159

Does it ever trouble you that the righteous seem to suffer, while the wicked seem to escape suffering? Have you ever gotten the bad end of a deal while somebody else—perhaps even a professing Christian—came out on top after doing something he shouldn't have done? If so, this passage will encourage you: "The righteous shall rejoice when he sees the vengeance . . . so that men will say, 'Surely there is a reward for the righteous; surely He is God who judges in the earth.'"

When someone else hurts us, when we get the bad end of a deal, we must first *accept the burden and realize there is no real justice in the world today*. Oh, there's some justice, of course. We are grateful for what the law is doing. But fundamentally, it seems that those who are doing good are being persecuted, while those who are doing evil are being promoted. Accept the burden of this seeming inequality. That's the way things are in this world.

Second, *leave the situation with the Lord*. When someone does something that shouldn't be done, we immediately want to right the wrong and punish the wrongdoer. But we must leave it with God. He says, "Vengeance is Mine, I will repay" (Rom.12:19).

That leads to a third word of counsel: *Wait on the Lord*. Your reward is yet to come. This world is heaven for the unsaved. They never will experience the joys and blessings in the glory of eternity with the Lord. But a believer's heaven is yet to come. Heaven is a place of unmixed joy; hell is a place of undiluted sorrow. In this world we have a mixture of sorrow and joy. Wait, for your reward is yet to come.

At times this world appears to lack justice. You need not fret over this. When you are faced with inequality, leave your burden with the Lord and wait patiently for Him to resolve the issue. For God's people, the best is yet to come.

DAY

160

Read Psalm 59:1-17

WHO'S WATCHING YOU?

Have you ever been in a public place and noticed that someone was watching you? I've been in restaurants when my wife has said, "Those people at that table keep watching us. I wonder if we know them." It usually turns out that we don't know them, and they don't know us, but maybe we look like someone they know.

In this psalm David records his experience when Saul's men were watching his house. They wanted to arrest and kill him. But David was rejoicing in the Lord. He was singing in a time of danger. And he was crying out to the Lord for mercy.

What God is to you determines what He does for you. "I will sing of Your power" (v.16). David knew that God is a God of power. Saul could not overthrow Him. "I will sing aloud of Your mercy" (v.16). That's what David needed more than anything else. We need to pray all day long that the mercy of God will sustain us. David discovered mercy in the morning (v.16). Start your day by singing to the Lord and drawing upon His mercy.

"To You, O my Strength, . . . God is my defense" (v.17). Those are words of security and dependability. When God is your Power, when God gives you mercy, when God is your Strength and Defense, then you can face any enemy. You can face any circumstance, because God is going to see you through.

God responds according to your faith and surrounds you with His mercy. Is yours the kind of faith that can sing to Him in times of danger? The next time you face threatening circumstances, trust the Lord. He will protect you and deliver you from your enemies.

Read Psalm 59:1-17

DEFENSE AND DELIVERANCE

DAY **161**

Have you ever had to escape danger by going out through a window? Paul escaped from Damascus that way (Acts 9), and David through a window as well (I Sam.19). One day David went home and discovered that he was being spied on. His wife let him down through a window, and he escaped from his enemies. As we read this psalm, we notice four assurances that kept David going.

First, *David knows that God sees, so he prays* (vv.1-5). David needed to be defended and delivered. His enemies were lying about him. Suffering is hard to take when you haven't sinned. But God is on the throne and is watching us. He knows our difficulties. The next time you're in trouble, remember that God sees you. Pray to Him—He's listening.

Second, *David is sure that God hears, so he waits* (vv.6-9). While we wait, God accomplishes many things, and we regain our strength (v.9; Isa.40:31).

Third, *David is sure that God rules, so he trusts* (vv.10-13). God meets David with mercy and the enemy with judgment. David prays that God will scatter his enemies, stop them and consume them.

Fourth, *David is sure that God delivers, so he sings* (vv.14-17). We cannot always stop people's actions. David's wife warned him that he had to leave or he would be dead by morning (I Sam.19:11), yet he was able to sing about God's mercy in the morning (v.16). Always thank God after He answers prayer.

How do you exercise your faith when the enemy is pursuing? Respond by praying, waiting, trusting and singing.

DAY 162

Read Psalm 60:1-12

AFTER THE VICTORY

"Through God we will do valiantly, for it is He who shall tread down our enemies" (v.12). Psalm 60 is unusual because David didn't write it in the midst of trouble. So many of his psalms were written from a cave or a battlefield. But this psalm was written after a great victory. The army had achieved a tremendous victory in Edom for the people of God.

What do we learn from this psalm? First, *we must be cautious after a victory*. "O God, You have cast us off; You have broken us down; You have been displeased; oh, restore us again!" (v.1). David was crying out to God and saying, "O God, we have just won a great victory. But there are battles yet to fight." Some of God's great people had their biggest defeats after their victories. Elijah won a great victory on Mount Carmel, and then he became discouraged and suffered a great defeat. We must be careful to win the victory after we have won the battle.

Second, *we are always carrying God's banner*. Even after the victory has ended, we are still His ambassadors. "You have given a banner to those who fear You, that it may be displayed because of the truth" (v.4). We carry a banner of truth because we are standing for the Word of God. After we've won the victory, let's not put down the banner. Let's continue to carry it to the glory of God.

Third, *we must give God the glory.* David gave Him all of the glory for what He had done. It's so easy to claim the victory for yourself. It's so easy after the victory to say, "This is what I have done." Pride moves in, and that can lead to defeat.

One of your most vulnerable times comes after God has given you a victory, for you may let down your guard. And the Devil stands poised to attack again. How do you seal the victory? Always carry the banner of God and be sure to give Him the glory. The next time God gives you a victory, stay grounded in the truth of His Word and avoid entertaining any prideful thoughts. God deserves all the glory.

FIGHTING BATTLES

About the time one problem is solved, another one begins. That's the situation David found himself in when he wrote this psalm. He was leading one battle and praying about another. In your own battles, seek to imitate David's four responses in this psalm.

First, *he surveys the situation* (vv.1-3). David always looked at situations through the eyes of a poet. He pictures this predicament as a sudden flood, an earthquake and staggering, drunken people. David thinks God will prevent the Moabites from invading the land, but He allows them to come in. David then asks the Lord to forgive and restore the people and stop the flood. The Jews think the mountains and the earth are sure and steadfast, but David feels everything trembling and breaking open. He sees the people staggering as though drunk. The cup of wrath, of judgment, has come. David looks at the situation and says, "Can things get any worse?"

Second, *he lifts the banner of God's truth* (vv.4,5). David fought these wars because he was God's king and the Israelites were God's people. We need to realize that even though there are problems, struggles and battles in life, God still loves us (Rom.8:35). His love cannot change and will not fail, *no matter how we feel*. David lifts the banner of God's truth. That is one of God's names: "The-Lord-Is-My-Banner" (Ex.17:15). David was capable, but he was depending on God's right hand. The Lord rallies His troops around His banner.

Third, *he listens to the Commander* (vv.6-8). David knew he was second in command, for God was the Leader of the armies of Israel. God says, "Wherever you go in Israel, it all belongs to me; lawn the land. So stop worrying." When David heard the Commander talk like that, he knew he didn't have to be afraid. He rested in the victory of the Lord (I Cor.15:58).

Finally, *he launches out by faith* (vv.9-12). David says, "I don't have any confidence in myself. God has to lead me to victory." Almighty God always goes before us. He gives us help and the victory (Ps.118:8).

On whose strength you draw, the Lord's or your own, will determine victory or defeat. If you let Him lead, He will take you to victory.

Read Psalm 61:1-8

FEEL LIKE GIVING UP?

When his son Absalom rebelled against him, David had to flee from Jerusalem to save his life. Out of that experience he wrote this psalm. "Hear my cry, O God; attend to my prayer. From the end of the earth I will cry to You, when my heart is overwhelmed; lead me to the rock that is higher than I. For You have been a shelter for me, and a strong tower from the enemy" (vv.1-3).

David was asking for God's help and strength. He may have been in a cave when he wrote these words or hiding in a shelter in the wilderness. We don't know. But his true Rock was God. His true Shelter and his true Strong Tower was God. It's good to know that when we are away from the safety of home and city, we still have the safety of the Lord.

David was abiding. "I will abide in Your tabernacle forever; I will trust in the shelter of Your wings" (v.4). This means the Holy of Holies, where the wings of the cherubim overshadowed the Ark of the Covenant. We might ask, "How can you abide in the tabernacle, David, when you're out there in the wilderness? You're running away." He would say, "My God is always with me. As long as I abide in Him, I am abiding in His tabernacle." David realized he didn't need city walls for protection. God was his Rock. He didn't need the tabernacle for his worship. God was his Tabernacle.

David was rejoicing. "So I will sing praise to Your name forever, that I may daily perform my vows" (v.8). When you bring your requests to the Lord and rely on Him, you discover you can rejoice in Him. "For You, O God, have heard my vows . . . You will prolong the king's life" (v.5). God answered David's prayer.

What is God to you? Is He your Rock, your Shelter, your Strong Tower, your Tabernacle? Are you trusting Him to meet your specific needs today?

God never intended that His people "throw in the towel." Remember these truths. He is always listening to your cry. He is always with you and never forsake you, whatever your circumstances. You can always rejoice in God's protection. Apply the truths of this psalm to your situation today.

The Accomplishments of
PRAYER

Whenever David found himself in a tight spot, he instinctively turned to God in prayer. Prayer is the natural breath of the believer. It enables you to accomplish what you cannot accomplish by yourself.

First, *prayer enables you to reach farther* (v.2). David was homesick. Although he was away from Jerusalem, he was not away from God. No matter where you are, you can reach out through prayer and touch the lives of family, friends and missionaries.

Second, *prayer enables you to go higher* (v.2). David was overwhelmed and wrapped in gloom. When he prayed, God lifted him up and put him on a high rock, in a tower that He built for him (v.3). Prayer puts you on the mountaintop and enables you to get a clear perspective of your situation.

Third, *prayer enables you to come closer* (v.4). "The shelter of your wings" is not referring to a mother hen gathering her chicks before a storm breaks; it is talking about getting under the wings of the cherubim in the Holy of Holies. Through Jesus you can enter into the presence of God and dwell under His wings.

Fourth, *prayer enables you to grow richer* (v.5). In prayer you draw upon the heritage you have in Jesus Christ (Eph.1:3).

Fifth, *prayer enables you to live fuller* (vv.6,7). It's not the length of life that counts but the depth. Prayer puts depth into your life. I pity people who depend upon worldly entertainment instead of the fullness of life in Christ.

Finally, *prayer enables you to be happier* (v.8). Prayer and praise always go together. David starts out crying and ends up praising. He starts out praying and ends up rejoicing. Spend time with the Lord in prayer. It will change your life.

Evaluate your praying. Is it accomplishing in your life what it accomplished in David's? If not, spend more time in prayer and determine to experience its accomplishment in your life.

Read Psalm 62:1-12

TRIPLE ASSURANCE

Verses 2, 5 and 12 contain three assurances that help us wait: God is our Salvation. God is our Expectation. God is our Vindication. Let's look closer at these three assurances.

God is our Salvation. David refers to salvation not from sin but from danger. "He only is my rock and my salvation; He is my defense; I shall not be greatly moved" (v.2). David's enemies were pursuing him as usual. Saul was trying to kill him as usual. And yet David says, "I'm going to wait on the Lord. I'm not going to run around and lose control of myself. I'm going to wait on the Lord because from Him comes my salvation." That's true today also. We live in a dangerous world. We never know what may be just around the corner, but we have the assurance that God is our Rock and our Defense.

God is our Expectation. Where do you look for your expectation? To yourself, your wallet, your bankbook, your friends? Where do you look when the future seems bleak and dark? David looked to God. "My soul, wait silently for God alone, for my expectation is from Him" (v.5).

God is our Vindication. It relieves us of a great deal of pressure and burden to know that we are not judges but witnesses. We are not here to vindicate ourselves. Our vindication comes from God, "who will render to each one according to his deeds" (Rom.2:6). Today, as you face difficulties with people or things or circumstances, wait on the Lord. From Him come your salvation, your expectation and your vindication.

In troubled times, how often do you first look to yourself or others for answers before looking to God? If you look to God and wait for Him, He will see you through. Put God first and wait for Him to act on your behalf.

Read Psalm 63:1-11

ARE YOU THIRSTY?

DAY 167

King David wrote this psalm when he was in the wilderness of Judah. I never really appreciated what he wrote until my wife and I visited the same spot. What a dry and, barren place it is! Look at what David wrote, "O God, You are my God; early will I seek You; my soul thirsts for You; my flesh longs for You in a dry and thirsty land where there is no water" (v.1). In other words, David says, "Here I am in this dry, hot, dangerous wilderness, and I really would love to have some water. However, what I really want is God."

When you find yourself in a dry wilderness situation in life, what do you do? Follow the stages in David's experience. First, *he seeks God.* He wanted to see God's power and glory as he had seen it in the sanctuary. He wanted to see that wilderness turned into a sanctuary. David had been in the tabernacle. He had seen the glory of God, but he wasn't satisfied with that. We are satisfied to hear about God and sing about Him in church. Then we come to the wilderness. We should be like David and say, "I want to see God's glory through this wilderness experience just as though I were worshiping God in the church service."

Next, he *blesses God.* "Thus I will bless You while I live" (v.4). David also *is satisfied with God.* Satisfaction doesn't come from circumstances on the outside. It comes from blessing on the inside. "When I remember You on my bed, I meditate on You in the night watches" (v.6). Finally, he *rejoices* in *God.* "But the king shall rejoice in God" (v.11). That's what God wants from us, even in the wilderness.

Wilderness experiences are good for you, for they teach you an important truth: You draw satisfaction from blessing on the inside, not from circumstances on the outside. When you face a wilderness experience, follow David's response. God will meet your needs.

Read Psalm 64:1-10

FREE FROM FEAR

Most of us live relatively safe and secure lives, but David was in exile. He was being hounded by King Saul, who wanted to kill him. Here David prays for protection, and he closes the psalm by saying, "The righteous shall be glad in the Lord, and trust in Him. And all the upright in heart shall glory" (v.10). We find three key concepts in this verse that encourage us: joy, faith and glory.

Are you glad in the Lord today? So many times we are not glad because of circumstances. David prayed, "Hear my voice, O God, in my meditation; preserve my life from fear of the enemy" (v.1). I would have said, "Preserve my life from the enemy." But David said, "Preserve me from fear of the enemy." In other words, instead of fear he had faith. Instead of fear he had joy. Instead of fear he wanted to bring glory to God.

Most of our problems are not on the outside but on the inside. When the disciples were in the boat in the middle of the Sea of Galilee on a stormy night, Jesus came to them and rebuked them for their unbelief. Their problem wasn't the storm on the outside—it was the storm on the inside. Likewise, your problem today may not be the circumstances around you or the people against you. It may be the fear that's inside you.

"All men shall fear, and shall declare the work of God" (v.9). David sang praises to the Lord. He was glad in the Lord. He trusted in and gave glory to Him. "All the upright in heart shall glory" (v.10). It's easy to read this verse but much more difficult to practice it. Take your eyes off the circumstances and put them on the Lord. Trust in His promises, not your own power. And most of all, seek to bring Him all the glory.

Fear can rob you of your joy and trust in God. Don't allow fear or circumstances to take your eyes off the Lord. Let the truth of the Word of God control your mind and heart.

THE THREE Ps

"Praise is awaiting You, O God, in Zion; and to You the vow shall be performed" (v.1). David was a great soldier. But he also was a great singer and a great saint. In spite of difficulties and problems and even dangers, he was able to praise the Lord.

He continues, "O You who hear prayer, to You all flesh will come" (v.2). Some people only pray. They don't really praise. And yet praise and prayer belong together. Prayer means coming to God and telling Him your needs. David says, "All flesh will come." Anyone who knows the Lord can pray anywhere in the world anytime. All the world can come to God, and all the world can pray.

The more we pray, the more answers we have to praise the Lord for. But sometimes we can't pray because sin is in the way. This is why David says, "Iniquities prevail against me; as for our transgressions, You will provide atonement for them" (v.3). The more we praise the Lord, the more we see how needy and dirty we are. And so we come for purging, confessing our sin to God.

"Blessed is the man whom You choose, and cause to approach You, that he may dwell in Your courts. We shall be satisfied with the goodness of Your house, of Your holy temple" (v.4). That's the experience God wants us to have—to approach Him, to dwell with Him, to be satisfied with Him. How do we do this? By prayer, praise and purging of sins. Then we will draw near to Him as He draws near to us.

Do you have a close relationship with God? You can, draw nearer to Him. Confess any sins you may be harboring. Then praise Him and come to Him in prayer.

DAY

170

Read Psalm 66:1-7

AN INVITATION

Psalm 66 contains several invitations that are tied to the word *come*: "come and sing"; "come and see"; and "come and hear." Let's look at the first two invitations.

The first invitation is *come and sing*, or praise the Lord. "Sing out the honor of His name; make His praise glorious" (v.2). Sometimes we act as if praise is tedious. Sometimes we praise Him in a tired fashion. But the psalmist asks for glorious praise. Why? "Through the greatness of Your power Your enemies shall submit themselves to You. All the earth shall worship You and sing praises to You" (vv.3,4). This is missionary zeal. We aren't to praise the Lord by ourselves. We come and sing, and we invite the whole world to join us.

The second invitation is *come and see* the works of God. Today people call the works of God natural law or scientific law. We try to explain everything, but we can't. Come and see the works of God—what happens in the heavens, what happens in your body and what happened in history. This is the work of God. I like verse 7: "He rules by His power forever." Satan is not ruling this world system—God is. He is allowing Satan to do some things, but He's going to use even that to glorify Himself. God is ruling by His power, and He will rule forever,.

If you want to enjoy today, come and sing. If you've lost your song, come and see the works of the Lord. You'll be singing before long.

Have you lost your song of praise? Come and see the works of God; it will restore your song. His works reveal His greatness and His love. If you are walking with the Lord, praise Him and tell others what He is doing in your life.

WHY THE TRIALS?

This psalm is for the discouraged. "Oh, bless our God, you peoples! And make the voice of His praise to be heard" (v.8) Why? "Who keeps our soul among the living, and does not allow our feet to be moved" (v.9). God holds our life in His hand. "In Him we live and move and have our being" (Acts 17:28). So let's praise Him.

"For You, O God, have tested us; You have refined us as silver is refined" (v.10). The reason God tries us and tests us is to prove us. He's proving nothing to Himself. He knows us from top to bottom. Instead, He's proving something to us. God considers us as valuable as silver, and He puts us into situations that test and strengthen us.

Notice the images in these next two verses. "You brought us *into the net*; You laid affliction *on our backs*. You have caused men to ride *over our heads*; we went through fire and through water; but You brought us out to rich fulfillment" (vv.11,12, italics mine). This indicates total defeat. We go through fire and water, but we are brought out into a wealthy place. That word *wealthy* means "an abundant place, a moist place, a place of running water and fruitfulness." The wilderness of Judea, where David so often found himself, was dry and barren.

The psalmist does not say, "Well, here I am in trouble again." No, he says, "God brought me *in*, and God's going to bring me *through*. And when He brings me *out*, I'm going to be in a wealthy place." God always enriches us when we go through difficulty. He proves us and tries us to make us more like Jesus.

The trials of God have a refining and strengthening effect. The result is they make us more like Jesus. Are you discouraged today by trials? Be encouraged that God will see you through and that He will use your trials to build you.

DAY

172

Read Psalm 67:1-7

WILL YOU SHARE?

The author of this psalm is unknown, but it was someone who had a vision of the whole world. God had blessed him, and he wanted to share that blessing with everyone. He writes, "God be merciful to us and bless us, and cause His face to shine upon us" (v.1). That sounds like a priestly benediction, doesn't it? "The Lord bless you and keep you; the Lord make His face shine upon you, and be gracious unto you" (Num.6:24,25).

Three times in verse 1 the psalmist uses the word *us*. He refers to the Jewish people, but he doesn't stop there. "That Your way may be known on earth, Your salvation among all nations" (v.2). So many Old Testament Jews wanted to keep what they had for themselves. They did not want to share it. How unlike God's plan! After all, why did He call Abraham? That he might be a blessing to the whole world. Why did Jesus die? That the Gospel message might go out to the whole world.

Why has the Lord blessed us? That we might share the Gospel with others. We have no problem praying verse 1: "Oh, be merciful to us and bless us and make Your face shine upon us." But what about verse 2? Do we want to be blessed so that we might be a blessing? That's the reason God blesses us in the first place. Likewise, He answers our prayers so that we might become an answer to someone else's prayer.

The result of making God's salvation known among all the nations is praise. "Let the peoples praise You, O God; let all the peoples praise You" (v.3). This doesn't mean just the Israelites. Even the Gentiles are included. "Oh, let the nations be glad and sing for joy!" (v.4). "Let all the peoples praise You" (v.5).

Notice how the psalm ends: "Then the earth shall yield her increase; God, our own God, shall bless us. God shall bless us, and all the ends of the earth shall fear Him" (vv.6, 7). The sequence in this psalm is significant. The psalmist begins by saying, "Lord, bless me so that I may bless others." He does become a blessing to others, so God blesses him again. What a marvelous experience of God's grace.

Are you part of God's sequence of blessing? If you will share, He will bless you so that you may be a blessing. Experience the fullness of His grace by telling others about Him.

Read Psalm 68:1-6

LIKE SMOKE AND WAX

DAY **173**

Someone has said that a person is known not only by the friends he keeps but also by the enemies he makes. The Lord Jesus had enemies. David had enemies. Anyone who stands up for what is right will have enemies. But notice what these enemies are like—"as smoke is driven away" (v.2). Who's afraid of smoke? It can smother us, but if we keep fresh air coming in—the fresh wind of the Holy Spirit—it can't bother us. David also compares his enemies to melting wax (v.2). A burning candle is a picture of what will happen to God's enemies. The smoke is quickly blown away, and the wax quietly melts. God gets the victory.

"So let the wicked perish at the presence of God. But let the righteous be glad; let them rejoice before God" (v.2,3). Why? Because of what God does for us. "Sing to God, sing praises to His name, extol Him who rides on the clouds" (v.4). I like that picture. God is the Great Conqueror, riding upon the heavens.

He also is "a father of the fatherless" (v.5). He comes right where we are to comfort and heal our broken hearts. Furthermore, God is Judge and Redeemer. He frees those who are bound with chains.

Are you feeling oppressed by your enemies? Leave the burden with your Father, and let Him be your Conqueror.

DAY 174

Read Psalm 68:7-18

SHARING THE WEALTH

Here David describes the victories of God. "You have ascended on high, You have led captivity captive; You have received gifts among men" (v.18). This is a picture of our Lord's ascension. We find this verse quoted in the New Testament, referring to Jesus Christ (Eph.4:8).

Look at what Jesus has performed for us. First, *He went before us.* "O God, when You went out before Your people" (v.7). Wherever you are today, if you're in the will of God, He has already gone before you. The picture here is of the nation of Israel going through the wilderness. God didn't expect the Israelites to figure out the logistics for themselves. By night He led them by a pillar of fire and by day by a cloud. The Ark of the Covenant—the presence of the Lord—went before them. He also went before us and bore our sins on the cross.

Second He *has gone above us.* "You have ascended on high" (v.18). The Lord Jesus has ascended to glory, and He is seated there at the right hand of the Father in majesty. He who went before us to win the victory has now gone above us to share the victory.

Now He *dwells among us.* Notice the end of verse 18: "That the Lord God might dwell there." And what is He doing? He is giving gifts to His people. It's a picture of the Conqueror distributing the Spoil. How wealthy we are! How much we have to thank Him for. Will you trust the Victor today?

Because of Christ's death and Resurrection, you are wealthy. God freely shares with you the spoils of His victory at the cross. You need never be defeated in this life.

Read Psalm 68:19-27

BURDENS AND BENEFITS

DAY 175

"Blessed be the Lord, who daily loads us with benefits, the God of our salvation!" (v.19). We can translate that verse, "Blessed be the Lord, who daily bears our burdens." Let's think about benefits and burdens. God is the One who gives us the burdens of life. Sometimes we bring burdens upon ourselves by our disobedience, rebellion, sin, unbelief, lack of love and unkindness. But if we are walking in the will of God on the path of His choosing, and if we have burdens to bear, He is the One who has given them to us. Let's view the burdens of life as benefits.

Perhaps the greatest example of this is the Apostle Paul. How he was burdened with his thorn in the flesh! He prayed three times that God would take it away. Instead, God turned that burden into a benefit. He told Paul, "I'm going to give you the grace that you need" (see II Cor.12:7-9). Sometimes God answers prayer by taking things away. Sometimes He answers prayer by adding things to us. That's what he did for Paul, and the burden became a benefit.

"But," you say, "I have some heavy burdens. I don't see much benefit to them." Notice the word *daily* in verse 19: "Blessed be the Lord, who daily loads us with benefits." We live a day at a time. To think of all of life's burdens coming at once can be crushing. Remember what you have been through in your life. You've been through circumstances you never thought you would get through. But God brought you through. "Give us this day our daily bread" (Matt.6:11). "And, Lord, give us this day our daily burdens and benefits."

God knows how much we can bear, and His grace is sufficient for each day. But there is another dimension to our burdens. God can turn them into benefits. Has He given you a heavy burden? Perhaps He wants to turn it into a benefit and do something special for you.

DAY **176**

Read Psalm 68:28-35

HOW STRONG IS GOD?

We don't go far on our own strength. Here, David instructs us how to understand and appropriate the strength of God. He tells us to *ascribe strength to God*. Realize that He is a God of strength. "His excellence is over Israel, and His strength is in the clouds" (v.34). That means His strength is high up. God can get strength even from the clouds (nothing but rolling vapor). We think of God as loving, gracious and merciful. But let's also think of Him as strong.

We also need to *ask for strength from God*. "Strengthen, O God, what You have done for us" (v.28). We have every privilege to come and ask God for the strength we need today. "But those who wait on the Lord shall renew their strength; they shall mount up with wings like eagles, they shall run and not be weary, they shall walk and not faint" (Isa.40:31). God has already determined what He wants to do. He'll do it when we request it. "You do not have because you do not ask" (James 4:2).

Next, we need to *acknowledge our strength is from God*. "The God of Israel is He who gives strength and power to His people. Blessed be God" (v.35). If you need strength today, don't look to yourself or to anyone else. Look up, because God is the God of strength, and He wants to command strength for you if you'll ask Him.

····◆····

Often Satan will tempt you to draw your strength from the world's substitutes. When that happens, remember the truths of this psalm. When you need strength to continue the battle, spend time in prayer with God. Ascribe strength to Him, ask Him for strength and acknowledge that your strength is from Him.

THE WORST DEATH

I was chatting about death with a neighbor once, using it as an opportunity to witness to him. We were discussing what the most difficult way to die would be. I finally said, "Perhaps the most difficult way to die would be to be smothered—to be sinking in quicksand and be smothered."

David had that kind of experience spiritually. "Save me, O God! For the waters have come up to my neck. I sink in deep mire, where there is no standing; I have come into deep waters, where the floods overflow me" (vv.1,2). It's bad enough to be sinking in quicksand, but David also had the floods coming over him. What did he do? He did what every Christian should do. First, *he waited.* "My throat is dry; my eyes fail while I wait for my God" (v.3). "Let not those who wait for You, O Lord God of hosts, be ashamed" (v.6). David knew the situation was in God's control. Yes, he did cry out to God for rescue. Nothing is wrong with that. But he also waited.

Second, *he wept.* "When I wept and chastened my soul with fasting, that became my reproach" (v.10). *Reproach* is used again and again in Psalm 69. (This is a messianic psalm that talks about the reproach Jesus endured for us.) Nothing is wrong with weeping. Pain hurts, and some situations can break your heart. David waited and wept, and he knew that God was going to see him through.

Third, *he watched.* "Let not those who wait for You, O Lord God of hosts, be ashamed because of me; let not those who seek You be confounded because of me, O God of Israel" (v.6). In other words David says, "It's not important what happens to me. But I don't want to create any problems for anybody else." Throughout this psalm David becomes more and more like the Lord. When you find yourself sinking, wait, weep, watch and let God work.

When you find yourself sinking in the quicksand, there is little else you can do but cry to the Lord. Sometimes He allows the "quicksand" experiences to turn you to Him. Wait for God. Acknowledge that He is in control. Give Him the pieces of your broken heart and watch Him work for you. You can depend on His faithfulness.

DAY **178**

Read Psalm 69:13-21

NO COMFORTERS

"Reproach has broken my heart and I am full of heaviness; I looked for someone to take pity, but there was none; and for comforters, but I found none" (v.20). When we read Psalm 69, we meet Jesus Christ, for many verses from this psalm are quoted in the New Testament, relating to Him. For example, "I have become a stranger to my brothers, an alien to my mother's children; because zeal for Your house has eaten me up, and the reproaches of those who reproach You have fallen on me" (vv.8,9; John 2:17). David is going through difficulty, and it is making him more like Jesus. Therefore, it enabled him to reveal the Lord to us.

What breaks your heart? Is it broken when you can't have your way? Is it broken when something is taken away from you? Jesus and David both said, "Reproach has broken my heart" (v.20). What can you do about a broken heart? David prayed, "Deliver me. Hear me. Draw near to my soul. Redeem me" (vv.14, 16, 18). And God answered him.

Sometimes you bear reproach because of others. You feel heavy, brokenhearted and alone. But Jesus went through all of this for us. Be thankful that you can share in the fellowship of His sufferings (Phil.3:10). Also, while others are going through this experience, be an encouragement to them. If you've known what it's like to have a broken heart, and if you've looked for someone to take pity, then you know how much it means to have a friend. Today, find someone with a broken heart and start to bring healing to him.

When your heart is broken, be encouraged that Jesus knows what you are going through and that you are becoming like Him. But there's another purpose: You can help others whose hearts are broken. God will use you to help bring healing to them. Don't waste your experiences; they have great value.

RECIPE FOR REJOICING

"I will praise the name of God with a song and will magnify Him with thanksgiving." This verse seems out of place here, because this psalm has an atmosphere of trial and sorrow. Six times we find the word *reproach* in Psalm 69. David cries out to God for help, so it's strange to find him saying, "I will praise the name of God with a song, and will magnify Him with thanksgiving." When you are sinking, when you think that everything has gone wrong, when others are persecuting you and smiting you, *praise the name of God with a song.*

Paul and Silas must have thought of verse 30 when they were suffering in jail in Philippi (see Acts 16:16-34). They were in the stocks. They had been humiliated and arrested. Their rights were taken from them. They had been beaten with rods, and their bodies ached. But they began to sing and praise God. The concert brought down the house, and the jailer was saved. When you find yourself sinking, start singing.

Magnify the Lord. When I hurt, I have a tendency to magnify myself. I think, *Nobody ever felt the way I feel. Nobody's ever been through what I've been through*. But David said, "I'm not going to do that. I'm going to magnify the Lord."

Thank the Lord. Anyone can thank Him when things are going well. Anyone can thank Him in the sunshine. But when you are sinking in the deep mire, it's difficult to give thanks to God. But we need to do so.

Here you have a threefold recipe for rejoicing when you are sinking: Praise the name of the Lord, seek to magnify Him and bring your thanksgiving from your heart.

Are you overwhelmed by your circumstances? Trust the Lord and follow this recipe. He will cause you to rejoice.

DAY **180**

Read Psalm 70:1-5

HURRY UP, GOD!

Has God ever been slow in your life? He was in David's. This undoubtedly was one of the psalms written when David was being harassed by King Saul. So he cries out, "Lord, why don't You do something? You're being awfully slow."

Have you ever pondered the delays of God? He is never in a hurry, but once He starts to work, watch out! He patiently accomplishes His work. David pleads, "Make haste, make haste" (v.1). He repeats his plea in verse 5: "I am poor and needy; make haste to me, O God! You are my help and my deliverer; O Lord, do not delay." If right now it seems as though God is tarrying instead of working, if it seems as though He is delaying instead of acting, what should you do? Seek Him and wait on Him and love Him. Verse 4 says it beautifully: "Let all those who seek You rejoice and be glad in You; and let those who love Your salvation say continually, 'Let God be magnified!'" We've seen that phrase before. David, when he was sinking, said, "I . . . will magnify Him with thanksgiving" (Ps.69:30).

Here's a good lesson for us. When God is not moving as rapidly as we think He should, when our timetables do not coincide, what should we do? Rejoice in Him, love Him and magnify Him. Let Him worry about the timetable. God is always working, and we know that all things are working together for good (Rom.8:28). But He waits for the right time to reveal His victories. Let Him watch the clock.

God's delays are a part of your character-building process. The next time God gives you a delay, encourage yourself by remembering that He never stops working for you, and He knows when and how to help you. Submit to His timetable and His care.

Read Psalm 71:1-11

WHEN I AM OLD

DAY **181**

The older I become, the more I appreciate this psalm. It focuses on God's special blessings for those who are getting older. "Do not cast me off in the time of old age; do not forsake me when my strength fails" (v.9).

What does God do for us as we get older? He helps us meet and solve some of the problems that we encounter in our later years. Take the problem of *weakness*, for example. That's what David talks about in verse 9: "Do not forsake me when my strength fails." The outward man is failing, but the inward man can be renewed day by day. God will provide you with the spiritual strength that you need.

Another problem we face as we get older is *confusion*. "In You, O Lord, I put my trust; let me never be put to shame [confusion]" (v.1). We can't always keep up with so many rapid changes in this world. As we get older, we might say, "I don't quite know what's going on." But God says, "Look, don't worry about it. You trust Me, and I'll never allow you to be confused."

A third problem we experience is that of *living in the past*. Too often we say, "Back in the good old days . . ." I've concluded that perhaps the good old days were not that good. David acknowledges, "For You are my hope, O Lord God" (v.5). He was living in the future. We don't know what the future holds, but we do know that God holds our future.

Finally, we may face the problem of *complaining*. How easy it is to complain as we grow older. But David said, "Let my mouth be filled with Your praise and with Your glory all the day" (v.8). When we're walking with the Lord, He takes care of weakness and confusion. He takes care of our fear of the future. He also substitutes praise for complaining, and therefore, we grow old graciously.

Each phase of life has unique advantages and problems. And God stays with you through each phase. Are you facing the problems of old age? Are you struggling with weakness, confusion, living in the past and complaining? Bring your fears to God. He delights in caring for His people.

DAY
182

Read Psalm 71:12-24

FOR THOSE WHO FOLLOW

As we get older, things change. We must drop some things, and we must start others. Not much goes on continually—except in Psalm 71. David uses the word *continually* three times. First, he tells us that we can continually resort to the Lord in prayer: "Be my strong refuge, to which I may resort continually" (v.3). No matter how old we get, we can pray, because the Lord never fails. We also can have continual praise. "My praise shall be continually of You" (v.6). If prayer is without ceasing, then praise will be without ceasing. David also tells us, "I will hope continually" (v.14).

"Now also when I am old and grayheaded, O God, do not forsake me, until I declare Your strength to this generation, Your power to everyone who is to come" (v.18). Notice that David's focus is not simply on his needs. He wants to have his needs met so he can share the Lord with others. "You shall increase my greatness and comfort me on every side . . . I will praise You" (vv.21,22).

If we are resorting to the Lord continually in prayer, if we are rejoicing in Him continually in praise, if we are hoping in Him continually and laying hold of His promises, if we are saying that the best is yet to come and praise Him more and more, then we can grow old and gray-headed without fear. We'll be able to glorify the Lord, and we'll be able to share Him with others in the next generation. What kind of heritage are you leaving for future generations? What are you teaching them by word and example about God's strength and power? Will others put their faith in the Lord on the basis of your life and testimony?

You can always live to bring glory to God no matter what your age is. Those of us who are older can do that in a special way; we can teach the younger generation about His faithfulness. Preserve your Christian heritage for future generations. Let your life be a continual testimony for God.

Read Psalm 72:1-11

GREATER THAN SOLOMON

DAY 183

Psalm 72 was written for Solomon, probably when he became king. But looking beyond this psalm, we will see someone who is greater than Solomon—Jesus Christ. Notice what the writer says, "Give the king Your judgments, O God, and Your righteousness to the king's Son" (v.1). In fact, he mentions *righteousness* several times in this psalm. "He will judge Your people with righteousness" (v.2). "The mountains will bring peace to the people, and the little hills, by righteousness" (v.3). "In His days the righteous shall flourish" (v.7). Jesus is to us the righteousness of God. The psalmist wants Solomon to be a righteous man, to have the kind of integrity and honesty that it takes to exercise kingly judgment. Jesus Christ has never made a mistake. He is our righteousness, and He does what is righteous.

Next, the writer talks about *peace*. "The mountains will bring peace to the people" (v.3). "In His days the righteous shall flourish, and abundance of peace, until the moon is no more" (v.7). We can have righteousness without peace. We can turn soldiers loose and let them execute people who are breaking the law. But we can't have peace without righteousness. We must first have righteousness with God before we can have peace with Him.

The righteousness and peace of our Lord are emphasized in the Book of Hebrews, in the person of Melchizedek. Jesus is the King of righteousness and peace. He also brings refreshment. "He shall come down like rain upon the mown grass, like showers that water the earth" (v.6). We have days when our hearts are dry like a desert. But the Lord showers blessings upon us and produces fruitfulness in us, and all of this leads to victory. "All kings shall fall down before Him; all nations shall serve Him" (v.11). We worship and obey Him who is infinitely greater than Solomon.

One day Christ will establish His kingdom on the earth. Through His righteous rule He will bring peace. Today, He establishes His kingdom in the hearts and lives of believers. Because of His righteousness, you may have the peace of God in your heart. Do you have this peace?

WHAT A NAME!

"His name shall endure forever; His name shall continue as long as the sun. And men shall be blessed in Him; all nations shall call Him blessed" (v.17). Originally, that was written about Solomon. But as we read this verse, we see that it also refers to Jesus.

It speaks of His name. "You shall call His name Jesus, for He will save His people from their sins" (Matt.1:21). That's what His name means—Savior. What kind of a name is it? It is enduring: "His name shall endure forever" (v.17). I'm a student of biography. When I go to used-book sales, I buy books about old people—old preachers, missionaries and statesmen—folks who have been forgotten. Have you ever read an old edition of an encyclopedia and thought, *Who are these people? I've never heard of them.* Their names did not endure. In fact, some of the names in the headlines today will be forgotten a few months from now. But not so with Jesus. He has the *enduring name*, a name that "is above every name" (Phil.2:9).

Jesus also has an *enriching name*. "Men shall be blessed in Him." The names of some people don't bring blessing—they bring cursing. You certainly wouldn't call your son "Judas" or your daughter "Jezebel." But Jesus has an enriching name. It brings blessing. We have been blessed in Him "with every spiritual blessing" (Eph.1:3).

His name also is an *enabling name*. "Blessed be the Lord God, the God of Israel, who only does wondrous things!" (v.18). God enables us, through the name of Jesus, to do wonderful things. In the Book of Acts we find the name of Jesus on the lips of the apostles. "In the name of Jesus Christ of Nazareth rise up and walk" (3:6). What a privilege it is to know His name. What a privilege it is to have the authority of His name as we pray and serve Him.

There is no other name like Jesus. It is full of power and authority. It is enduring and brings blessing and enablement to those who know His name. Do you know Jesus as your Savior? "Whoever calls on the name of the Lord shall be saved" (Rom.10:13).

Read Psalm 73:1-28

THANKSGIVING MESSAGE

DAY 185

Asaph begins by standing true in what he believes about God, but he slips because he starts to look at neighbors and becomes envious. He wonders why the wicked prosper. When he loses his praise, he starts stumbling and suffering. He should have sought answers by looking up, not by looking around or within.

Asaph understands the end of the evil ones. The key question is not "Where are you?" but "Where are you going?" Are you taking the broad road that leads to destruction or the narrow road that leads to life (v.20)? The psalmist looks to God and makes several discoveries. First, he discovers that we can be thankful for *the guarantee of His presence*. His name is Immanuel, which means "God with us" (Matt.1:23; Isa.41:10; 43:2; Ps.23:4).

Second, we have *the grasp of His hand*. We see God's powerful hand in creation. We see His gentle hand lead us beside the still waters. And we see His pierced hands on the cross as He dies for us.

Third, we have *the guidance of His counsel*. God's commands and commissions are for everyone, but He knows each of us personally. He knew us in the womb and has arranged for us the lives He wants us to live. Live one day at a time and walk one step at a time (Prov.4:18). That counsel comes from the Word of God and through prayer.

Finally, we will have *the glory of His heaven*. As Christians, we know we are going to heaven because of the price Jesus paid on the cross (I Thess.5:10), the promise He made (John 14:2,3) and the prayer He prayed (John 17:24). We may not understand completely today, but we have a future glory (I Pet.1:3; II Pet.1:11; Phil 4:4).

As a Christian, you have much for which to be thankful. God is with you. When you find yourself becoming frustrated by the world's inequalities, stop, look up and give thanks to God for His blessings.

Read Psalm 73:1-12

DISTORTED VISION

When we are burdened and bothered by what we see in this world, we need to read this psalm. It starts with a wonderful affirmation of faith. "Truly God is good to Israel, to such as are pure in heart" (v.1). Asaph believes in the God of Israel, and he believes that God honors and rewards those who keep their lives clean. But in verse 2 he turns his eyes off of God, and he starts looking around at other people. "But as for me, my feet had almost stumbled; my steps had nearly slipped. For I was envious of the boastful, when I saw the prosperity of the wicked" (vv.2,3).

Let's look at his two major problems. First, *something is wrong with his vision*. He is not looking to God. He is looking at the wicked people around him. Who are these people? He describes them in verses 4-9. "For there are no pangs in their death, but their strength is firm" (v.4). They don't get sick; they don't have the bills others have. They're not troubled. They are proud and violent. "Their eyes bulge with abundance; they have more than heart could wish" (v.7), yet they are corrupt. They set their mouth against God. In verse 10 he says, "Waters of a full cup are drained by them." Asaph was drinking a bitter cup. His vision was distorted. This is what happens when we walk by sight instead of by faith.

Second, *something is wrong with his values*. "I was envious . . . when I saw the prosperity of the wicked" (v.3). Does he think that people without God are prosperous? Has his values suddenly changed? The psalmist is living by the values of the world, not the values of the world to come. "They increase in riches" (v.12)—but what kind of riches? When your feet start to slip and you start questioning God's goodness and His government in the world, check your vision and your values.

To live the life of faith, you need to understand God's perspective on the world. You must walk by faith, not sight. Keep your eyes on the Lord and don't conform to the values of this world. God is faithful to provide. "Seek first the kingdom of God and His righteousness, and all these things shall be added to you" (Matt.6:33).

Read Psalm 73:13-17

GOD'S PERSPECTIVE

DAY **187**

Is it really worth it to be a dedicated Christian? Is it worth it to obey the Lord when those who disobey Him seem to be more prosperous than we are? That's what Asaph wondered when he wrote Psalm 73. In the first 12 verses he thought he had really missed the good life: "I have cleansed my heart in vain, and washed my hands in innocence. For all day long I have been plagued, and chastened every morning. If I had said, 'I will speak thus,' behold, I would have been untrue to the generation of Your children" (vv.13-15). How does it all end? "It was too painful for me—until I went into the sanctuary of God; then I understood their end" (vv.16,17). Asaph's perspective was wrong, and that made him question his life until he sought God.

If you look at a distant mountain from one vantage point, you see one thing. But if you move closer or farther back, you see something else. The same thing is true with pictures, such as a beautiful painting or a photograph in a gallery. Your perspective doesn't change the painting or the facts, but it does change your *reaction* to the facts. So we need to go into the sanctuary of God. We need to know from His point of view what it means to live for the Lord.

Have you cleansed your heart in vain? Of course not. We all want a clean heart. Have you washed your hands in innocence? We all want clean hands. Is your tongue speaking something it shouldn't speak? According to verse 15, don't be afraid. Tell God exactly how you feel. Is your mind perplexed? Is your heart pained? Then you need to go to the sanctuary of God. That means getting God's point of view by spending time with Him in the Word, in prayer and in meditation.

Check your values with God's values and your vision with His point of view. Make sure your perspective is the perspective of heaven. That will keep your feet from slipping, and you'll walk with God in victory.

In times of need, your point of view can make a big difference. God wants us to gain His perspective. To do that, you must enter His sanctuary. Meditate on the Word, and fill your heart and mind with it. Then bring your burden to the Lord. He will help you gain His point of view.

Read Psalm 73:18-28

SEEING BEYOND

"You will guide me with Your counsel, and afterward receive me to glory" (v.24). Asaph wrote this verse after he had gone through a period of doubt, and it was a wonderful conclusion to his severe depression. He came out of his experience with several certainties.

First, *God holds us.* "Nevertheless I am continually with You; You hold me by my right hand" (v.23). The wicked may have violence, bounty, prosperity and a full cup of apparent blessing. But we have God, and He holds us.

Second, *God guides us.* "You will guide me with Your counsel, and afterward receive me to glory" (v.24). That's the important thing—the afterward. What is going to happen afterward? We can be sure that we will be with Him forever. It makes little difference what happens to us materially and physically in this life as long as we have riches in the next life. Some who are rich in this world will be poor in the next world. But many who are poor in this world will be rich in the next world.

Third, *God strengthens us.* "My flesh and my heart fail; but God is the strength of my heart and my portion forever" (v.26). Fourth, *God helps us in every stage of life.* "But it is good for me to draw near to God" (v.28). Wherever we are, whatever we're going through, we must draw near to God. "I have put my trust in the Lord God, that I may declare all Your works" (v.28).

The promise of an eternal home in heaven with the Lord encourages you in this life. God purchased you with a great price, and He keeps and protects you through everything. What assurances you have!

Read Psalm 74:1-11

DAY 189

A NEW TEMPLE

It must have been difficult for the Jewish people to watch the Babylonians destroy their city and temple. No wonder Asaph wrote, "O God, why have You cast us off forever? Why does Your anger smoke against the sheep of Your pasture?" (v.1). Keep in mind that this happened because the people had sinned. They had their great city. They had their beautiful temple. The problem was they trusted the city and the temple, but they did not obey the Lord. In their sin, they had defiled the temple. Jeremiah said they had turned it into a den of thieves (Jer.7:11). God would not permit this, so He allowed the Babylonians to destroy the city and the temple. Psalm 74 reveals the heartbreak of Asaph.

Even today the Enemy is destroying God's work. "They seem like men who lift up axes among the thick trees" (v.5). What can God's people do? Notice what Asaph said about God's people. We are the sheep of His pasture (v.1). He's the Good Shepherd, and He has given His life for the sheep. What defense do sheep have against a Babylonian army? Jesus, the Shepherd.

We are also God's congregation. "Remember Your congregation, which You have purchased of old, the tribe of Your inheritance which You have redeemed" (v.2). We are a purchased and redeemed people. "Remember . . . this Mount Zion where You have dwelt"(v.2). God lives with us. Jerusalem and the temple were destroyed, but He had even greater things in store. Jesus came to earth and revealed the glory of God. Now He's building a new temple, His Church, and it can never be destroyed.

God is your trust. If you trust Him, you will want to obey Him. Be careful that you don't misplace your trust in the world's substitutes. The Enemy will do all he can to divert your trust in God. Keep trusting in the Lord and rejoice that He never fails.

DAY

190

Read Psalm 74:12-23

A NIGHT SEASON

"For God is my King from of old, working salvation in the midst of the earth" (v.12). Asaph wrote those words after surveying the damage the Babylonians wrought in Jerusalem and the temple. In verses 1-11 he looked around and saw perpetual desolations. He saw the enemy had wrecked the sanctuary of God. The Babylonians had removed God's banners and set up their own. All the beauty, all the splendor of Jerusalem had gone up in smoke. When you look around and see the Enemy's destructive influence, remember: "God is my King from of old, working salvation in the midst of the earth" (v.12).

In verse 12 Asaph stopped looking around and looked up. He realized that *God was on the throne*. At times we cry, "How long, O Lord? How long? Why are these things happening? Why don't You do something?" We know why He permitted the Babylonians to destroy Jerusalem and the temple: The spiritual leaders of the people had led the nation into idolatry and blasphemy, so God disciplined them. Asaph looked up and said, "God is King. He has never failed, and *He is working salvation*. The Enemy may be working destruction; but my God is King, and He is working salvation in the midst of the earth."

Asaph had a third encouragement. He remembered *what God had done in the past* (vv.13-23). God divided the Red Sea. He broke the armies that attacked His people. He led His people through the wilderness. He opened the rock and provided water. He dried up the rivers. I like verse 16: "The day is Yours, the night also is Yours." We like the day but not the night. Remember, God controls the night as well as the day. Asaph was going through a night season in his soul as he saw everything around him falling apart. What was his solution? Trust. "For God is my King from of old, working salvation in the midst of the earth" (v.12).

Has the Enemy been doing his destructive work in your life? Lay hold of the encouragements of this psalm: God is on the throne; He is helping to deliver you; and He is faithful to act as He has in the past. Start by acknowledging His control in your life. Ask Him to help you and courageously place your trust in Him.

Read Psalm 75:1-10

WHO PUT THEM THERE?

DAY **191**

In this day when people promote themselves and take care of "number one," it's good to read verse 7: "But God is the Judge: He puts down one, and exalts another." This *rebukes our pride*. Who is the One who allows people to be where they are? God. John the Baptist said, "A man can receive nothing unless it has been given to him from heaven" (John 3:27). Peter wrote: "Therefore humble yourselves under the mighty hand of God, that He may exalt you in due time" (I Pet.5:6). Who is the One who exalts people to places of leadership? God. Who is the One who removes people from certain positions? God. Who is wise enough to know when to do all of this? God. No one in any position should think that he is there because God *needs* him.

Let's realize that we are where we are because God put us there. But verse 7 not only rebukes our pride—it also *encourages our patience*. Think of Joseph, waiting for God to put down his enemies and set him up where he was supposed to be. Consider Moses or Nehemiah. Oh, how we need patience! Sometimes God allowed His people to be under the tyranny of bad leaders or foreign dictators. Just as He did in the Old Testament, God allows us to go through difficult situations to break our wills and make us more like Him.

Third, this *relieves the pressure in our lives*. Are you in a place of leadership? God put you there. And because He put you there, He will keep you there for as long as He wants. He will use you the way He chooses. Be careful of pride. When we become proud and haughty and think we have all the answers, God says, "It's time to put you down." But if we put ourselves down, He will exalt us. If we humble ourselves under His hand, that hand will turn over and lift us up. "God resists the proud, but gives grace to the humble" (I Pet.5:5).

Have you been struggling because you are under bad leaders at your workplace or in your church? Did poor decisions by others put them there? Bring your burden to God and talk to Him about it. Ask for His strength to continue and remember that He is the Judge.

DAY
192

Read Psalm 76:1-12

DUE RESPECT

We read and hear so much about the love of God that we sometimes forget the fear of God. "You, Yourself, are to be feared; and who may stand in Your presence when once You are angry?" (v.7) What is this fear Asaph mentions? It's the fear of the Lord, that reverent respect and awe that we show to Him because of His greatness and power. We are God's children, and the Holy Spirit in our hearts says, "Abba, Father." We can pray, "Our Father, who art in heaven." We can draw close to God, and He will draw close to us. But remember that God is God and we are human beings. He is in heaven, and we are on earth. He is eternal, and someday we will be with Him in heaven. Meanwhile, our earthly existence is temporal.

The fear of God is not like the dread of a prisoner before a judge. It's not the cringing of a servant before a master. It's the reverent respect and awe of a child realizing the greatness and the glory of God. We fear Him because He is so *great*. "In Judah God is known; His name is great in Israel" (v.1). Oh, what a great name He has! How sad that the people of the world take His great name in vain. We also fear Him because He is *glorious*. "You are more glorious and excellent than the mountains of prey" (v.4).

We also fear God because of *who He is* and *what He has done*. "At Your rebuke, O God of Jacob both the chariot and horse were cast into a dead sleep" (v.6). What is the result of fearing Him? God fights our battles. He goes before those who fear Him. We can stand before Him because Jesus intercedes for us. God will not be angry because of our sins. Jesus has taken care of that. Let's fear the Lord, and He will fight our battles for us.

God deserves your reverent respect. And you have many reasons for giving it to Him. Do you give God His due respect? Take time to meditate on who He is and what He has done for you. Come into his presence and worship Him. "The fear of the Lord is the beginning of wisdom" (Prov.9.1).

Conversations
IN THE NIGHT

It doesn't have to be dark outside for us to be in the middle of the night. Sometimes the darkness is in us. Discouragement moves in, and we are like Asaph, who said, "My hand was stretched out in the night without ceasing; my soul refused to be comforted" (v.2). Some translations read, "My sore was running in the night." What do you do when your soul refuses to be comforted?

Asaph tells us what we should do. First, *talk to God*. "I cried out to God with my voice—to God with my voice; and He gave ear to me" (v.1). Someone has suggested that when you can't sleep at night, instead of counting sheep, talk to the Shepherd. That's what Asaph did. Sometimes approaching the Lord is painful. "I remembered God, and was troubled" (v.3). What did he remember about God that troubled him? Perhaps he disobeyed a commandment or doubted a promise. Or perhaps he realized how holy God is and how sinful he is.

But talking to the Lord also brings reassurance. "I have considered the days of old, the years of ancient times" (v.5). In other words, God can be trusted. He has cared for you in the past, and He will care for you in the future.

Second, *talk to yourself*. "I meditate within my heart, and my spirit makes diligent search" (v.6). Talk to yourself about the Lord. Examine your life and your Christian walk. Your discouragement will be replaced by a song. "I call to remembrance my song in the night" (v.6).

When you feel discouraged, get your eyes off your circumstances and onto the Lord. Also, examine your life. Have you disobeyed the Lord? Talk to Him and let Him encourage you. Then talk to yourself and encourage yourself with the things of God. He will give you a song in the night.

DAY

194

Read Psalm 77:7-10

UNANSWERED QUESTIONS

Asking questions is much easier than answering them. If you have children or grandchildren, you know how true that is. These verses contain a series of questions from a discouraged man. "Will the Lord cast off forever? And will He be favorable no more? Has His mercy ceased forever? Has His promise failed forever more? Has God forgotten to be gracious? Has He in anger shut up His tender mercies?" (vv.7-9). Then he concludes by saying, "This is my anguish; but I will remember the years of the right hand of the Most High" (v.10).

It's normal to ask questions when we are going through difficulty and pain. David prayed, "My God, my God, why have You forsaken Me?" (Ps.22:1). Jesus also quoted those words on the cross (Matt.27:46). When we are going through difficulty, we expect God to move in, help us and deliver us. And when we are waiting for that deliverance, we get impatient. That's when the questions come.

Don't be afraid to be open and honest with God. Tell Him how you feel and what you're thinking. He would rather you be honest about your feelings than hypocritical. But remember this: As Christians, we do not live on explanations; we live on promises. Suppose God started to answer these questions. Will the Lord cast off forever? No. Will He be favorable no more? Of course, He's going to be favorable. Is His mercy completely gone forever? No. If God answered all of these questions, would it make any difference? It might ease your mind a little bit, but it wouldn't really change your situation. Live by faith, not by sight. Trust the promises of the Lord. He will not change.

God does not always provide explanations for your difficulties, but He does provide the promises of His Word. The next time you find yourself in the midst of discouragement, bring your questions and concerns to Him in prayer. Then rely on the promises of His Word. God knows your needs and will meet them.

HOLY AND HIDDEN

Asaph refused to be comforted. He asked a lot of questions of the Lord. At the close of his discouragement, he came to two wonderful conclusions. First, "Your way, O God, is in the sanctuary; who is so great a God as our God?" (v.13). And second, "Your way was in the sea, your path in the great waters, and your footsteps were not known" (v.19).

What an unusual way to express faith! First, Asaph tells us that *God's way is in the sanctuary*. His way is a way of sanctification and holiness. God leads us in grace and from grace to glory. He makes no mistakes—His way is the best way and always has been. If we are living in the Holy of Holies, we will be able to discover God's way. If we are in the Holy Word of God, we can have a holy walk with Him.

Second, *God's way is in the sea*. His way is hidden. We may not understand all of God's leading, but this we can know: God *is* leading. Asaph said, "You led Your people like a flock by the hand of Moses and Aaron" (v.20). His way is in the sea, and if He has to, He will open up the sea for you. If necessary, He will help you walk on the water. But the psalmist came to the right conclusion. God's way is holy, so obey Him. His way is hidden, so trust Him.

Perhaps you're going through a difficulty today and asking the Lord a lot of questions—why, how, when, how long—the questions Asaph asked. Let God bring you closer to Himself by following His guidance.

DAY 196

Read Psalm 78:1-8

SERVANTS OF TOMORROW

We have a responsibility to the next generation. The psalmist wrote, "We will not hide them from their children, telling to the generation, the praises of the Lord, and His strength and His wonderful works that He has done" (v.4).

Why should we share the *Word of the Lord* with the generation to come? "That they may set their hope in God, and not forget the works of God, but keep His commandments" (v.7). That's preparing them for the future, because hope looks to the future. Christians are born again unto a living hope by the Resurrection of Jesus Christ. We know that our Lord is going to return and take us home to heaven. Too many people in the younger generation are setting their hope in money, in government or in their abilities. So we share the blessing of the Lord with the next generation to help them set their hope in Him.

Second, we want the next generation to remember the *works of God*. How easy it is to forget what He has done for us! Yet if we keep reminding the next generation, they will remember, too. The past must not be forgotten. Those who forget the past are condemned to repeat its mistakes.

Finally, we must share the *things of the Lord* with the younger generation so they will keep His commandments. The psalmist wasn't talking about a legalistic life. He was talking about a loving obedience to the Lord. Yes, we do have a responsibility to the new generation, and we fulfill that responsibility by being a good example, by teaching, sharing and encouraging.

You are entrusted with your Christian heritage. When you share with the next generation the Word and works of God, you teach them valuable lessons about how He still works in the lives of His people. Strive to be an example that encourages the next generation to obey the Lord.

ALWAYS FAITHFUL

The children of Ephraim mentioned in Psalm 78 failed the Lord, and they failed their fellow Israelites when their help was badly needed. "The children of Ephraim, being armed and carrying bows, turned back in the day of battle. They did not keep the covenant of God; they refused to walk in His law, and forgot His works and His wonders that He had shown them" (vv.9-11).

What a tragedy it is when people fail in their warfare. Jesus warned us about those who look back and do not fulfill the will of God (Luke 9:62). If we are looking back, we cannot plow ahead. And if we look back, we cannot fight as we ought. Yes, there is a spiritual battle going on, and we need every soldier. But something was wrong with these warriors. They were *unfaithful*. Even though they were armed, they turned back in the day of battle.

Something was wrong with their walk. "They did not keep the covenant of God; they refused to walk in His law" (v.10). That's where failure always starts. God wanted them to walk in His law that He might help them win the battle, but they would not obey Him.

Finally, they *forgot what God had done for them*. "And forgot His works and His wonders that He had shown them" (v.11). Can you imagine forgetting a miracle? If a miracle took place in your life today, you would talk about it until the day the Lord called you home. You'd call a press conference! Think of the miracles God did for His people. But they forgot them. The Ephraimites were undependable on the battlefield because they forgot what He had done for them. They turned against the law of God, and they turned from the works of the Lord. Consequently, they were unable to help in His work.

Unfaithfulness is common in people. But not so with God. Faithfulness is part of His character. This truth ought to encourage you if you know the Lord. Be faithful in your walk with Him. Remember His works and be a faithful soldier in your battle for Him.

DAY

198

Read Psalm 78:21-33

FUTILITY AND FEAR

The history of Israel in the Old Testament is really the history of all Christians. Like Israel, we have been redeemed through the blood of the Lamb. And like the people of Israel, we are heading for the Promised Land.

What is the one thing you need most on the journey from earth to heaven? Love? Yes, that's important. Hope? That's important, too. But I think faith is needed most. The one thing you must do is trust God. That's what the psalmist talks about in this passage. The people would not believe in God and continued to sin. We see the consequence in verse 33: "Therefore their days He consumed in futility, and their years in fear." When the Israelites got to the edge of the Promised Land, they refused to go in. They were at Kadesh-Barnea and would not trust God to lead them. So they had to wander around for some 40 years in vanity and emptiness, struggling with problem after problem.

Unfortunately, many of God's people are betweeners—they are living between Egypt and Canaan. They have been delivered from bondage by the blood of the Lamb, but they have never entered into their inheritance. They are living between Good Friday and Easter Sunday. They believe that Jesus died on the cross, but they are not living in the power of His Resurrection.

Don't be a betweener today. Consider how God blessed the people of Israel. He sent them manna and fowl to feed them. He provided them with water. But also consider how God disciplined them because of their unbelief. In His patience, however, He finally brought them through. We are like the people of Israel. Our greatest need is to believe God. We don't live by explanations; we live by promises. Today, while you hear His voice, don't harden your heart.

Unbelief leads to futility and fear. Perhaps you are a "betweener" today refusing to trust God's leading. When Israel believed the promises of God, He blessed them. Trust Him, obey Him and believe Him, and His blessing will come!

Read Psalm 78:34-39

FLATTERY GETS YOU NOWHERE

DAY **199**

Flattery is not communication; it is manipulation. We flatter people because we want something from them. It's bad enough to flatter people, but it's even worse to flatter God. "Nevertheless they flattered Him with their mouth, and they lied to Him with their tongue; for their heart was not steadfast with Him nor were they faithful in His covenant" (vv.36,37).

How do we flatter God? First, *when we praise Him but don't mean it.* It's so easy to stand in church and sing songs of praise with our minds somewhere else and our hearts not in our singing. We are simply going through an empty ritual. We also flatter God *when we make promises to Him that we don't intend to keep*. We do this sometimes in our praying.

We flatter God a third way *when we pray to Him but don't really seek His Will.* It's easy for us to go through routine prayers and make promises. "Dear Lord, today I'm going to witness," or, "Dear Lord, today I'm going to read my Bible, or, Dear Lord, today I am not going to yield to that temptation." But in our hearts we have no intention of following through. We lie to God. So often the Israelites lied to Him. They brought sacrifices, hoping to buy God's blessing. They went through the ritual and the routine of worship, hoping that He would somehow deliver them. They were flattering Him—their hearts were not right with God.

What does it mean to have a heart right with God? It means we are honest and open with Him. We are sincere, not lying. We tell Him just how we feel and exactly what we're going through. That's what God wants. He wants us to walk in the light as He is in the light (I John 1:7), not trying to cover up or excuse our sins, but confessing them. To have our hearts right with the Lord, we must stop flattering God and always deal with Him in truth.

God wants you to be open and honest with Him. Never flatter Him with dishonesty, insincerity or deception. One way to be honest in your relationship with God is to keep your heart clean. Confess your sins instead of trying to cover them. He knows your heart, so be truthful in your praying.

DAY
200

Read Psalm 78:40-53

FLAWED MEMORY

The older we get, the more we forget. This is especially true when it comes to our relationship with God.

The people of Israel often remembered what they should have forgotten and forgot what they should have remembered! "They did not remember His power: the day when He redeemed them from the enemy, when He worked His signs in Egypt, and His wonders in the field of Zoan" (vv.42,43). How amazing. The Jews had seen God perform ten miracles on their behalf in Egypt. Moses even pointed out that this was the hand of the Lord, yet they forgot all about it. After they were delivered from Egypt and living in the desert, the first time they were thirsty, they complained. The first time they were hungry, they complained.

Their constant cry was, "Let's go back." What did they remember about Egypt? The bondage? The taskmasters? Being beaten and whipped? Carrying the heavy burdens? They didn't remember those things. They remembered the leeks and the onions and the garlic and the cucumbers. They remembered the things that satisfied their stomachs. They did not remember the spiritual victories that God had given, His deliverance or His guidance. He had fed and led them, protected and provided for them; and they forgot about it. The same is often true of us. We forget what God has done for us, and when we forget, we start to go backward.

Forgetfulness has consequences. "Yes, again and again they tempted God, and limited the Holy One of Israel" (v.41). Imagine—feeble, unbelieving man limiting Almighty God! But that's what happens when we forget Him. Don't limit God in your life today. He has unlimited wisdom and unlimited power, and your life has unlimited potential in His hands. Don't turn back. Look ahead. Don't test Him. Trust Him and remember his mercies.

The same God who worked miracle after miracle for Israel is the One who is working for you today. Don't live with a flawed memory. Meditate on God's faithfulness and goodness.

Read Psalm 78:54-64

TEMPTING GOD

DAY 201

There is only one direction for Christians to travel—forward. We must not think back or look back or turn back. We must move ahead, out of the old life and into the new.

That's the picture of the Israelites. God delivered them from Egypt. He brought them into the Promised Land, yet when they got there, they failed Him. "Yet they tested and provoked the Most High God, and did not keep His testimonies, but turned back and acted unfaithfully like their fathers; they were turned aside like a deceitful bow. For they provoked Him to anger with their high places, and moved Him to jealousy with their carved images" (vv.56-58). They ignored all of God's greatness. He defeated the other nations. He gave the Jews houses they did not build. They drank from wells they did not dig. They ate from trees they never cultivated. They ignored God's goodness, and then they deliberately tempted Him.

How do you tempt God? When you deliberately disobey Him and dare Him to do something. You are not walking in ignorance—you know what you are doing. To tempt God means to sin with your eyes wide open. This provokes Him.

The people of Israel even adopted the idolatrous worship of the people they had defeated! We do this today, too. How easy it is for us to accept the idols of this world, to trust in money and position, to trust in the words of men instead of the words of God. And the result? "He forsook the tabernacle" (v.60). God moved out. He said, "If you don't want me, I'm leaving." As a consequence, the people of Israel went into captivity.

What a tragedy to enter into the blessing God has for us and get so confident and selfish we forget the One who gave us the blessing.

Be careful never to place your trust in God's blessings rather than in God. Enjoy the Blesser—the God who gives and guides you—rather than the blessing.

Read Psalm 78:65-72

FROM SERVANT TO RULER

We know that David committed adultery and that he made a man drunk and had him murdered. In addition, he once took a census of the Israelites out of disobedience to God—70,000 people died as a result. But David is still a great man. God forgave him and used him in a wonderful way.

David was a man of humility. "He also chose David His servant, and took him from the sheepfolds; from following the ewes that had young He brought him, to shepherd Jacob His people, and Israel His inheritance" (vv.70,71). David began as a servant, and God made him a ruler. That's always God's pattern. There are those who make themselves leaders, but God's blessing is not upon them. David had God's blessing because he was faithful in his job. That's what Jesus said in one of His parables. "Well done, good and faithful servant; you were faithful over a few things, I will make you ruler over many things. Enter into the joy of your lord" (Matt.25:21). If you want to be a leader, learn how to be a follower. If you want to be a ruler, learn how to be a servant, faithfully doing what God has called you to do.

David was a man of integrity. "So he shepherded them according to the integrity of his heart" (v.72). *Integrity* means having one heart, whereas a double-minded man is unstable in all his ways (James 1:8). David's sole purpose was to serve the Lord.

David was a man of ability. He "guided them by the skillfulness of his hands" (v.72). Integrity ties your heart and your hands together. Your heart serves the Lord, and your hands are busy for Him. We need people like that today. No amount of dedication can compensate for a lack of skill, but no amount of skill can compensate for a lack of dedication. We need both.

David exhibited the traits of a true ruler—humility, integrity and ability. They also are required of you for faithful service. Where has God placed you for service? Are you a faithful leader or follower? He rewards His faithful servants. Dedicate yourself to the Lord today and serve Him faithfully.

Read Psalm 79:1-13

WHEN ALL SEEMS LOST

DAY 203

There are days when we look around and it seems as though the Enemy has won. That's the way Asaph felt when he wrote Psalm79.

He looked around and saw *defilement*. "Oh God, the nations have come into Your inheritance; Your holy temple they have defiled; they have laid Jerusalem in heaps" (v.1). Asaph refers to the destruction of the temple and the city of Jerusalem. We, too, can look around today and see defilement in people's minds and hearts.

Then Asaph saw *death*. "The dead bodies of Your servants they have given as food for the birds of the heavens . . . Their blood they have shed like water all around Jerusalem" (vv.2,3). Our world is basically a cemetery. The wages of sin is death. We see it wherever we look.

Asaph also saw *derision*. "We have become a reproach to our neighbors, a scorn and derision to those who are around us" (v.4). People today don't magnify the Lord; they laugh at Him. They laugh at the Church, at God's people. We are a derided people because so often it looks as though we are losing and they have won the battle.

Finally, Asaph saw the enemy *devouring*. "For they have devoured Jacob, and laid waste his dwelling place" (v.7): Yes, the devouring, destroying hand of Satan was at work. But Asaph says, "Help us, O God of our salvation." Why? "For the glory of Your name; and deliver us" (v.9). How? "And provide atonement for our sins, for Your name's sake!" Asaph isn't concerned so much about his own comfort as he is about God's glory. So he prays, "Help us."

God helps by purging us from our sins. In addition, verses 11 and 12 tell us that He will come and save us. How wonderful that day will be when Jesus Christ comes to deliver us! Meanwhile, in the world we see defilement, death, derision, destruction and devouring. Now is the time to cry and say, "O God, for the glory of Your name, help us do Your will."

Satan is at work in the world, but one day God will be glorified, and He will deliver His people from this world. God promises to be with you and to be your Salvation. Rest on that promise.

Read Psalm 80:1-7

RESTORATION

"Restore us, O God; cause Your face to shine, and we shall be saved" (v.3). We find this prayer three times in Psalm 80. Christians ought to pray this every day.

We certainly ought to pray this in times of *affliction*. The people of Israel were going through the affliction of God. He was angry with them and had to chasten them. The psalmist says, "You are feeding us with the bread of tears. We are drinking our tears. We are a strife to our neighbors. Our enemies are laughing at us" (vv.5,6). Asaph doesn't pray for the Lord to change his circumstances. Rather, he says, "Lord, restore us. We have wandered away. We are not what we ought to be. Turn us right again."

We also ought to pray Asaph's prayer in times of *rebellion*. God's people were rebelling against Him, and that's who He was chastening them. But in spite of their failures, in spite of their unbelief, God never changes. The psalmist prays, "O Lord God of hosts, how long will You be angry against the prayer of Your people?" (v.4).

What was wrong with their prayers? They were praying selfishly for their own comfort and deliverance. They weren't thinking about the glory of God. But Asaph is different. He prays for their restoration. When you look at your failure, immediately look for God's favor and His salvation.

There are times when you need God's restoration. Sometimes He afflicts you and chastens you because His glory is at stake. He wants you to glorify Him. Have you failed God? Do you need His restoration? Pray Asaph's prayer today from your heart.

Read Psalm 80:8-13

DAY 205

Bloom Where YOU'RE PLANTED

One of the greatest tragedies in life is wasted opportunity—not making the most of what God has given us. We came into this world with certain abilities, and when God saved us, He gave us gifts and the grace to exercise those gifts to help others, to build our own lives and to glorify His name.

This is why God puts us through certain experiences. Asaph said, "You have brought a vine out of Egypt; you have cast out the nations, and planted it. You prepared room for it, and caused it to take deep root, and it filled the land" (vv.8,9). That vine, of course, was the nation of Israel. God delivered Israel from Egypt and planted her like a luxurious vine in the land of Canaan. But soon He had to break that vine. He had to discipline His people. The vine was not producing the fruit God wanted it to produce.

God blesses us to make us a blessing. He planted the people of Israel in the land that they might, by their life and testimony, bear spiritual fruit, letting the Gentile nations know about the true and living God. He gave them an opportunity to show the other nations what He could do for those who would trust and obey Him. Instead, the vine became like all the other vines. The Israelites compromised and sinned. So God had to cut down His vine and discipline His people.

Remember, God has planted you where you are that you might be a blessing. He wants you to take deep root. He wants you to bear rich fruit. And if you will draw upon His spiritual power, He will enable you to be a blessing. Bloom where you are planted and bear fruit to the glory of God and the enrichment of others.

God has blessed you with certain abilities so you may invest them in others and bring glory to Him. As you use your God-given talents, you glorify Him and bless others. Draw from God's spiritual resources and let Him use you to enrich others.

DAY
206

Read Psalm 80:14-19

REVIVE US AGAIN

Look at two important words in Psalm 80. One is *return*. "Return, we beseech You, O God of hosts; look down from heaven and see, and visit this vine" (v.14). The other word is *revive*. "Then we will not turn back from You; revive us, and we will call upon Your name" (v.18).

God had departed from His people. He had planted this vine, the nation of Israel, in the land of Canaan. He had cast out the other nations to make room for Israel. The vine took root and began to bear fruit. But the people of Israel began to sin against the Lord. Instead of being distinctively separate, they began to imitate the other nations and visit their altars and participate in their sacrifices. So God said, "If that's the way you want it, you can have it." God left His people. The word *Ichabod* means "the glory has departed" (I Sam.4:21).

Jesus said, "I will never leave you nor forsake you" (Heb.13:5). God will never take away His presence, but He will take away His power and His blessing. If necessary, He will withhold that extra anointing He wants to give us. Verses 18 and19 are a prayer for revival: "Revive us, and we will call upon Your name. Restore us, O Lord God of hosts; cause your face to shine, and we shall be saved!"

God will never leave you, but there are times when He may need to withhold His power and blessing because of sin in your life. Are you in need of God's restoration? He hears the prayer of revival. Ask Him to clean your heart and then pray Asaph's prayer.

Read Psalm 81:1-16

WHAT MIGHT HAVE BEEN

DAY 207

Life is made up of things that were, things that are and things that might have been. We find all three in Psalm 81.

First, we find *the things that were* (vv.1-10). The psalmist talks about the God of Jacob and says, "Let's get our orchestra together. Let's get our trumpets and let's sing to the Lord. He gave us a statute. He delivered us from Egypt." He reflects on and rejoices in the past. But the things that *were* did not last long, because the people rebelled against the Lord.

Next, we see *the things that are*. "But My people would not heed My voice, and Israel would have none of Me. So I gave them over to their own stubborn heart, to walk in their own counsels" (vv.11,12). The things that *were* brought rejoicing: The things that *are* spoke of rebellion. The people of God rebelled against Him. They wouldn't listen to Him, call upon Him or obey His Word. So they lost all that He had for them.

Finally, we see *the things that might have been* (vv.13-16). "Oh, that My people would listen to Me, that Israel would walk in My ways! I would soon subdue their enemies, and turn my hand against their adversaries. The haters of the Lord would pretend submission to Him, but their fate would endure forever. He would have fed them also with the finest of wheat; and with honey from the rock I would have satisfied you." What might have been? Victory, satisfaction, joy, the finest wheat and honey out of the rock.

Don't rebel against God and thus miss the blessings He wants to give you.

Dwelling on past failures only turns life into regret. If you have failed the Lord, come back to Him and pray for forgiveness. Dedicate yourself to Him and start experiencing those things that might have been. God has the best plan for you.

DAY
208

Read Psalm 82:1-8

THE ULTIMATE JUDGE

When we watch the news on television or read it in a magazine or newspaper, we may think that the unjust are winning and the just are losing. We get the same idea when we read Psalm 82. But this psalm also says that God is part of the judicial system.

God attends court. "God stands in the congregation of the mighty; He judges among the gods" (v.1). The word *gods* means "the judges." When the judges get together in court, God is there whether they recognize Him or not.

God admonishes the judges. "How long will you judge unjustly, and show partiality to the wicked?" (v.2). He tells them what to do: "Defend the poor and fatherless; do justice to the afflicted and needy. Deliver the poor and needy; free them from the hand of the wicked" (vv.3,4).

God judges the judges. The judges think they are trying others, but God is trying them. "They do not know, nor do they understand; they walk about in darkness; all the foundations of the earth are unstable" (v.5). When the law is not being upheld, all the nations fall apart. "I said, 'You are gods, and all of you are children of the Most High. But you shall die like men, and fall like one of the princes'" (vv.6,7). The psalmist believes that God will one day make everything right. "Arise, O God, judge the earth; for You shall inherit all nations" (v.8).

Yes, there is going to be injustice in this world until Jesus comes. But when the King of kings is reigning and the Lord of lords is supremely in control, we finally will have justice in this world.

In spite of the world's injustice, God is in control, and He sees all that happens. Until Jesus comes to reign, we must live here. In the meantime, trust Him, obey Him and do His will.

Read Psalm 83:1-18

DAY 209

ENEMIES OF THE KING

Christians are strangers living in enemy territory. Our enemies are those who do not love Jesus Christ, His Church or His Word. What shall we do about our enemies, who also are God's enemies? Follow the example of the psalmist and turn them over to the Lord. "For behold, Your enemies make a tumult; and those who hate You have lifted up their head" (v.2). He refers to Israel's enemies—the Edomites, the Ishmaelites, the Moabites and other heathen nations around her. Through the centuries Israel has had many enemies, and God has defeated them. But He has blessed those nations that have blessed Israel.

What is God going to do about our enemies? The psalmist says He will judge them, though we don't know where or when. He paints some vivid pictures. "O my God, make them like the whirling dust" (v.13). One translation says "like a wheel of whirling dust." When a wheel goes down a dusty road, it stirs up dust. The enemies are nothing but dirt, like whirling dust that blows away, "like the chaff before the wind! As the fire burns the woods, and as the flame sets the mountains on fire" (vv.13,14). One day God's fire of judgment is going to sweep through them, and they will be destroyed. Verse 15 compares this to a storm: "So pursue them with Your tempest, and frighten them with Your storm."

Why does God judge His enemies? "That men may know that You, whose name alone is the Lord, are the Most High over all the earth" (v.18). God is the King. Turn your enemies over to Him. He knows how to take care of them.

For centuries God has dealt with the enemies of Israel. He takes an active part in dealing with your enemies, too. When they surround you, turn them over to the Lord and rest in His care.

DAY **210** Read Psalm 84:1-4

DESIRING GOD

Psalm 84 expresses the thoughts of a man who wants to go to Jerusalem for a feast but cannot. We do not know why. Perhaps he is ill, or there is some problem at home. He writes, "How lovely is Your tabernacle, O Lord of hosts! My soul longs, yes, even faints for the courts of the Lord; my heart and my flesh cry out for the living God" (vv.1,2).

His great desire was not to go to Jerusalem solely to observe a holy day. Instead, he wanted to go to the temple and meet God. "Even the sparrow has found a home, and the swallow a nest for herself, where she may lay her young" (v.3). In other words, God's house is to his soul what a nest is to a swallow—a place of rest and security and satisfaction. The psalmist even envies the priests. "Blessed are those who dwell in Your house; they will still be praising You" (v.4). Outsiders were not allowed to live there, and they were limited in where they could go inside. Only the priests could enter the Holy of Holies.

We have the privilege of fellowshiping with God without going through a priest. Do you have a great desire to worship Him today? Or are you happy for an excuse to stay home from God's house?

If you have been saved by God's grace, you ought to have a strong desire to worship Him and fellowship with Him. You have the privilege of attending God's house and worshiping with His people. Do you desire to be with them? Does your heart cry out for the living God?

Read Psalm 84:5-7

THE ROAD TO ZION

DAY 211

At the time this psalm was written, every Jewish man was required to go to Jerusalem to celebrate the feast three times a year. Whole villages would make their pilgrimage together, singing along the way. "Blessed is the man whose strength is in You, whose heart is set on pilgrimage. As they pass through the Valley of Baca, they make it a spring; the rain also covers it with pools. They go from strength to strength; everyone of them appears before God in Zion" (vv.5-7).

As they traveled down the road, the men looked in three different directions. First, *they looked within* (v.5). "Blessed is the man whose strength is in You, whose heart is set on pilgrimage," or, "in whose heart are the highways to Zion." Everyone has a road map in his heart that takes him where he really wants to go. Look within yourself today. What kind of road map do you have? Where does it lead? Have you limited yourself, or are you entering into all the fullness of walking with the Lord?

They looked back (v.6). They passed through a valley, Baca, which means "weeping." As they passed through Baca, they left behind a blessing for someone else. Sometimes on our pilgrimage we go through the valley of weeping. When you go through it, do you leave behind a blessing for somebody else? Or do you expect others to give you a blessing?

Then they looked ahead. "They go from strength to strength; every one of them appears before God in Zion" (v.7). They were looking forward to meeting with the living God as they went to celebrate the feast. We, too, go from strength to strength. You may look ahead and say, "I'll never make it." But you will. He gives you the strength to keep going as you make your pilgrimage.

You, too, look in three directions in your pilgrimage. It is often a difficult journey, but God will give you the strength to continue and progress. In your heart you have a road map to Zion. Follow it, and one day you will meet the living God face to face.

DAY

212

Read Psalm 84:8-12

GRACE AND GLORY

The psalmist yearns to go to the courts of the Lord. But as he meditates on Him, he realizes he can have God's blessing right where he is. He does not have to go to the temple. "The Lord God is a sun and shield; the Lord will give grace and glory; no good thing will He withhold from those who walk uprightly" (v.11).

Grace—that's how the spiritual journey begins. We are saved by God's grace. We trust Jesus, and in grace God saves us. *Glory*—that's how it ends. One day we will be in heaven and share the glory of the Lord forever.

But between grace and glory, life can be rather difficult. We read in I Peter 5:10 that the "God of all grace, who called us to His eternal glory by Christ Jesus, after you have suffered a while, [will] perfect, establish, strengthen, and settle you." Whatever begins with grace leads to glory, but how do we make the journey between grace and glory? "For the Lord God is a sun and shield" (v.11). He is a *Sun*. That's provision and sufficiency. He is a *Shield*. That's protection and security. We start the journey with grace; we continue the journey trusting God's provision and protection; and we end the journey by entering into the glory of the Lord.

What does it mean to walk uprightly? It means walking in the light, obeying His word, loving Him and trusting Him.

Psalm 84:11 is a great verse to claim for your pilgrim journey. Begin with God's grace and end in His glory. Along the way you have the promise of His provision and protection. Do you qualify for God's provisions for the journey? Determine always to walk uprightly by obeying the Word of God and trusting its promises.

Read Psalm 85:1-13

THE REVIVAL PEOPLE

DAY **213**

"Will You not revive us again, that Your people may rejoice in You?" (v.6). This prayer has been set to music in the song "Revive Us Again," and it's a prayer we need to pray.

Who needs revival? Unsaved people can't be revived because they never had life to begin with. The unsaved person is dead in trespasses and sins. But Christians, through faith in Jesus Christ, have been raised from the dead. We've been given eternal, abundant life. Unfortunately, sometimes we turn away from the Lord and lose that spiritual vibrancy. We don't lose our salvation, but we lose the joy of our salvation, its power and the overflowing blessings we give each other.

God's people are *the revival people*. We desperately need to be revived. The psalmist cries out to God for new life. Someone has said that our church services start at eleven o'clock sharp and end at twelve o'clock dull. How we need the breath of God to blow upon us! How we need His life to touch us!

What is *the revival purpose*? A. W. Tozer used to say, "It's difficult to get Christians to attend any meeting where God is the only center of attraction." We have to have entertainment, food and all sorts of distractions. But the psalmist wants God's people to rejoice in Him alone.

God's people should live with a vibrancy that comes from the joy of their salvation. Does your life still sparkle as it did when you came to know the Lord? Pray that He will revive the Church. And pray that your testimony will bless others and glorify the Lord.

DAY **214**

Read Psalm 86:1-10

ENCOURAGEMENTS TO PRAY

"For You, Lord, are good, and ready to forgive, and abundant in mercy to all those who call upon You" (v.5). What a promise to claim today! Just two verses later the psalmist says, "In the day of my trouble I will call upon You, for You will answer me" (v.7).

The psalmist gives a number of encouragements to pray. First, *remember who God is*. Never forget His attributes. The better we know Him, the better we are able to pray. What kind of God are we praying to? One who is good, merciful and ready to forgive. You may say, "I can't pray to God. My hands are dirty. My heart is dirty. I'm not what I ought to be." Then come to Him and say, "I know You are ready to forgive; You are abundant in mercy." And God will forgive you. He hears all who cry out to Him.

Second, *remember what God does*. "For You are great, and do wondrous things; You alone are God" (v.10). "Call to Me, and I will answer you, and show you great and mighty things, which you do not know" (Jer.33:3).

Third, *remember what God promises*. He promises to answer us. Jesus said, "Ask, and it will be given to you" (Matt.7:7). "You do not have because you do not ask" (James 4:2).

Remember who God is, the kind of God to whom you are praying. Remember the great and wonderful things He does. He can do the impossible for you today. And remember, He promises to answer.

These are wonderful encouragements to pray. When you pray, keep them before you. Contemplate God's character. Remember what He has done in your life. Recount His faithfulness to you. And be sure to claim the promises of the Bible.

Read Psalm 86:11-17

DAY 215

MIND, HEART AND WILL

Here is a good prayer for you today. "Teach me Your way, O Lord; I will walk in Your truth; unite my heart to fear Your name" (v.11). The whole person is wrapped up in this prayer.

First, we see *an open mind.* "Teach me Your way; . . . I will walk in Your truth." Is your mind open to God's truth? Do you really want Him to teach you His way? He revealed His ways to Moses and to the Israelites. He will do the same for you also. We need people today who will say, "Lord, I have an open mind. I want you to show me Your way and truth."

But that's not enough. We need to have *an obedient will.* The psalmist makes a promise in verse 11: "Lord, if you show me your way, I will obey it." Jesus said, "If anyone wants to do His will, he shall know concerning the doctrine, whether it is from God or whether I speak on My own authority" (John 7:17).

Finally, we see *a united heart.* "Unite my heart to fear your name." A united heart is wholly fixed upon the Lord. A divided heart is dangerous. Jesus said, "No one can serve two masters; for either he will hate the one and love the other, or else he will be loyal to the one and despise the other. You cannot serve God and mammon" (Matt.6:24). James 1:8 says a double-minded man is unstable in all of his ways.

If you want God to guide and bless you today, follow the example of this prayer. Give to Him an open mind and say, "Teach me." Give to Him an obedient will and say, "I will do what you want me to do." And give to Him a united heart. Fear His name, and you'll end up praising Him, glorifying Him and enjoying His blessings.

Is your mind open to the truth of God's Word? Does your will respond to truth and obey it? Is your heart undivided, fixed upon the Lord? Today, dedicate your mind, heart and will to God.

Read Psalm 87:1-7

CITY OF GOD

Most of us have places in this world we love in special ways. It might be an old home or perhaps a school. It might even be a church or a place in that church building where God met you in a significant way. God also has a place He loves especially. "The Lord loves the gates of Zion more than all the dwellings of Jacob" (v.2). The psalmist refers to the city of God.

Zion is important to Christians also. Of course, our citizenship is in the heavenly Zion (Phil.3:20), where one day we shall walk the golden streets. But we can give thanks for Jerusalem, the earthly city of God.

First, *our foundations are in Zion*. This means the foundations of our spiritual life. The Word of God, the Bible, originated from the Jewish nation. The knowledge of the true God came from the Jewish nation. And the Son of God, the Savior of the world, came from the Jewish nation.

Second, *our family is in Zion*. The psalmist speaks about one who was born there. People born in Jerusalem are proud of their birthplace, just as we are proud of our birthplace. But Christians have been born from above. We have been born again spiritually because we trust Christ as our Savior.

Third, *our fountains are in Zion*. "All my springs are in you" (v.7). The word springs means "fountains"—our refreshment, our strength, our spiritual power. They all come from our heavenly Zion.

Believers in Christ are citizens of heavenly Zion. Are you a citizen of the city of God? If not, why not trust Him as your Savior and begin your pilgrimage to Zion?

HOLDING ON

There are days when it's difficult to rejoice. Oh, we talk about having the joy of the Lord and walking in the sunshine of His countenance. We are grateful for days like that, but there are also difficult days. The author of Psalm 88 penned these words when he was having one of those difficult days. He tells us about his problems.

First, he is struggling with unanswered prayer. "O Lord, God of my salvation, I have cried out day and night before You. Let my prayer come before You; incline Your ear to my cry" (v.1). This is not an unsaved man crying out to a God he doesn't worship. This is a true believer pleading with God for help. And so far, He hasn't done anything.

He also is coping with *trouble* and *sickness*. "For my soul is full of troubles, and my life draws near to the grave. I am counted with those who go down to the pit; I am like a man who has no strength . . . You have put away my acquaintances far from me; You have made me an abomination to them; I am shut up, and I cannot get out" (vv.3,4,8). Some scholars think that the psalmist had leprosy, since he was segregated from everyone else.

The foundations of his life seem to be slipping away, and the possibility of death looms before him. In his desolation, what does he do? He holds on to God's power, lovingkindness and faithfulness.

What do you do on difficult days? Hold on to all that God is and all that He does. God is still working for you. All things are still working together for good (Rom.8:28). Don't turn away from Him. Wait. He will bring you out of your affliction.

Whenever you experience a difficult day, encourage yourself by focusing on God's character and His attributes—power, lovingkindness and faithfulness. Remember what He has done for you in the past. In spite of what you see around you, trust the Lord. He will see you through your affliction.

DAY 218

Read Psalm 88:13-18

LIGHT IN THE DARKNESS

When nothing seems to go right, when people are neglecting you and God seems to have forgotten you, *don't stop praying*. This troubled psalmist did not cease to pray. "Lord, I have called daily upon You; I have stretched out my hands to You" (v.9). Even though the light is not shining, don't stop praying, because God will answer.

Start each day with the Lord. "But to You I have cried out, O Lord, and in the morning my prayer comes before You" (v.13). Always begin your day with the Lord, and He will give you the strength to finish it.

Look to God alone. We have a tendency to trust circumstances, ourselves and other people. Not the psalmist. He said, "I'm going to look to God alone. I'm going to trust the Lord of my salvation."

Yes, there are those dark, dismal, disappointing days. But God is still on the throne. Trust Him to see you through.

How well do you fare when the days are dark? Follow the example of the psalmist. Start your day with God in prayer and draw strength from His Word. Keep your eyes on the Lord, not on your circumstances, and He will deliver you.

Read Psalm 89:1-10

GREAT IS HIS FAITHFULNESS

DAY 219

Have you thought lately about the faithfulness of God? Too often we are prone to focus on our own faithfulness and our own faith. Our living a victorious Christian life indicates that we are trusting a faithful God who cannot fail, not that we are faithful to Him.

How should we respond to the faithfulness of God? First, *sing of His faithfulness.* "I will sing of the mercies of the Lord forever; with my mouth will I make known Your faithfulness to all generations" (v.1). Are you praising God today for His faithfulness? When you find yourself unfaithful to the Lord, consider His faithfulness. After all, "He is faithful and just to forgive us our sins and to cleanse us from all unrighteousness" (I John 1:9).

Second, *share God's faithfulness with others.* "With my mouth will I make known Your faithfulness to all generations." In giving our testimonies, we sometimes brag about ourselves. I was in a meeting once where the leader said, "Let's give praise to the Lord, and let's be careful not to give praise to ourselves." The psalmist said, "I'm going to share the faithfulness of God—not what I have done, but what He has done; not what I am, but what He is."

Third, *submit to His faithfulness.* "God is greatly to be feared in the assembly of the saints, and to be held in reverence by all those who are around Him" (v.7). Our God is faithful.

Can we trust Him today? Yes, we can. Is His Word going to fail? No, not one word of all His promises has failed. Is His grace going to run out? No, He has vast riches of His grace. God is faithful in everything.

Have you learned to respond to God's faithfulness? Praise Him for His faithfulness, share it with others and submit to it. He can be trusted.

DAY

220

Read Psalm 89:11-29

THE JOYFUL SOUND

"Blessed are the people who know the joyful sound! They walk, O Lord, in the light of Your countenance. In Your name they rejoice all day long, and in Your righteousness they are exalted" (vv.15,16). That describes how God's people ought to be.

We *should walk in joy*. Throughout the year the people of Israel heard joyful sounds. The trumpets would call them to a feast or remind them of the faithfulness and goodness of God. The psalmist is talking here about that festal blowing of the trumpet. Today we might hear a joyful sound—the sound of the trumpet, the voice of the archangel—and meet the Lord. God's people should be walking in joy. Every day should be a joyful experience of anticipation, excitement and enrichment.

We *should walk in the light*. "But if we walk in the light as He is in the light, we have fellowship with one another, and the blood of Jesus Christ His Son cleanses us from all sin" (I John 1:7). When you walk in the light, you see things as they really are. You don't stumble or cause someone else to stumble.

We *should walk in faith*. "In Your name they rejoice all day long" (v.16). Why? His name can be trusted. Those who know God's name know victory and blessing.

We *should walk in the heights*. "In Your righteousness they are exalted" (v.16). There's not only excitement and enrichment in our life with God, we are also exalted, lifted high. This doesn't mean that we are glorified instead of God. It means that He lifts us up.

Keep your ears tuned. You might hear that joyful sound today.

Do others know you are a Christian by your life? If you walk with joy and in the light, you will bless others and glorify God. Do you find your walk with God enriching? Enjoy Him to the fullest. Let Him exalt you.

UNBREAKABLE COVENANTS

There is one thing that God cannot do—He cannot lie. When He makes a covenant, He keeps it, and we can hold on to His Word forever. This is what God said concerning David and his family: "If his sons forsake My law and do not walk in My judgments, if they break My statutes and do not keep My commandments, then I will visit their transgression with the rod, and their iniquity with stripes. Nevertheless My loving kindness I will not utterly take from him, nor allow My faithfulness to fail. My covenant I will not break, nor alter the word that has gone out of My lips" (vv.30-34).

God is faithful to His Word. He's not going to alter what He has said. "Forever, O Lord, Your word is settled in heaven" (Ps.119:89). "Heaven and earth will pass away, but My words will by no means pass away" (Matt.24:35). God's Word is not going to change, but it should change us.

God is faithful to chasten. He said, "If David's descendants don't live as they ought to live, I'll chasten them. My promise won't fail even though they fail." Even if we are not faithful, God is still faithful. He will not deny His Word. He is faithful to discipline us when we need it.

God is faithful to forgive. When we ask Him for His forgiveness, He forgives our sins and cleanses us from all our unrighteousness (I John 1:9). I'm glad I don't have to figure out every day what God's attitude is toward me. He doesn't change; He is faithful.

Have you experienced God's faithfulness in your life lately? Trust His Word, submit to His chastening and ask His forgiveness.

DAY 222

Read Psalm 89:38-45

DOWN, DOWN, DOWN

God did wonderful things for the people of Israel, and He gave them wonderful promises. We would expect the Israelites to be loyal followers of God, but they were not. They turned their back on Him and sinned, so God had to discipline them. This passages depicts His chastening.

What really happens when God disciplines His people? "You have renounced the covenant of Your servant; you have profaned his crown by casting it to the ground" (v.39). God wants us to reign in life. Jesus Christ has made us kings and priests. But when God chastens us, He takes our crowns from us. Our authority is gone; the glory is gone; and the honor is gone. Instead of acting like kings, we live like slaves. When God chastened the Israelites, their crowns were cast down.

In verse 40 the walls were broken down. "You have broken down all his hedges; you have brought his strongholds to ruin." There is no security in what we build. God casts it down.

In verse 43 the soldiers were smitten down. "You have also turned back the edge of his sword, and have not sustained him in the battle." When we disobey the Lord, everything falls apart.

In verse 44 the glory ceased, and God cast down the king's throne.

Yet God will forgive. Don't lose your joy in the Lord. Let's live today with authority and security because we are walking with Him. If you find yourself down, look up. Ask Him to raise you up and restore you to victory again.

Sometimes God's discipline can be hard. Have you lost your joy in life because of His chastening? Regain the reign in your life. Look to God for forgiveness and restoration.

A FEW REMINDERS

"How long, Lord? Will You hide Yourself forever? Will Your wrath burn like fire?" (v.46). These questions come from the broken heart of a man who wondered why God's people were going through so much trouble. Several times we see the word *remember* in these verses. "Remember how short my time is; for what futility have You created all the children of men?" (v.47). What could the psalmist possibly remind God about?

He reminds Him that *life is short.* God did not make us in vain. Sometimes we receive His grace in vain. Sometimes what He does for us is in vain. But that's our fault, not His. Life is short. That's good to remember the next time you are tempted to sin. Why waste time disobeying God?

Then *he reminds God of His promises.* "Lord, where are Your former lovingkindnesses, which You swore to David in Your truth?" (v.49). This refers to the covenant God had made with David. It looked as though God had broken His promise. He doesn't break His promises, but He likes to have us remind Him of them.

Next, *he reminds God of their reproach.* "Remember, Lord, the reproach of Your servants—how I bear in my bosom the reproach of all the many peoples, with which Your enemies have reproached, O Lord" (vv.50,51). Remember our reproach. Why? Because it detracts from the glory of God.

Let's remind ourselves that we are here to bring glory to His name. The psalmist ends on the mountains: "Blessed be the Lord forevermore! Amen and Amen" (v.52). He starts with burdens and ends with blessing. He starts with sighing and ends with singing, because he lifts his broken heart to the Lord in prayer.

When you go through troubled times, remember God's promises and remind Him of them. He is faithful to His Word.

DAY 224

Read Psalm 90:1-6

TIME AND ETERNITY

First there were sundials. Then came water clocks, hourglasses and mechanical clocks. Now we have digital clocks and watches that split time into hundredths of a second. Our culture certainly is concerned with time. That's why it's good to read what Moses says: "Lord, You have been our dwelling place in all generations. Before the mountains were brought forth, or ever You had formed the earth and the world, even from everlasting to everlasting, You are God. . . . For a thousand years in Your sight are like yesterday when it is past, and as a watch in the night" (vv.1,2,4).

It's good to contemplate God's eternity in the light of man's frailty. We are creatures of time, but God is eternal. He is our dwelling place from generation to generation. The eternity we face is in His hands.

The psalmist also tells us that God is faithful. From generation to generation, from everlasting to everlasting, He has been faithful, and He will continue to be faithful. He's the God of Abraham, Isaac and Jacob. He's the God of individuals, the God of different personalities. He's the One we can trust.

Let Him be God in your life today. When you abide in Him and live for His glory, you are partaking of the eternal. The Bible says, "He who does the will of God abides forever" (I John 2:17).

When you compare time with eternity, you gain a bit of God's perspective. You can incorporate eternal values into this life. You can partake of the eternal by allowing God into your life. Is He your dwelling place? Have you partaken of His faithfulness?

Read Psalm 90:7-11

DEATH: A REASON FOR LIFE

DAY 225

Life expectancy in the United States is up to 75 years. That's good news; 25 years ago it was only 70 years. Perhaps it will keep going up, but in comparison to eternity, the human life span is short. That's why we read, "The days of our lives are seventy years; and if by reason of strength they are eighty years, yet their boast is only labor and sorrow; for it is soon cut off, and we fly away" (v.10).

That sounds like a rather doleful statement, but it's true. The setting of Psalm 90 is found in the events recorded in Numbers 14. God had brought the Jews directly to Kadesh-Barnea. He said, "Now go in and possess the land." And they would not do it. They doubted God's promise and questioned His wisdom. They did not believe He would enable them to conquer the land. As a consequence, God said, "All right, everybody 20 years and older is going to die within the next 40 years." And that's what happened—the world's longest funeral march. For the next 40 years the nation wandered in the wilderness, while that older generation died. Then God took the younger generation on a whole new crusade, and they conquered the Promised Land.

The older people knew they were going to die before they got to the Promised Land. But Christians today know that when we die we'll go to the place Jesus is preparing for us. It's important to make our lives count while we are on earth. Yes, our lives have their difficulties, and if the Lord doesn't return soon, our lives will end in death. But death will lead to eternity. And we can live a life of the eternal today. The Bible says, "He who does the will of God abides forever" (I John 2:17). Let's touch the eternal today by abiding in the Almighty and doing His will.

You need not die to bring eternity to the present. You do so by abiding in God and doing His will. Determine to make your life count. Invest it in eternity.

Read Psalm 90:12-17

A HEART OF WISDOM

"So teach us to number our days, that we may gain a heart of wisdom" (v.12). Moses' words summarize what we need to know if we want to make our lives count.

We live a day at a time. Usually, we don't number our days; we number our years. When you have a birthday and someone asks how old you are, you tell them your age in the number of years. But we'd better number our days, because we live a day at a time. "Give us this day our daily bread" (Matt.6:11). God has ordained that the entire universe functions a day at a time.

We live from the heart. "So teach us to number our days, that we may gain a heart of wisdom." We need to take care of the heart. That's why Solomon wrote in Proverbs 4:23, "Keep your heart with all diligence; for out of it spring the issues of life." What is in your heart will direct your life.

We also live by God's wisdom. Wisdom is knowing and having discernment, so that we can apply the truth of the Word of God at the right time, in the right way, with the right motive. Wisdom comes from the Word of God and from getting to know Him and ourselves better.

Moses gives the secret of making life count—live it a day at a time. You need God's help to apply His Word to your life. Live as though this may be your last day. Ask God for the wisdom you need and apply it by faith.

SAFETY IN THE SHADOW

I wonder what the safest place in the world is. A bomb shelter? A bank vault? Perhaps a prison surrounded by an army? According to Psalm 91, the safest place in the world is a shadow. "He who dwells in the secret place of the Most High shall abide under the shadow of the Almighty" (v.1). "He shall cover you with His feathers, and under His wings you shall take refuge; His truth shall be your shield and buckler" (v.4).

What does this mean? The psalmist refers to the Holy of Holies in the tabernacle and the temple. In the Holy of Holies, two cherubim were over the mercy seat, and their wings touched each other. "Under his wings" means at the mercy seat, where the blood was sprinkled, there in the presence of the glory of God. The Holy of Holies was God's throne. It was the place of God's glory. In other words, the safest place in the world is in fellowship with God—not just visiting the Holy Place, as the high priest did once a year, but *dwelling* in the Holy Place. The psalmist is urging, "Live in the Holy of Holies."

According to Hebrews 10, we have an open invitation to come right into the presence of God and dwell in the secret place—under His wings, at the mercy seat. This is where God meets with us where His glory is revealed, where He gives us His guidance and shows us His will. My shadow is not much protection for anyone. But when it belongs to the Almighty, a shadow is a strong protection. Live in the Holy of Holies, under the shadow of the Almighty.

God invites you to fellowship with Him—to live in the Holy of Holies. What an invitation! You may come into the safety of His presence and receive His mercy, guidance and protection. Do you live under God's shadow?

DAY 228

Read Psalm 91:9-16

GUARDIAN ANGELS

"For He shall give His angels charge over you, to keep you in all your ways" (v.11). This is the promise Satan quoted to Jesus when he tempted Him in the wilderness.

This promise speaks about our *security*. We can't see the angels. But they are God's messengers, servants sent to help us. If we are in the will of God, we have the protection of His army. He is called the "Lord of Hosts" (the Lord of the armies). The hosts of the heavens are under His control—the stars and planets and all the universe. But so is the great host of angels—thousands and thousands of angels, God's creation, His army sent for our ministry.

When the child of God is in His will, then he is immortal until his work is done. This suggests that we have a *responsibility*—"to keep you in all your ways"—to be in the will of God. "Because you have made the Lord, who is my refuge, even the Most High, your dwelling place" (v.9). When you are dwelling with God, abiding in Him, then He says, "No evil shall befall you" (v.10). It doesn't say we won't be hurt; it says we won't be harmed. We may have to go through the valley, go through the battle or go through difficulty. But it will not bring evil to us.

Our security and our responsibility lead to our *victory*. What kind of victory does God give us? "You shall tread upon the lion and cobra; the young lion and the serpent you shall trample underfoot" (v.13). Satan is the lion and the serpent. The psalmist tells us that because we are abiding in the Lord, because His truth is our shield and our buckler, we have victory. We can call upon Him, and He will answer. It's wonderful to know that God gives us security as we fulfill our responsibility.

Angels are God's messengers sent to help and protect you. As you think about angels and their ministry, keep in mind your responsibility to stay in the will of God and abide with Him. Thank God for the "invisible" ministry of His angels and for the part they have in your victory over Satan.

Read Psalm 92:1-6

AN IDEAL DAY

DAY **229**

As we begin each day, we trust we'll still be around at the end of the day. What happens in between depends on how we start in the morning and how we end in the evening. Verses 1 and 2 describe an ideal day: "It is good to give thanks to the Lord, and to sing praises to Your name, O Most High; to declare Your lovingkindness in the morning, and Your faithfulness every night."

That's how we ought to live each day. When you wake up in the morning, *remember His lovingkindness*. Don't wake up grouchy, saying, "Oh my, another day." Wake up saying, "Today the Lord loves me, and His lovingkindness endures forever. God has my life in His hands. There's nothing to be afraid of."

During the day offer *praise* and *thanksgiving*. "It is good to give thanks to the Lord, and to sing praises to Your name, O Most High." Find every reason you can to praise Him—even for little things like parking places, phone calls that bring a blessing to you or perhaps news of a friend.

At the close of the day, *remember God's faithfulness*. In the morning we look forward to lovingkindness. During the day we experience that lovingkindness. And at the end of the day, we can look back and say, "God has been faithful." No matter how difficult this day may be for you, when you get to the end, you're going to be able to look back and say, "Great is Thy faithfulness."

Each day has its own set of burdens, blessings and challenges. How you begin and end a day determines what kind of day you will have. Begin your day with lovingkindness. Praise God and thank Him during the day. In the evening, remember His faithfulness during the day. What a great recipe for living a day at a time!

DAY
230

Read Psalm 92:7-15

FRESH AND FLOURISHING

Someone has said that there are three stages in life: childhood, adolescence and "My, you're looking good." We can't stop aging. But no matter how old we grow, we ought to continue growing in the Lord. "The righteous shall flourish like the palm tree; he shall grow like a cedar in Lebanon. Those who are planted in the house of the Lord shall flourish in the courts of our God. They shall still bear fruit in old age; they shall be fresh and flourishing" (vv.12-14). I am greatly encouraged by those words, because as I get older, I want my life to count more and more for Jesus.

God tells us to be like palm trees. That means we should be *planted*—"planted in the house of the Lord." We must abide in Christ, whose roots are in the spiritual. What a tragedy it is to get older and move into the world and into sin, abandoning what you were taught from the Word of God.

We should also be *productive*. "They shall be fresh and flourishing"—fruitful trees to the glory of God. Palm trees stand a lot of abuse, storms and wind. The wind that breaks other trees bends the palm tree, but then it comes back up. Palm trees have roots that go down deep to draw up the water in the desert area. They can survive when other trees are dying. And palm trees just keep on producing fruit. The fruit doesn't diminish; it gets better and sweeter.

Finally, we should be *flourishing* "in the courts of our God." When some people get old, they get grouchy, mean and critical. Let's not be like that. Allow the Lord to make you fresh and flourishing. Have roots that go deep. You can stand the storms and still be fruitful, feeding others from the blessing of the Lord.

God wants you to grow like strong, productive trees that bear much fruit. He wants your roots to grow deep to draw nourishment from His hidden spiritual resources. Are you planted and feeding on the Word of God daily? Are you producing fruit and bringing glory to Him? Are you flourishing and feeding others?

Read Psalm 93:1-5

LOOKING ABOVE THE FLOOD

DAY 231

While I was ministering at a Bible conference in the Pacific Northwest, I watched the ocean as it moved in. The last day of the conference was rainy and stormy. The ocean waves looked as though they were right at our back door. The scene reminded me of verse 3 in today's passage: "The floods have lifted up, O Lord, the floods have lifted up their voice; the floods lift up their waves."

What do you do when you find yourself threatened by the floods of wickedness? Do what the psalmist did. He looked at God's throne. "The Lord reigns, He is clothed with majesty. The Lord is clothed, He has girded Himself with strength. Surely the world is established, so that it cannot be moved. Your throne is established from of old; You are from everlasting" (v.1). No waves or floods can disturb the throne of God. But often we don't look high enough. We see the floods, but we don't see God. We see the waves getting higher and higher, and we don't lift up our eyes by faith and see the eternal, established, secure, strong throne of God.

The psalmist also heard God's testimonies. He didn't listen to the sound of the waves. Today, you might hear a lot of threatening sounds. Don't pay any attention to them. "Your testimonies are very sure" (v.5). The psalmist heard God's testimonies and said, "I can trust the Word of God."

This psalm also reminds me of Peter when he walked on the water (see Matt.14:28-31). He took his eyes off the Lord and forgot His promise. Jesus said to him, "Come." That's all Peter needed. He should have said to himself, "If Jesus says, 'Come,' I can come"—because His commandments are always His empowerments.

God's throne is established, and His testimony is sure. When you see the flood approaching, lift your eyes higher to see the throne of God and open your ears to hear His Word. Put your faith to work and trust His promises of strength and power.

DAY

232

Read Psalm 94:1-10

TRUST GOD'S TIMING

"Lord, how long will the wicked . . . triumph?" (v.3). I'm sure you also have asked that question. This sentiment is expressed many times in Scripture. The great saints of God cried out, "O Lord, how long?" When David was being chased by King Saul, many times he said, "How long, O Lord, before I get my throne? You've promised it to me."

The psalmist tells us that God has His plan. He hears our prayers and sees our need. He knows exactly what is going on. The wicked think that they have everything under control. "Yet they say, 'The Lord does not see, nor does the God of Jacob understand'" (v.7). "God can't see what we're doing; God's not going to do anything." That's the false confidence of the wicked. But the psalmist answers that with inspired logic. "He who planted the ear, shall He not hear? He who formed the eye, shall He not see? He who instructs the nations shall not He correct, He who teaches man knowledge?" (vv.9,10). In other words, is God dumber than we are? He sees what's going on in this world. He hears the cries of His own people and disciplines those who need discipline.

Our tendency, of course, is to take things into our own hands. Moses tried that approach, and it sent him to the wilderness for 40 years to learn how to trust God's timing and method. When you find yourself crying out, "How long, O Lord, how long," focus on God and remember that He knows as much about the situation as you do—probably more. Then wait on Him. Watch and pray. You can be sure that He will keep His promises.

Learning to trust God's methods and timing is a lifelong course. When you need to wait patiently for God to act, first look to Him and lay hold of His promises in Scripture. Then rest in His care. He knows your situation, and He keeps His word. He will act at the right time.

Read Psalm 94:11-23

PRAY, WAIT OR ACT?

DAY 233

"Who will rise up for me against the evildoers? Who will stand up for me against the workers of iniquity?" (v.16). I wonder what kind of an answer we would give to these questions.

There are times when we only *pray* about a problem. There are times when we *wait*. There are times when God says, "Not now—I'll take care of it later." But there are times when we must *act*, as when Moses had to stand up and lead the people out of Egypt, or when David had to perform the judgment of God. There are times when we who are the light of the world must stand up and shine, when we who are the salt of the earth must apply that salt to the decay in the world today.

How easy it is to be a spectator and say, "Well, I'll pray about it." Good—be sure you do. But God says, "Who's going to stand up for Me against the workers of iniquity?" The answer: those who know that God is their Help. "Unless the Lord had been my help, my soul would soon have settled in silence" (v.17). "But the Lord has been my defense, and my God the rock of my refuge" (v.22). When God is your Help, when you have the strength of God that comes from His Word, you can stand up against the sin in this world.

Those who are separated from sin are also called to action. "Shall the throne of iniquity, which devises evil by law, have fellowship with You?" (v.20). We have laws today that provide defense from a lot of sin. Yet those who are separated from sin must stand up with God against iniquity—those who believe that He will give us the ultimate victory. We may lose a few battles, but thank God we're going to win the war!

Christians are never to become complacent about evildoers. We deal with them by praying, waiting and acting. God wants you to be an influence for Him. Be an active witness where He has placed you. Ask for His leading in knowing when to pray, wait or take a stand.

DAY **234** Read Psalm 95:1-7

RESPONDING TO GREATNESS

"For the Lord is the great God, and a great King above all gods" (v.3). That's a great affirmation of faith the psalmist wrote as he looked at the heathen gods of other nations.

In his book *Your God Is Too Small*, J. B. Phillips affirms the greatness of God. If you have a small God, you'll have small faith; if you have a great God, you'll have great faith—not great faith in your faith but great faith in a great God. If God truly is a great God, then how should we respond to His greatness?

First, *thank Him*. "Let us come before His presence with thanksgiving; let us shout joyfully to Him with psalms" (v.2). Be thankful that He is a great God. Note that His greatness extends to creation. "In His hand are the deep places of the earth; the heights of the hills are His also" (v.4). Isn't it good to know that God is a God of the depths as well as a God of the heights? When we're living on the mountaintop, He is there. When we're down in the valley, He is there. "The sea is His, for He made it; and His hands formed the dry land" (v.5). I'm glad that my God is God of the changing places, such as the sea, and of the stable places, such as the dry land. No matter where we are, we can experience His greatness.

Second, *sing to Him*. "Oh, come, let us sing to the Lord! Let us shout joyfully to the Rock of our salvation" (v.1). And *worship Him*. "Oh, come, let us worship and bow down; let us kneel before the Lord our Maker" (v.6).

The greatness of God is the answer to the smallness of man. When you see great sin and great disappointment or when you have a great burden to carry, remember that you are worshiping a great God. As you kneel before Him, He becomes even greater.

HARDENED HEARTS

We find a warning in today's passage. "Today, if you will hear His voice: Do not harden your hearts" (vv.7,8). The context is the nation of Israel in the wilderness. From Egypt to Canaan, they saw God at work. He led them out of Egypt, through the wilderness and into the Promised Land. And what did they do in return? They hardened their hearts.

How do we harden our hearts? It's a process that occurs gradually as we complain about God's work and ignore His Word. The Israelites complained about the way He led them and the way He fed them. They heard God's Word and deliberately disobeyed. This is called tempting God. "When your fathers tested Me; they tried Me, though they saw My work. For forty years I was grieved with that generation" (v.9).

When you see God at work and you complain instead of rejoice, when you hear His Word and deliberately disobey it—you're tempting Him. It's like a little child just daring mom or dad to discipline him. When you harden your heart, you miss God's best for your life. The people of Israel saw the miracles. They heard the messages. They were fed day after day. But in a period of 40 years, that whole older generation died. They did not enter into the fullness of their inheritance.

What should you do to prevent a hard heart? Repent. Listen to God's Word and respond to it tenderly. Watch God's work and respond to it thankfully. Stop complaining and disobeying. Worship the Lord and keep a tender heart before Him.

When you take God and His provisions for granted, you become less thankful and less responsive to Him. Heed the warning of these verses: Keep your heart open to God's Word and obey Him.

Read Psalm 96:1-6

STRENGTH AND BEAUTY

Early one spring morning I walked out that front door of my home and saw a spiderweb. It was beautiful, but it wasn't strong. Before the day was over, the web was gone.

Some things are beautiful but not strong. And other things are strong but not beautiful. A concrete slab is strong, but you're not likely to want one in your living room. Similarly, a steel girder exists to support, not to be seen. There was a beauty about the tabernacle and temple. "Honor and majesty are before Him; strength and beauty are in His sanctuary" (v.6). The tabernacle was a tent—it had beauty but not a great deal of strength. The temple had both strength and beauty.

Our God is practical, but not so practical that He leaves out the beautiful. He gave both strength and beauty to His creation, such as trees, mountains and rivers.

God also wants us to have beauty. He wants us to have the kind of strength that is beautiful and the kind of beauty that is strong. We can "worship the Lord in the beauty of holiness" because "strength and beauty are in His sanctuary."

God's works have both beauty and strength. If you are walking in fellowship with Him, your life will have a beauty that is strong and a strength that is beautiful. You'll become more and more like Jesus.

TRUE HOLINESS

"Oh, worship the Lord in the beauty of holiness!" (v.9). God desires holiness for His people. "Be holy, for I am holy" is repeated several times in the Old Testament. And the apostle Peter used it in one of his letters (I Pet.1:16). It means to be separated, unique and distinct.

God the Father, God the Son and God the Holy Spirit work together to lead us into a life of holiness. The cross of Jesus indicates that God wants us to be holy. On the cross Jesus died for our sins to make us holy, to bring us to God. The Holy Spirit within us urges us to a holy life by His power. The Word of God helps us grow in holiness. Jesus said to His Father, "Sanctify them by Your truth; Your word is truth" (John 17:17).

True holiness is beautiful; false holiness is not. The Pharisees had a false holiness—an artificial, manufactured piety. Jesus had true holiness, and He attracted people. The Pharisees repelled them. The fruit of the Spirit—love, joy, peace, patience and the rest—make for a beautiful life.

True holiness is beautiful, and this beauty comes from worship. Did you know that you become like what you worship? If your god is selfish, you become selfish. If your god is ugly, you become ugly. The person who worships money becomes hard. The person who worships pleasure becomes soft. But the person who worships the true and living God becomes beautiful—more and more like Christ.

God has given you the necessary resources to live a holy life. Allow His Word to teach you and the Holy Spirit to guide you. Live so that you may become more like Christ.

Read Psalm 97:1-12

BALANCING LOVE AND HATE

A friend of mine likes to quote a beatitude that he has either invented or borrowed: “Blessed are the balanced.” It’s a good point. We can’t easily walk unless we’re balanced. When I was learning how to ride a bicycle, my parents put me on one and gave me a push, but I could not keep balanced. To roller skate, ice skate or ski, you’ve got to maintain balance.

This is also true of the Christian life. That’s why the psalmist says, “You who love the Lord, hate evil!” (v.10). There’s a balance for you. Christians are not supposed to hate one another, but they are supposed to hate evil.

We can have one of several attitudes toward the evil in the world today. First, we can defend it. I don’t see how Christians can do that, but there are those who do. There are even those who promote it. They’re playing right into the hands of Satan. Or, we can close our eyes and ignore it, like the priest and the Levite in the parable of the Good Samaritan, who passed by on the other side. Or we can endure it and say, “Well, it’s here, and I’ll just grit my teeth and clench my, fists and put up with it.” But the Word of God says we should *hate it* and *oppose it.*

We hate evil because we love the Lord. If we love Him, we love the things He loves and hate the things He hates. This is also true in human relationships. When you love someone, you love the things he or she loves, and you want to share those things. When God judges evil, we want to be on His side. We don’t want to be like Lot, who, though it grieved his soul, tolerated the evil in Sodom. Everything Lot lived for was burned up when Sodom went up in smoke (Gen.19). “He preserves the souls of His saints; He delivers them out of the hand of the wicked.” God is on our side. And if God is for us, who can be against us?

What is your attitude toward evil in the world? If you love the Lord, you cannot remain neutral. You must hate evil and oppose it, for it is dangerous to tolerate it. Ask God for the strength to take a stand against evil and be a witness to those who practice it.

A SINGING FAITH

One of my seminary professors was a missionary in Africa for many years. When he first arrived on the field by riverboat, from the banks of the river he could hear screaming and wailing and the beating of drums. But 25 years later, when he went down to the river to leave the field, people lined the banks and were singing, "All hail the power of Jesus' name, let angels prostrate fall." What a difference!

The Christian faith is a singing faith. Christians ought to be singing people. We are admonished in the Word of God to sing to the Lord. "Oh, sing to the Lord a new song! For He has done marvelous things; His right hand and His holy arm have gained Him the victory" (v.1).

Sing about God's victories. If you think you have no victory in your life, start singing about the victory of the Lord, and you'll be surprised what He'll do for you.

Sing about His salvation. "The Lord has made known His salvation; His righteousness He has revealed in the sight of the nations" (v.2). We should proclaim the message of salvation to people today.

Sing about His mercy and faithfulness. "He has remembered His mercy and his faithfulness" (v.3). The Lord has been merciful to us and His faithfulness endures to all generations.

Sing about His coming. Verse 9 tells us that the hills are rejoicing before the Lord, "for He is coming to judge the earth. With righteousness He shall judge the world, and the peoples with equity." Sing about His coming, for Jesus may come back today!

Are you singing the praises of God in your life? If you've lost your song, it may mean that you've lost something else—your vision of God, faith in His Word—or perhaps sin has come into your life. Follow the instructions of this psalm and "sing to the Lord a new song."

DAY **240**

Read Psalm 99:1-9

Prerequisites of ANSWERED PRAYER

One of the greatest joys in the Christian life is the joy of answered prayer—to be able to say to someone, "God answered my prayer today," or to hear someone say, "Thank you for praying—let me tell you what God did." The psalmist writes about this: "Moses and Aaron were among his priests, and Samuel was among those who called upon His name. They called upon the Lord, and He answered them" (v.6). Moses called upon the Lord many times when he had the burdens of the people on his shoulders. Aaron, as the high priest, also called upon the Lord. Samuel had some disappointments in his life. His family was not all it ought to have been, and Israel was not all it ought to have been. So he cried out to the Lord as well.

If we call upon the Lord, will He answer us? Yes, if we have met the conditions that Moses, Aaron and Samuel met. First, *they listened to God's Word*. "He spoke to them in the cloudy pillar" (v.7). "If you abide in Me, and My words abide in you, you will ask what you desire, and it shall be done for you" (John 15:7). We want to talk to God and tell Him about all of our problems. He wants to talk to us and tell us about all of His promises. We should listen to Him first, and then He will listen to us.

Second, *they obeyed Him*. They kept His testimonies and the ordinances. Obedience is important to answered prayer. If we're abiding in Christ, we will obey His Word, and then we will be able to call upon Him.

Third, *they confessed their sin*. God forgave their sins, and He enabled them to do what He wanted them to do. As a result, they wanted to exalt the Lord. The purpose of prayer is to glorify God. "Exalt the Lord our God, and worship at His holy hill; for the Lord our God is holy" (v.9).

How glad I am to know that my High Priest in heaven is interceding for me. I can come to Him any time for the grace that I need.

Do you enjoy answered prayer? Do you listen to God's Word and obey it? Is your heart clean of unconfessed sin? Meet God's conditions for answered prayer and let Him bless you.

Read Psalm 100:1-5

THE HIGHEST OCCUPATION

DAY 241

The next time you sing the doxology in a worship service, remember that you are singing Scripture, a version of Psalm 100. This psalm is a digest of instructions on how to worship the Lord.

Who should worship the Lord? "Make a joyful shout to the Lord, all you lands!" (v.1). God wants the whole world to worship and give thanks to Him. Why are we to go into all the world and preach the Gospel? So that all the world will one day be able to make a joyful shout to the Lord.

How should we worship the Lord? First, *by serving*. "Serve the Lord with gladness; come before His presence with singing" (v.2). We are to serve the Lord with gladness because there's joy in our hearts and because the joy of the Lord gives strength.

Second, we worship Him *by singing*. "Come before His presence with singing." I fear that too often in our services, singing becomes routine. We hold the hymnal and sing the songs that we know so well, but our minds and hearts are a million miles away. Think about and rejoice in the words you sing.

We also worship the Lord *by submitting to Him*. "Know that the Lord, He is God; it is He who has made us, and not we ourselves; we are His people and the sheep of His pasture" (v.3). Submit to Him. Follow Him. Obey Him.

Finally, we worship the Lord *by sacrificing*. "Enter into His gates with thanksgiving, and into His courts with praise" (v.4). You don't need to sacrifice animals on an altar, but you can give your time, money and skills.

Why should we worship the Lord? "For the Lord is good; His mercy is everlasting, and His truth endures to all generations" (v.5).

The highest occupation of the Christian life is worshiping the Lord. Never allow your worship to become routine or artificial. Worship Him with a joyful and thankful heart by serving, singing, submitting and sacrificing.

DAY 242

Read Psalm 100:2

PRAISE THROUGH SERVICE

Joyful noise leads to joyful service. If we are to serve the Lord joyfully, our words must become deeds. Jesus warns against hypocritical worship (Matt.15:8). How are we to serve the Lord genuinely?

First, *we serve willingly.* We are redeemed to do what God wants us to do. This verse was meaningful to Old Testament Jews, because they knew about servitude. God delivered them from slavery in Egypt so they might serve Him.

Second, *we serve exclusively.* We cannot serve the Lord and someone else at the same time (Matt.6:24; Ex.20:2,3). But we can serve others for Jesus' sake. Our goal is to please Him alone. Our power, wisdom and the plans for our lives come from Him alone.

Third, *we serve joyfully.* Sometimes we are like the elder brother in the parable of the Prodigal Son; we may do the Father's will and work, but we are far from His heart. God doesn't want our service to be drudgery or to be done grudgingly. That tears us down. When we serve Him joyfully, we enjoy growth, development and excitement. Are you happy serving the Lord?

We praise God most effectively through our service to Him. Are you engaged in service to the Lord in your church or community? When you offer your service to the Lord willingly and joyfully, you glorify His name. Let your words of praise lead to acts of praise!

Read Psalm 100:3, 4

DAY 243

PRAISE THROUGH SUBMISSION

Psalm 100 is God's instruction sheet for praise. Praise is both an action and an attitude of the heart, and one way we praise God is to submit to Him. This passage suggests three acts of submission that bring praise to God.

First, *we submit as creatures to the Creator* (v.3). Satan wants us to think he is God. Some people behave as though they are God. But only Jehovah is God (Isa.46:9; Ps.46:10; I Chron.16:25). A man once said to his girlfriend, "I'm a self-made man." She replied, "It's nice of you to take the blame." We are not self-made. God, in His wisdom, power and patience, has made us. In man is a mingling of dust and deity, for God made us in His image.

Second, *we submit as children to the Father.* We are chosen by grace (Ex.19:5,6). He died for us and saved us because He loves us. When we believe on the Lord Jesus Christ as Savior, we enter into a spiritual family, with God as our loving Father. As we develop in our relationship with Him, we submit to His authority.

Third, *we submit as sheep to the Shepherd.* We need a shepherd. Jesus is the Good Shepherd (John 10:11) and the Great Shepherd (Heb.13:20), and we are the sheep of His pasture (Ps.73:13). It's important to feed on the green pastures of the Word of God.

When you submit to God the Creator, God the Father and Christ the shepherd., you are praising God. Submitting to Him is aligning your will to His will and obeying His Word. Submit to God—He will love and guide you.

DAY **244**

Read Psalm 100:4

PRAISE THROUGH SACRIFICE

In Old Testament days, God's people brought animal sacrifices to the altar. Today, instead of bringing the Lord dead sacrifices, we present living sacrifices to Him. The Bible speaks of several sacrifices that praise God.

We have the *sacrifice of praise* (Heb.13:15). When our lips thank God for what He has done and for who He is, our praise pleases Him. We have the *sacrifice of a broken heart* (Ps.51:17). We are to present our bodies as a *living sacrifice* to Him (Rom.12:1,2). There is the *sacrifice of good works* (Matt.5:16; Heb.13:16). And there is the *sacrifice of finances* (Phil 4:18). When we share our money, time, possessions and energy with others, we bring a sacrifice to God.

Examine your life to see if you are making sacrifices for His glory. Many jobs are waiting to be done, and you might be the person for a specific job.

Have you found that place of ministry God has for you? Are you using the gifts He has given you? Offer your sacrifices of praise to God, that you may bring glory to Him and minister to others.

Read Psalm 100:5

Why We Should

PRAISE THE LORD

DAY 245

Praise is the highest use of man's faculties. When we contemplate the attributes of God, we can't help but thank and praise Him. This verse speaks of three of God's attributes that make Him worthy of our praise.

First, we see *His goodness*. It's part of God's nature to be kind and benevolent. He is not frowning upon us; He's smiling on us through Jesus. We see His goodness in creation (Gen.1:31; Ps.33:5), even though man has wrecked it (Rom.8:19-23). God even shows His goodness to the unsaved nations of the world (Acts 14:17). His goodness ought to lead to man's gladness.

His goodness keeps us from fainting (Ps.27:13). He gives us courage (v.14). God wants to guide us (25:8,9) and protect us (31:19,20). We should respond to His goodness in three ways: (1) We should be repentant; (2) we should want to enjoy Him; and (3) we should draw near to Him.

Next, we see *His mercy* (Ps.23:6). When God is merciful, He does not give us what we deserve, which is eternal death for our sins. Mercy is forever a part of His nature (Heb.4:16; I Pet.1:3; Ps.107).

Last, we see *His faithfulness*. This attribute speaks of God's reliability and stability. He is faithful to chasten us (Ps.119:75). He is faithful to confirm us (1 Cor.1:9). He is faithful to care for us and give us victory over temptation (I Cor.10:13). He is faithful to forgive us (I John 1:9). God is not going to change (Heb.13:8). He is faithful in all He does. Share with your children and your grandchildren that God is good, merciful and faithful.

God's goodness, mercy and faithfulness reveal much about Him. The more you contemplate His attributes, the more you can praise Him.

DAY

246

Read Psalm 101:1-8

HEART AND HOME

A pleasant elderly couple who attended the first church I pastored came to me one day and said, "Pastor, we have moved into a new house, and we'd like you to come and dedicate it." So my wife and I went to the house, read Scripture, prayed and dedicated that house to the glory of the Lord.

What is the most important part of a house? At first you might say the foundation, the heating system or the plumbing. But the most important part of a house is the home. And the most important part of that home is the hearts of the people who live there.

That's what David said when He was dedicating his house to the Lord. "I will behave wisely in a perfect way. Oh, when will You come to me? I will walk within my house with a perfect heart" (v.2). If you want to wreck your house, start wrecking your home. And if you want to wreck your home, start wrecking your heart. But if you want your house and your home to be all that God wants them to be, then make your heart perfect.

What is a perfect heart? It's one that has integrity, wholeness and oneness—a heart that is not divided. Nobody can serve two masters. No one can plow and look back. You need to have a heart that is integrated and united. "Unite my heart to fear Your name," David said (Ps.86:11). He walked around his new house and said, "I want my heart to be perfect, to be wholly fixed upon the Lord. I want Him to reign supremely in my home, because He reigns supremely in my heart."

Can you say the same?

Your heart affects your home. Both need to be dedicated to the Lord. Are you fixed upon the Lord? Does He reign in your home? Determine to walk with integrity always and to make yours a united heart that serves God.

Read Psalm 102:1-11

DAYS OF TROUBLE

DAY 247

One day I phoned a friend of mine who is in the ministry and asked, "How's it going?" His quiet reply was, "Well, I'm having one of those days." The next time you're having one of those days when everything seems to be going wrong—your plans are falling apart, you don't feel well, there are problems and burdens, and it seems as if all of the forces of the enemy are against you—read this psalm. "Hear my prayer, O Lord, and let my cry come to You. Do not hide Your face from me in the day of my trouble" (vv.1,2). What kind of a day was the psalmist having? A day of trouble. In fact, he compares himself to a lonely bird. "I am like a pelican of the wilderness; I am like an owl of the desert. . . . I am like a sparrow alone upon the housetop" (vv.6,7). That's the way he feels—like a bird alone on a housetop. He wants to go into the house and enjoy some fellowship, but he's alone.

The psalmist's enemies were reproaching him (v.8). But in a day of trouble and reproach, he says, "I'm going to change this by the grace of God." And it becomes a *day of prayer*. He tells God how he feels and what he sees. He cries out, "God, You are the only one who can change things." God can change things for you also. He may not change the circumstances on the outside, but He does change your feelings on the inside. Then the day of trouble becomes a day of triumph.

Everyone has days of trouble. When circumstances entrap you and trouble closes around you, pray to the Lord. He knows how to turn your trouble into triumph. Although He may not answer your prayers the way you expect, He will do what is best for you and for His glory.

DAY 248

Read Psalm 102:12-28

More Sure Than THE WORLD

Have you heard the phrase, "It's as sure as the world"? In fact, nothing is more *unsure* than the world. "Of old You laid the foundation of the earth, and the heavens are the work of Your hands. They will perish, but You will endure" (vv.25,26). The "sure" world will perish. Jesus said, "Heaven and earth will pass away, but My words will by no means pass away" (Matt.24:35): What is the surest thing in your life? On what are you building your life? You'd better be building it on the Lord; He's the only One who is sure.

Jesus always is the same. "But You are the same, and Your years will have no end" (v.27). Jesus Christ is the same yesterday, today and forever. God has made this universe, and everything around us looks so certain. We are so sure of the way things work. We can send people from the earth to the moon. God's universe is precisely crafted, but He says that all of this will perish.

What should you do, knowing that you live in a temporary world? Trust God, who is sure. Pray to Him. "He shall regard the prayer of the destitute, and shall not despise their prayer" (v.17). Trust His Word and praise Him. Prayer and praise go together. "This will be written for the generation to come, that a people yet to be created may praise the Lord" (v.18).

Many people foolishly build their entire lives on the cracked foundations of this world and will one day perish with it. But God is changeless and eternal. He wants you to build your life on Him. When you pray, praise Him for His creation and for His work in your life.

Read Psalm 103:1-5

DAY 249

DON'T STOP PRAISING

I wonder how long we could talk to the Lord without asking for something. "Bless the Lord, O my soul; and all that is within me, bless His holy name! Bless the Lord, O my soul, and forget not all His benefits" (vv.1,2). Psalm 103 has no requests. It is nothing but praise; David is blessing the Lord.

What are some of these benefits David sings about? They are ones we may have forgotten or that we may be taking for granted. First, *the Lord saves.* "Who forgives all your iniquities, who heals all your diseases" (v.3). The last part of that statement is an illustration of the first part. He forgives all our iniquities in the same way He heals the human body. Often in the Bible, sin is compared to sickness, and salvation is compared to health. God brings saving health to our souls.

Second, *He keeps.* "Who redeems your life from destruction, who crowns you with loving kindness and tender mercies" (v.4). He keeps us and protects us from the destruction around us. He puts a crown on our heads and makes us kings.

Third, *He satisfies.* "Who satisfies your mouth with good things" (v.5). In fact, David says God so satisfies us that our youth is renewed like the eagle's. The eagle molts, loses its old feathers, gets a new coat and soars again.

Do you pray to God for the sole purpose of praising Him? You have much for which to praise Him, for His love and care never cease. He saves, keeps and satisfies you. Never take God for granted; always take time to praise Him.

DAY
250

Read Psalm 103:6-12

Great Things
HE HAS NOT DONE

We usually praise the Lord for something He has done for us. Today, let's thank the Lord for something He has *not* done. "He has not dealt with us according to our sins, nor punished us according to our iniquities" (v.10).

Everyone knows the plague of his heart—not only the occasional sins but those that try to get us into bondage. What's more, God knows all about it, too. In fact, He knows our sins better than we do. God sees the origin and the outcome of our sins. One reason He hates sin so much is that He is holy, and He sees where sin leads. James tells us that lust, when it conceives, produces sin. And then sin, when it's full grown, produces death (1:15). Sin is pictured as an evil pregnancy.

But the psalmist says that God "has not dealt with us according to our sins." On what basis does He deal with us? On the basis of the cross, the grace of God. Jesus Christ died for our sins, and God forgives them through the blood of His Son. We can come to Him and ask Him to forgive any sin.

But the knowledge that God does not deal with you the way you deserve to be dealt with should not tempt you to tempt Him. Do not be fast and loose with sin. Hate sin, and rejoice today that you're walking with the Father on the basis of the cross of Jesus Christ.

Rejoice today that God does not deal with you according to your sin but according to the cross of Jesus Christ. Your forgiveness comes at a great cost. The next time you're tempted to sin, consider its wages and cost. You are greatly indebted to Christ, so live to please Him.

Read Psalm 103:13-18

DAY 251

DUST AND DESTINY

Our God remembers what we often forget. Sometimes we forget the things He wants us to remember, and that gets us into trouble. Have you remembered lately what you are made of? "As a father pities his children, so the Lord pities those who fear Him. For He knows our frame; He remembers that we are dust" (vv.13,14). God took the dust of the ground and made Adam. Then He breathed into Adam the breath of life, and he became a living soul. Physically, we are made from the dust. But we have the mark of deity upon us, for we are made in the image of God.

When we think of dust, we think of something common and ordinary. You can walk out the back door and find dust. Perhaps you don't even have to go that far. You might just want to look on top of the radio or the dining room table. Dust speaks of *weakness* and *frailty*. But it also speaks of tremendous *potential*. God made us from dust that we might be weak in ourselves but strong in Him. God took the dust and made clay, and then He took the clay and made a man. Where there is dust, there is potential. He is the Potter; we are the clay.

You have to say, "Lord, You made me out of dust but full of potential. And you made me this way that I might be weak in myself but strong in You. 'Mold me and make me after Your will, while I am waiting, yielded and still.'" Paul said, "I can do all things through Christ, who strengthens me" (Phil.4:13). He also said, "We have this treasure in earthen vessels, that the excellence of the power may be of God and not of us" (II Cor.4:7).

Where there is dust, there is potential. Where there is dust, there is opportunity for growth. Continue to yield to Him and His creative process in your life. Ask Him to mold you after His will.

DAY

252

Read Psalm 103:19-22

AT HIS COMMAND

No matter how difficult your situation may be today, no matter how discouraging the news, you can still lean on this: "The Lord has established His throne in heaven, and His kingdom rules over all" (v.19).

God is enthroned in heaven and in control of everything that happens. Sometimes it may not look like it. If you're walking by sight, you may wonder if there is a God at all. Or if there is a God, does He care? Or if He cares, can He do anything? The psalmist tells us, "Don't walk by sight; walk by faith."

God has an army. "Bless the Lord, you His angels, who excel in strength, who do His word, heeding the voice of His word" (v.20). The angels act at His command. If we read and study the Word of God and obey it, everything in the universe will work with us. If we disobey the Word of God, everything will work against us—just as it did against Jonah, who was running in the wrong direction, going on the wrong ship, with the wrong motive, for the wrong purpose. God finally brought him to a place of obedience.

Don't be like Jonah. Have faith that God is in control and working on you in every situation.

No matter how difficult your day or how discouraging the news might be, lean on the wonderful assurance that God is on His throne. He is ruling, and His servants are at work accomplishing His Word. Obey God's Word today and keep walking by faith.

Read Psalm 103:1-12

ENGRAVED BLESSINGS

DAY 253

Someone has said that memory is a sepulcher of broken bones. Someone else has said that memory is a nursery in which children who have grown old play with their broken toys. Memory is the library and the treasury of the mind. Psychiatrist Rollo Mays says, "Memory is not just the imprint of the past upon us; it is the keeper of what is meaningful for our deepest hopes and fears."

Memory is selective. Often we forget what God has done for us. Charles Spurgeon said, "We write our blessings in the sand, and we engrave our complaints in the marble." Memory becomes impressed with burdens. The word *remember* is used 14 times in Deuteronomy, and 9 of those warn of forgetting.

True praise ought to come from the heart, not the memory (Matt.15:8). Worship is the believer's adoring response to all that God says and does.

Engrave God's blessings in your heart, and you'll never grow weary of praising Him.

Never forget God's blessings. Praise Him for all He has done. Don't load your mind with past burdens but enrich it with a memory of His blessings.

DAY 254

Read Psalm 103:1-12

ILLUSTRATED BLESSINGS

This psalm has no petitions, only praise: Verses 3 through 5 are Hebrew poetry with parallel construction. Each verse has two statements. The idea that is presented in the first statement is repeated, illustrated or amplified in the second statement of the verse. The second statements in verses 3 through 5 are illustrations of three blessings: forgiveness, redemption and satisfaction.

The first blessing is *forgiveness* (v.3). The psalmist illustrates forgiveness with the concept of spiritual healing,. God doesn't have to heal us, but He does, and every blessing He gives is an atonement. What healing is to the body, salvation (forgiveness) is to the soul. Jesus is our Great Physician (Eph.1:7).

The second blessing is *redemption* (v.4). *Redeem* refers to a "kinsman redeemer." The Book of Ruth illustrates redemption, with Boaz as a kinsman redeemer. God protects and provides, and He keeps us safe and saved. He has lifted us from slavery to sovereignty.

The third blessing is *satisfaction* (v.5). One translation reads, "[He] satisfies thy old age with good things." This verse applies to every stage in life. God restores and renews us. He keeps us young spiritually, for we find satisfaction in His Word.

Do you have God's blessings of forgiveness and redemption,? If so, do you enjoy the satisfaction that comes from knowing Him and obeying His Word? God restores, renews and blesses you that you might bless others.

Read Psalm 103:1-12

DAY 255

UNIVERSAL PRAISE

"Bless the Lord, O my soul" (v.1). The psalmist opens by addressing God on a personal level. He is praising God for what He does and for who He is. As we read this psalm, we discover why God is so wonderful.

He is the merciful Savior (vv.8-12). God in His grace gives us what we don't deserve and in His mercy doesn't give us what we do deserve. But He does have a holy temper, and we must not provoke Him by deliberately sinning.

He is the tender Father (vv.13-18). Why does God show mercy? Because it is His nature to exercise compassion and love. He is tender because He knows we are made of dust. We are frail. We're temporary, like a flower that soon fades and dies. Our response to God's tenderness should be praise and obedience.

He deserves universal praise (vv.19-22). We see in the Book of Revelation that praise for God increases and spreads over all the universe. We will be part of that someday.

Why do we praise Him? Because His throne is secure. We praise Him because we can keep His commandments, serve Him and please Him. We praise Him because His works are so wonderful, and He's allowed us to be part of them.

The psalm ends the way it begins—on a personal level. "Bless the Lord, O my soul." Follow the psalmist's lead and praise God for His wonderful attributes and deeds.

DAY
256

Read Psalm 104:1-4

GOD'S SECRET AGENTS

Have you thought lately about angels? We usually don't think about them because we don't see or hear them. But God's Word tells us they are His special messengers. "Who makes His angels spirits, His ministers a flame of fire" (v.4). We have a fire of God at work—His angels, accomplishing His will.

The angels have always served God. They sang at creation. They visited Abraham. They came to Hezekiah when Jerusalem was under attack, and one angel destroyed 185,000 soldiers. They announced the coming of the Messiah. They sang at Jesus' birth. They were with Him in the wilderness when He was tempted. They were with Him when He was in the Garden of Gethsemane. And now that Jesus has ascended to heaven, the angels worship and glorify Him there.

Angels also serve us. Hebrews 1:14 says, "Are they not all ministering spirits sent forth to minister for those who will inherit salvation?" Angels are God's invisible army, His servants, working for us.

I have a feeling that when we get to heaven we'll find out that there were many times when angels protected us from harm and strengthened us. Let's rejoice today that we are not alone. Greater are those who are with us than those who are against us.

God sends angels to minister to you. It should encourage you to know that they are working on your behalf. Today, thank him for His angels and for their ministry.

Read Psalm 104:5-13

QUENCHING THE THIRST

DAY 257

People who live in the city sometimes forget that God is the God of creation and nature. In the United States alone, more than 2700 acres of pavement are laid each day. Before long, God's creation might be completely covered by concrete and asphalt. We need to pause and get reacquainted with the God of creation. "You who laid the foundations of the earth, so that it should not be moved forever, You covered it with the deep as with a garment; the waters stood above the mountains. At Your rebuke they fled; at the voice of Your thunder they hastened away . . . You have set a boundary that they may not pass over, that they may not return to cover the earth" (vv.5-7,9). The psalmist refers to the Flood in Noah's day. It was God's judgment. But the next judgment He sends will be by fire, not water.

Water also is a blessing. "He sends the springs into the valleys; they flow among the hills" (v.10). This is a beautiful picture of the rivers and springs and hills, all of which enable animals to have food and drink. "They give drink to every beast of the field; the wild donkeys quench their thirst" (v.11). The birds of the heavens nest in the trees by these rivers. I like the phrase in verse 12—"they sing among the branches." God waters the earth. The crops grow, and man and beast are able to live. And as an extra blessing, He puts the birds in the branches to sing. All of creation is satisfied. "The earth is satisfied with the fruit of Your works" (v.13).

The God of creation also is the God of salvation, and He can satisfy your thirsty soul today.

As you observe nature, you are reminded of God's physical provision. He also provides for the spiritual needs of His people. Do you have a need today? Ask God to flood your soul with His blessing!

DAY

258

Read Psalm 104:14-18

A BALANCED DIET

The psalmists were captivated by the God of creation. Of course, the world they lived in was a little cleaner, a little purer, maybe a little more beautiful, because man had not yet exploited it. They recognized their dependence on Him for their sustenance: "He causes the grass to grow for the cattle, and vegetation for the service of man, that he may bring forth food from the earth, and wine that makes glad the heart of man, oil to make his face shine, and bread which strengthens man's heart" (vv.14,15).

Food, wine, oil, bread—these were staples for Jewish people in that day. Do not think that because the psalmist mentions wine he's talking about drunkenness. The Bible certainly warns against being drunk. Rather, he says that God supplies our every physical need and even above and beyond those needs. "God . . . gives us richly all things to enjoy" (I Tim.6:17).

In the Bible wine is a picture of the Holy Spirit. At Pentecost, when the people of God were rejoicing and worshiping and praising the Lord, the crowd said, "They are full of new wine" (Acts 2:13). Do you have the joy of the Spirit today? "Be not drunk with wine," Paul said, "but be filled with the Spirit" (Eph.5:18).

Oil also is a picture of the Holy Spirit, who makes the face to shine. Moses had a shining face because he fellowshipped with God. Stephen had a shining face because he gave his life for God. Jesus had a shining face on the Mount of Transfiguration.

Bread is a picture of the Word of God. It strengthens the heart. "Man shall not live by bread alone, but by every word of God" (Luke 4:4).

God wants to give us gladness; He wants to give us radiance; and He wants to give us strength. The Holy Spirit uses the Word of God to make the child of God more like Jesus.

Do you maintain a balanced spiritual diet with the staples God provides? Food, wine, oil and bread are symbols of how He nurtures and nourishes you. Feed on His Word and allow the Spirit to control your life.

CONSIDERING CREATION

After surveying God's work in creation, the psalmist wrote: "O Lord, how manifold are Your works! In wisdom You have made them all; the earth is full of Your possessions" (v.24). This verse shows us important traits of God.

First, *creation reveals God's wisdom.* We ought to take time to admire His wisdom in creation. I've read that if the proportion of gases in the air were changed ever so slightly, all of us would die. The way God tilted the earth, the way He arranged the seasons, the way He put creation together is a revelation of His great wisdom. It's logical that the God who is wise enough to run creation is wise enough to run our lives. If He can keep the stars and the planets and the seasons and all these things going as they should, can He not put our lives together and make them what they ought to be?

Second, *creation contains God's wealth.* "The earth is full of Your possessions" (v.24). Without His wealth, we could not exist. Not only are gold and silver and other precious stones measures of His wealth, but so are ore and rock, fruit and grain.

Third, *creation makes possible man's work.* "Man goes out to his work and to his labor until the evening" (v.23). Even Adam had work to do in the Garden of Eden. Work is a blessing, not a burden, if we're doing it for the Lord.

Fourth, *creation motivates us to worship the Lord.* "O Lord, how manifold are Your works!" We don't worship creation—that's idolatry. We worship the God of creation. We recognize that He gives every good and perfect gift (James 1:17). O let us adore Him, our great Creator, our great Savior.

Creation shows God's wisdom, so rejoice! Creation contains His wealth, so use it for His glory. Creation provides work for man, so view work as a blessing. But greatest of all, creation should move you to worship the Lord.

DAY **260**

Read Psalm 104:27-30

SPRING RENEWAL

Scientists tell us that our world is governed by what they call "natural law." Most of them forget that behind the law is the Lawgiver. Behind creation is a Creator, who cares for His creation and His people. Who unifies the universe? The God who made it. All of creation waits upon Him and trusts Him to supply what is needed. As the psalmist wrote, "These all wait for You, that You may give them their food in due season. What You give them they gather in; You open Your hand, they are filled with good" (vv.27,28).

God gives and we gather. He provides and we take. He is dependable; He takes care of His own. "I have been young, and now am old," David said. "Yet I have not seen the righteous forsaken, nor his descendants begging bread" (Ps.37:25). God is also generous. He does not give carelessly or selfishly. He opens His hand, and all of creation is filled with good.

God controls life and death and the changing seasons. "You hide Your face, they are troubled; You take away their breath, they die and return to their dust. You send forth Your Spirit, they are created; and You renew the face of the earth" (vv.29,30). Spring is so beautiful, summer so delightful and autumn so fruitful. Then winter comes, and it seems so dismal. But the same God of spring and summer and autumn is the God of winter. He brings the refreshing, renewing springtime again.

God can renew your life today. He can bring you seasons of fruitfulness and seasons of sunshine. Don't worry about the seasons of life. The God who runs this universe can manage the changing seasons of your life. If you are in a winter season, wait; when He is ready, God will send you a springtime.

Read Psalm 104:31-35

A NEW WORLD

DAY 261

When Jesus Christ is your Savior and God is your Father, when the Holy Spirit is within you and the Word of God is teaching you, all of creation takes on new beauty and new blessing. The sky is a deeper blue, and the earth is a richer green. You don't see just creation; you see the Creator. And you don't simply see a Creator; you see the Heavenly Father, who cares for you.

"I will sing to the Lord as long as I live; I will sing praise to my God while I have my being. May my meditation be sweet to Him; I will be glad in the Lord" (vv.33,34). The psalmist wrote these words after considering all of God's creation. He looked at the waters, the mountains springs and the rushing rivers. He heard the birds singing in the branches. He saw the cattle eating grass. He saw man baking bread and making oil. He watched the sun rise and set. "See all this?" he said. "I'm going to rejoice in this Creator, who is my God."

All creation is travailing in pain because of sin (Rom.8:22). But our Creator is still in charge, and His creation, in spite of sin, still has great beauty and great wealth. Did you know that God rejoices in His creation? "The glory of the Lord shall endure forever; the Lord shall rejoice in His works" (v.31). He rejoices to hear the birds sing. He rejoices to see the rivers flow.

Let's rejoice in His works also. And let's rejoice that God is glorified as we obey Him today.

God is glorified by His works, for they reflect His greatness. When you look at creation, do you see His greatness? Rejoice with Him as He rejoices in His creative works. "Rejoice in the Lord always. Again I will say, rejoice!" (Phil.4:4).

Read Psalm 105:1-4

SPIRITUAL HEALTH

Nutritionists remind us that we must have the minimum daily requirements of vitamins and minerals if we are to be physically healthy. Similarly, David gives God's minimum daily requirements we need if we are to be spiritually healthy.

The first requirement *is praise*. "Oh, give thanks to the Lord! ... Sing to Him, sing psalms to Him" (vv.1,2). Praise means giving thanks for all that God is, all that He does and all that He shares with us. Praise is rejoicing in the presence of the Lord because of who He is and because we are His children.

Prayer also is essential. "Call upon His name" (v.1). We call upon the Lord when we need strength and grace and help in a time of need. And He always hears us.

Witnessing is another element. "Make known His deeds among the peoples . . . Talk of all His wondrous works. Glory in His holy name" (vv.1-3). If we only praise and pray but don't present the Lord to other people, our lives will become narrow, shallow and selfish. We need to tell others that He is the only Savior.

The final requirement is *seeking* His *face*. "Seek the Lord and His strength; seek His face evermore!" (v.4). In other words, live in the light of God's countenance. Live with the smile of God upon your life and seek to please Him alone.

Just as your physical health requires care, so does your spiritual health. Are you taking proper care of your soul? God's minimum daily requirements help you maintain a healthy spiritual life. Make sure you meet your daily minimum. It will please Him and bring glory to Him.

Read Psalm 105:5-15

DAY 263

SPIRITUAL MEMORY

Your spiritual memory is vital to your spiritual health. Do you remember what God wants you to remember? Are you grateful for what He remembers? "Remember His marvelous works which He has done, His wonders, and the judgments of His mouth. . . . He has remembered His covenant forever, the word which He commanded, for a thousand generations" (vv.5,8).

We should remember God's words, His wonders and His works, but we often forget. How easy it was for the Israelites to forget what God had done for them. Each year they celebrated the Passover, and one reason for that celebration was to remind them that God had delivered them out of slavery in Egypt. Some things we ought to forget, such as "those things which are behind" (Phil.3:13). But the psalmist tells us to "remember His marvelous works" (v.5). Are you remembering God's blessings? The next time you are tempted to criticize or get angry with God, just remember His marvelous works.

God also remembers: "He has remembered His covenant forever" (v.8). He deals with us on the basis of His covenant promises, not on the basis of the Law, and He has sealed that covenant with the blood of His Son.

Finally, don't forget that His promises never fail. Not one word of all of God's promises has failed. Even when we forget, He remembers. Even when we neglect God's Word, He remembers it. God keeps His promises. He is faithful and will never lie.

Claim a promise from God's Word that especially encourages you today. As you remember that promise, remember also that God is ever faithful to keep His promises.

DAY 264

Read Psalm 105:16-23

PREPARED TO BE AN ANSWER

How wonderful it is to receive an answer to prayer. But there is something even more wonderful—to be an answer to prayer. Have you been an answer to prayer lately? Joseph was. In verse 17 we read, "He sent a man before them—Joseph—who was sold as a slave." At the time—Joseph—could not see what God was doing. But God was preparing him to be an answer to prayer. He was going to use Joseph to protect the people of Israel. If Joseph had not done this, the nation might have perished. If the nation had perished, we wouldn't have a Bible, and we wouldn't have a Savior.

God plans His work. We never have to worry about what is going on, because God knows. He is never caught off guard, and He is never surprised. God never says, "How did that happen?" He chose Abraham and Isaac and Jacob and Jacob's sons to accomplish some great purposes in this world—to bear witness of the true and living God, to give us the Bible and the Savior.

God also works His plan. He uses people to accomplish His purposes. We don't always know what God is doing. He didn't send an angel down to prison to explain to Joseph all of His plans. Joseph worked and walked by faith. He went through trials and dishonor, but he ultimately triumphed. From trial to triumph, from bondage to blessing, Joseph was an answer to prayer.

You may be wondering today, *Why am I going through this experience? Why doesn't God make life easier for me?* Remember Joseph. God chose him, prepared him and used him as an answer to prayer.

God doesn't waste your trials. He designs them for your good and His glory. Perhaps you are going through difficulties and trials today. Let God prepare you for what He has prepared for you. He might be planning to use you as an answer to prayer.

Read Psalm 105:24-45

SALT AND LIGHT IN "EGYPT"

DAY 265

Suppose you were an Egyptian during the time of Moses and Aaron. You lived through the plagues that came on your land because of the stubbornness of Pharaoh. What would be your response when you saw the Jews leave Egypt? The psalmist wrote, "Egypt was glad when they departed, for the fear of them had fallen upon them" (v.38). I have no problem believing that at all. Furthermore, I suspect that when God's people depart from this world, when our Lord comes again, the world will be glad.

Egypt is a picture of the world. To the people of God (Israel), it was a place of slavery and monotonous toil. It also is flat and barren in many areas. But Canaan is a land of hills and valleys, a land of rain and fruitfulness, milk and honey. When you were saved, God removed you from Egypt, spiritually speaking. He put you into Canaan and said, "Enjoy all of these blessings."

Why was Egypt glad when Israel left? One thing is sure—the Egyptians were afraid. Israel was worshiping the true God, and their true God was showing His power through the plagues. Israel was an irritant to Egypt—like salt in a wound, like light that exposes evil. God used Israel to witness to Egypt, but it did not receive that witness.

Christians are salt and light. Sometimes we irritate people. Sometimes by our conduct we expose what is wrong. One of these days we are going to be gone. It could be today. Jesus Christ might return today and take His people home to glory. No more salt. No more light. But what then? Judgment. Let's remember that we have a job to do while we are waiting for our Lord to come.

One of the Church's responsibilities is to be light and salt in the world. Sometimes you affect others without being aware of it. Other times you have obvious opportunities to impact others for Christ. Can you think of opportunities to be salt and light in your daily routine? Ask God to use you to make a difference in someone's life today.

DAY 266

Read Psalm 106:1-5

Who Can

PRAISE THE LORD?

"Who can utter the mighty acts of the Lord? Or can declare all His praise?" (v.2).

Who can truly praise the Lord? *Those who know God through faith in Jesus Christ.* "His mercy endures forever" (v.1). Only when we've experienced the mercy and the grace of God can we utter His mighty acts. We've been saved by His grace. This was God's greatest act—greater than bringing Israel out of Egypt and even greater than the creation of the universe.

Who else can praise the Lord? *Those who obey Him.* "Blessed are those who keep justice, and he who does righteousness at all times!" (v.3). If we are walking with the Lord and obeying Him, then we can praise Him and speak of His wondrous acts.

Also, *those who call upon the Lord* can praise Him. "Remember me, O Lord, with the favor You have toward Your people. Oh, visit me with Your salvation" (v.4). People who pray are people who praise. People who pray for God's will in their lives are those who rejoice in His work.

Finally, *those who trust His promises* can praise the Lord. "That I may see the benefit of Your chosen ones, that I may rejoice in the gladness of Your nation, that I may glory with Your inheritance" (v.5). God promised His people an inheritance in Canaan, and He gave it to them. We now have our inheritance in Jesus Christ. We are rich! We are richer than kings, and we can draw upon that inheritance: We are sharing in His goodness and His gladness, and one day we will share in His glory. Let's praise Him today.

Those who obey, trust and call upon the Lord know of the acts of God. They have claimed their inheritance in Jesus Christ. Are you among those who can praise the Lord? Have you claimed your inheritance?

Read Psalm 106:6-15

DAY 267

THANKS FOR NOTHING

Sometimes an unanswered prayer is the best thing for us. The psalmist says, "And He gave them their request, but sent leanness into their soul" (v.15). The Israelites had prayed selfishly. God was feeding them with manna from heaven, angel's food, but they wanted meat. All they had to do every morning was step our of their tents, stoop down and pick up the precious, clean, sweet, life-giving manna. But after a while their old appetites came back. They said, "Oh, if somebody would give us some meat to eat." So God sent them meat, but while they were eating it, many of them died (Num.11:31-33).

We can learn from this experience. First, *selfish prayers are dangerous.* How dangerous it is to say, "Oh, God, I simply have to have this." Such prayers are never beneficial. "You ask and do not receive, because you ask amiss, that you may spend it on your pleasures" (James 4:3).

Second, *prayer must change our character.* The Israelites got their request, but it didn't help their character. In fact, they were in worse shape spiritually after they got what they wanted. The prodigal son said, "Father, give me." He got what he asked for, and it almost ruined him. Then he came home and said, "Father, make me"—and his character changed. He began to be a real son (Luke 15:19). Selfish praying erodes our character, but praying in the will of God builds our character.

Third, *we must always pray for God's will.* The purpose of prayer, it has well been said, is not to get man's will done in heaven but to get God's will done on earth. Never be afraid to say, "Thy will be done."

God knows best how to answer your prayers—even whether or not to answer them! The psalmist has given three valuable guidelines for effective prayer. Do you apply these to your prayers? Let God use your prayer time to align you to His will and His point of view. Let Him prepare you for His answer.

DAY **268**

Read Psalm 106:16-23

STAND IN THE GAP

We often think of Moses as a great leader and a great legislator, and indeed he was one of the greatest. But have you ever thought of Moses as a great intercessor, a man of prayer? I was amazed to discover how many instances of prayer are recorded in the life of Moses. For instance, when the Israelites turned against God, made a golden calf and began to worship like the heathen, God was prepared to judge them. But Moses went up on the mountain and interceded, or "stood in the gap." "Therefore He said that He would destroy them, had not Moses His chosen one stood before Him in the breach, to turn away His wrath, lest He destroy them" (v.23).

The people of Israel had been delivered from Egypt and were standing at Mount Sinai, where God was giving Moses the Law. But they built an idol. How soon we forget what God has done for us; how soon we forget what He has said to us. We turn away and start living on substitutes.

Moses could have profited personally from their sin. God said, "Moses, I'll start with you and make a whole new nation, and no longer will the Jewish nation be the people of Abraham. It will be the people of Moses." But Moses replied, "No, Lord, you love these people. They are your people. Don't judge them. God did judge their sin, but He did not destroy the nation. Of course, the people did not appreciate what Moses had done for them, and they began to criticize him as well.

I thank God that today in heaven we have an Intercessor, the Lord Jesus Christ who ever lives to make intercession for us at the Father's throne (Heb.7:25). He and the Father love us and together are guiding and building our lives.

Intercession is one of the believer's most important ministries. Are you an intercessor? Others need your prayer support. Follow the example of Moses and stand in the gap.

A LEADER SINS

Moses wanted one thing that God would not give him: the privilege of entering the Promised Land. You'll remember that Moses had sinned against the Lord and therefore was not permitted to go into Canaan (Num.20). He brought the nation right up to the border and then had to go up on the mountain and die.

The Israelites were partly to blame for Moses' sin. "They angered Him also at the waters of strife, so that it went ill with Moses on account of them; because they rebelled against His Spirit, so that he spoke rashly with his lips" (vv.32,33). Moses and Aaron asked God for water for the thirsty people, and He said, "Speak to the rock, and the water will come out." But Moses lost his temper—the people provoked him—and he struck the rock. God gave them the water, but He said to Moses, "You have not sanctified me before the people in what you said or in what you did."

Leaders sin, and sometimes God's people encourage them to sin. If only the Israelites had gone to Moses and said, "Moses, we are praying for you," "Moses, we love you," or, "Thank you, Moses, for interceding for us. Thank you for all that you've done for us." But instead they complained and criticized. My heart goes out to pastors and Christian workers who are surrounded by people who cannot say thank you but constantly criticize and complain.

Many people don't realize the costs of being a spiritual leader. The higher we are in leadership, the greater our discipline. If Moses had been an ordinary citizen of Israel, God might not have stopped him from going into the Promised Land. But Moses was a leader. When leaders sin, they pay dearly for it. Let's not cause anyone else to sin today. Be an encouragement to the people of God.

Are you a leader in your church or group? You have an awesome responsibility to God and to those under your direction. The sin of a leader can cause widespread damage. Take special measures to avoid compromising situations and don't let others cause you to take your eyes off the Lord. Also, always pray for, encourage and support your leaders.

DAY 270

Read Psalm 106:34-48

THE COST OF MINGLING

It has been well said that the one thing we learn from history is that we don't learn from history. Anyone who has raised children or is trying to help raise grandchildren knows this. Somehow the new generation doesn't believe that the older generation knows anything.

Psalm 106 certainly bears this out. It is a record of how the people of Israel were blessed and then sinned. God helped them repeatedly, and they repeatedly sinned. We see one cause of their sin in verse 35: "But they mingled with the Gentiles." There's step one—they started mingling and breaking down the walls of separation. God had warned Israel not to mingle among the nations. They were not to get involved with them, but as verse 35 says, they "learned their works." First we mingle with the world, and then we start learning the world's way of doing things. And before long, Israel "served their idols, which became a snare to them" (v.36). They mingled, they learned, and they served.

The tragedy is that the families suffered the most. "They even sacrificed their sons and their daughters to demons" (v.37). Thus, they lost the next generation.

Many Christians today have broken down the walls of separation. They are mingling with and serving the world and are figuratively sacrificing their own children to demons. "Thus they were defiled by their own works, and played the harlot" (v.39). Israel was married to Jehovah God, but she was unfaithful to her marriage vows.

Don't be defiled by the world. Keep your walk with the Lord holy.

Sin contaminates. That's why you need "walls of separation." Don't mingle with the world, for one step of compromise will lead to another. Keep your heart clean of sin and do not entertain temptations. Let nothing come between you and your relationship with God.

Read Psalm 107:1-8

FROM WANDERER TO PILGRIM

DAY 271

One phrase is repeated four times in Psalm 107: "Oh, that men would give thanks to the Lord for His goodness, and for His wonderful works to the children of men!" (v.8). The psalmist gives us five vivid illustrations of what God has done for us and why we should praise His name. He talks about wanderers, prisoners, hospital patients, mariners and people seeking to build the city and sow the seed.

About wanderers the psalmist writes, "They wandered in the wilderness in a desolate way. They found no city to dwell in. Hungry and thirsty, their soul fainted in them. Then they cried out to the Lord in their trouble, and he delivered them out of their distresses. And He led them forth by the right way, that they might go to a city for habitation" (vv.4-7). God rescued them. Then there's that refrain. "Oh, that men would give thanks to the Lord for His goodness, and for His wonderful works to the children of men!" God has done this for you, so thank Him.

I was a wanderer before the Lord saved me—lonely, solitary, hungry, thirsty, aimless and wondering where to go next. Then someone told me about Jesus Christ—that He died on the cross for my sins, was buried, rose again on the third day and today is a living Savior for all who will call upon Him. So I cried unto the Lord in my trouble, and He delivered me out of my distresses. Now I'm delivered and guided and part of His family, no longer lonely, no longer hungry and thirsty, for Christ is the Bread of Life; He is the Living Water. I am a pilgrim on my way to a heavenly home.

Consider God's goodness to you and the guidance He gives. He deserves your praise. He saved you and delivered you from the penalty of your sins. Give thanks to God for changing you from a wanderer to a pilgrim.

Read Psalm 107:9-15

CONSEQUENCES OF REBELLION

It is dangerous to rebel against the will and the Word of God and to turn away from His path. Psalm 107 describes the fate of people who did. "Those who sat in darkness and in the shadow of death, bound in affliction and irons . . . therefore He brought down their heart with labor; they fell down, and there was none to help" (vv.10,12). Verse 11 tells us why this happened: "Because they rebelled against the words of God, and despised the counsel of the Most High."

This is the terrible and painful plight of all who rebel against God's will and Word—darkness, death and despair. Instead of being on that wonderful road that leads to glory, they are down in the dungeon in darkness and in bondage, under the shadow of death. People say, "I want to do my own thing. I want to do it my way." They shouldn't. The greatest judgment God might bring to our lives is to let us have our own way. Paul wrote that God gave mankind over to uncleanness, vile passions and a debased mind (see Rom.1:18-32). God says to those who rebel against Him, "Do you want to go in that direction? All right, I won't stop you, but neither will I change the consequences."

The people described in Psalm 107 who rebelled against God's Word ended up in darkness and death, in the dungeon of defeat and despair. But they cried out to God, and He delivered them. It's never too late for God's mercy. You can cry out to Him just as these people did. "Then they cried out to the Lord in their trouble, and He saved them out of their distresses. He brought them out of darkness and the shadow of death, and broke their chains in pieces" (vv.13,14). They received light and life and liberty because they called upon the Lord.

Some people need to realize that they have rebelled against God's will. If that is true in your case, call upon Him. He'll deliver you. Then you can praise the Lord "for His goodness and for His wonderful works to the children of men" (v.15).

Read Psalm 107:16-21

GOOD MEDICINE

DAY 273

Psalm 107 contains four vivid pictures of sin and salvation. In today's passage, the psalmist likens sin to a disease and God's Word to medicine: "Fools, because of their transgression, and because of their iniquities, were afflicted. . . . He sent His word and healed them" (vv.17,20).

Disease starts secretly. It enters your body secretly and grows secretly. Then it begins to sap your strength, rob your appetite and weaken you. Unless something is done, it will kill you.

So it is with sin. People play with sin without realizing its danger. That's like treating cancer or AIDS lightly. Sin brings death. To be healed, we need the medicine of God's Word.

Scripture can heal the brokenhearted. It can heal those who have been ravaged by sin, who have rebelled against the Lord. But the sick have to reach out by faith and admit their need (Matt.9:12). We have to admit that we can't help ourselves and that no one else can help us.

Medicine can be expensive and even hard to obtain sometimes. But the Word of God is free and available. If can cure every malady of the soul.

Perhaps your life has been ravaged by sin and you have yet to admit your need and reach out to the Lord for help. Never delay treatment for your soul. Read the Word of God and ask the Holy Spirit to apply its truths to your heart.

DAY 274

Read Psalm 107:16-21

THE GREAT PHYSICIAN

Yesterday we learned that the Bible is the only medicine that can cure the disease of sin. Now let's consider the Great Physician, who administers the medicine.

Jesus Christ came to call sinners to repent, and only He can save them. There are false physicians in this world today. What they offer does not solve the problems of the soul. The false prophets of Jeremiah's day were guilty of applying salves when they should have performed surgery (Jer.8:11,22). How would you like your doctor to lie to you about your health—to gloss over your physical ailments? That's what these "prophets" did to the Israelites regarding their spiritual condition.

Doctors are busy people and often cannot be there right when you need them. But Jesus comes when you call Him. His diagnosis is always accurate. He can cleanse every wound and heal every sickness. He won't force His medicine on you; He waits for you to admit your needs first. And the amazing thing is that He already paid the bill for your care on Calvary's cross.

Lost sinners deserve to die, but "whoever calls on the name of the Lord shall be saved" (Acts 2:21). If you've never trusted Him for your salvation, do so now.

The Great Physician administers the medicine of His Word to your ailing soul. He can save the unbeliever, heal a broken heart and restore a fractured relationship. Whatever your need, ask Jesus for His healing touch.

WEATHERING THE STORM

Quite frankly, I don't like large bodies of water. I don't like to be on them, and I don't like to be in them. I don't mind being by them; to sit by the ocean and watch the waves is fine.

When I read these verses I almost get seasick. They describe a storm at sea. "For He commands and raises the stormy wind, which lifts up the waves of the sea. They mount up to the heavens, they go down again to the depths; their soul melts because of trouble. They reel to and fro, and stagger like a drunken man, and are at their wits' end" (vv.25-27).

Storms do come to our lives. What causes them? Sometimes other people cause them. In Acts 27 Paul got into a storm because the people in charge of the ship would not listen to the Word of God. Sometimes God causes the storm to test us and build us. In Matthew 14 Jesus sent His disciples directly into a storm to teach them an important lesson of faith. Sometimes we cause the storm by disobedience—we are like Jonah running away from God, and the only way He can bring us back is to send a storm.

But the greatest storm that ever occurred was at Calvary. When the sun was blackened for three hours and God the Son was made sin for us, all of the waves and the billows of God's judgment came upon Jesus on the cross. Because He weathered that storm, you and I can cry out to God. He can deliver us from the storms of life or take us through them, giving us the strength and courage we need. The psalmist promises, "He calms the storm, so that its waves are still. . . . So He guides them to their desired haven" (vv.29,30).

Do you find yourself in a storm today? Ask God for the strength and courage to weather it and for the wisdom to understand it, not waste it.

DAY
276

Read Psalm 107:32-43

REMEMBER THE GIVER

It is dangerous for Christians to depend on comfortable circumstances. When God sees that we are depending on our circumstances and not on Him, He will change those circumstances in a hurry. "He turns rivers into a wilderness, and the watersprings into dry ground; a fruitful land into barrenness, for the wickedness of those who dwell in it. He turns a wilderness into pools of water, and dry land into watersprings. There He makes the hungry dwell, that they may establish a city for a dwelling place" (vv.33-36).

You can picture people saying, "My, we are blessed. We have these wonderful rivers and springs. We have all of this fruitful land. Let's just eat, drink and be merry." But God says, "Wait a minute. Are you enjoying the gifts and forgetting the Giver? Are you looking at My hand and forgetting My heart? Are you enjoying my wealth but neglecting My will?"

That's what often happens—we turn to idolatry. We start living on substitutes. The rivers and springs and fruitful land become our god. So God stops the rivers. He shuts off the water springs. He makes the fruitful land barren. Then we cry out and say, "Oh, God, what shall we do?" His answer is, "Start worshiping Me instead of your blessings. Start looking to the Blesser instead of the blessing. Don't be idolaters, who live on substitutes. Give thanks to Me for all the good things I have given you." In other words, get smart. "Whoever is wise will observe these things, and they will understand the lovingkindness of the Lord" (v.43).

Satan will do his best to get you to depend on the world's substitutes. When he succeeds, you forget God and trust in your resources and wealth—you become an idolater. Perhaps you enjoy comfortable circumstances. Thank God for them, but continue to draw your strength from the spiritual resources He has provided. If God has shut off His watersprings of blessings to you, start worshiping Him.

Read Psalm 108:1-13

DAY 277

What Is Your
HEART CONDITION?

"O God, my heart is steadfast; I will sing and give praise." David begins this psalm by reminding us of the importance of a steadfast or "fixed" heart in the Christian life.

What is a fixed heart? First, it trusts in the Lord for salvation. Jesus died for us on the cross. If we have trusted Him, we have fixed our hearts upon Him, and we have experienced His mercy. "For Your mercy is great above the heavens, and Your truth reaches to the clouds" (v.4).

A fixed heart is also *devoted*. Jesus said that we can't serve two masters. We're going to love one and hate the other or be loyal to the one and despise the other. We can't serve God and money—or, for that matter, God and anything else (Matt.6:24). So a fixed heart is devoted and loving—a heart that is devoted solely to the Lord.

Marriage is one of the many pictures of the Christian life found in the Bible. Those who trust Jesus Christ as Savior are married to Him. We are waiting for that day when the Bridegroom will come and claim His Bride, and we'll enter our heavenly home. Meanwhile, we want to be faithful to Him. We do not want to be guilty of spiritual adultery, being unfaithful to our Savior.

A fixed heart is *serving*. If your heart is fixed, you will be busy serving others. A person fixed upon the Lord in faith and love reaches out to serve others—to put others ahead of himself.

Finally, a fixed heart is *hopeful*. We anticipate the return of our Lord. When you love and trust someone, you look forward to being with that person. We wait and hope for the day when we will be in the Lord's presence.

The condition of a person's heart reveals much about the condition of his soul. A fixed heart is in tune with the Lord—trusting, devoted, serving and hopeful. What is your heart condition?

DAY 278

Read Psalm 109:1-13

WHY IS GOD SILENT?

What do you do when heaven is silent? What do you do when you cry out to God and there is no answer, or at least you can't hear it? This happened to David. He kept crying out to God, "Do not keep silent, O God of my praise!" (v.1). David was being attacked by the wicked—a frequent occurrence in his life. You must remember that when he prayed these prayers of judgment (v.13), he was not seeking personal revenge. No, he was praying as God's king over Israel. David wanted to see the wicked judged because they were attacking the people of God, the ones from whom God's Word and His Son would come.

Why is God silent at times? It may be because *we aren't listening or we don't want to listen*. Evangelist Billy Sunday used to say that a sinner can't find God for the same reason a criminal can't find a policeman—he's not looking. Sin makes us turn a deaf ear to God. When Adam and Eve heard the voice of God in the Garden of Eden, they ran and hid. Children often do that when they disobey.

Sometimes God is silent because *we aren't ready for the message*. He wants to talk to us about something, but we aren't ready. We have to go through refining trials to make us ready to listen.

God is sometimes silent because *He knows we aren't willing to obey*. He is always ready to show us His will, but He shows His will only to those who really want to do it. Jesus said in John 7:17, "If anyone wants to do His will, he shall know concerning the doctrine." Obedient people always hear the voice of God.

Finally, sometimes God is silent that He might test us—*to teach us the importance of silence*, the importance of waiting on Him. Waiting helps remind us of God's sovereignty.

The silence of God is one of the difficult tests of faith. What should you do when He is silent? Remember His faithfulness and past blessings. Live today on what He has already told you. Trust Him and wait. You will hear the voice of God again.

Read Psalm 109:14-20

CAREFUL CULTIVATING

DAY 279

What we love determines how we live. What delights us also directs us. David wrote about his enemies, "As he loved cursing, so let it come to him; as he did not delight in blessing, so let it be far from him."

What do you love? What do you delight in? You reap exactly what you sow. David's enemies were sowing curses, and he knew they were going to reap a harvest of misery. They were running away from the blessing of God, and David knew that in missing the blessing of God, they were going to miss the joys and purposes of life.

Let's be careful how we cultivate the appetites of our inner person. What we love we may get, and after we get it we may regret it. There may be some fun in sowing sin, but there's no joy in the reaping. Christians' tears and toil are in the sowing; our joy is in the reaping. But for those who live for the flesh and for the world, the joy is in the sowing, and the trial and the tears are in the reaping. If you take what you want from life, you pay for it.

How important it is to cultivate spiritual appetites—to have an appetite for the Word of God, for prayer, to be with His people and to delight in the worship and service of God!

Cultivate those appetites of your inner person that lead to spiritual growth. Keep them in check by feeding on God's Word and by walking with the Lord. He will use your appetites to bring blessing to your life and others.

DAY **280**

Read Psalm 109:21-31

PRAISE IN PERSECUTION

When David wrote this psalm he was being sorely persecuted by his enemies. He was praying for them; they were preying on him. Yet throughout this psalm he expresses some rather vehement thoughts. He calls upon God to bring judgment upon them because of the way they lived. Again, keep in mind that David was not seeking personal revenge. He was above that. Instead, he was praying as God's anointed king, concerned about the needs of his people.

I like the way Psalm 109 ends: "I will greatly praise the Lord with my mouth; yes, I will praise Him among the multitude. For He shall stand at the right hand of the poor, to save him from those who condemn him" (vv.30,31). Even though he sees all these enemies around him, even though they are persecuting the poor and needy, even though they love cursing, David says, "I'm going to praise God. I'm not going to look at them and walk by sight. I'm going to walk by faith and praise God." Praise can change a negative situation. It helps us see more clearly and lifts our hearts to the Lord when the world around us seems so difficult.

David not only praises God, he also witnesses. "I will praise Him among the multitude" (v.30). In other words, "I'm going to tell others about what God has done for me. Instead of focusing on the enemy, I'm going to go out and share the Word of God with others." That's a good way to get victory. Instead of thinking constantly about the problems in life, let's go out and tell others about the One who solves them.

Then he makes a third resolution. He says, "I'm going to trust my Advocate in heaven." God is standing at our right hand (v.31). At the right hand of God is Jesus Christ, our heavenly High Priest, our Advocate. So let's not be afraid. Let's not be bitter. Let's praise the Lord and realize that He is at our right hand, and we dare not trust anyone or anything but Him.

To trust God when you are surrounded by enemies requires that you walk by faith, not sight. Perhaps you are in a similar situation today. By a courageous act of your will, get your eyes off your enemies and begin praising God. It can change your situation.

Eavesdropping on

ETERNITY

It is not usually polite to listen in on other people's conversations, but in Psalm 110 we can do that. We hear God the Father speaking to God the Son. "The Lord said to my Lord, 'Sit at My right hand, till I make Your enemies Your footstool'" (v.1). This is quoted often in the New Testament. It talks about when our Lord Jesus Christ returned to heaven and was enthroned at the right hand of the Majesty.

What does this Father–Son conversation say to us? First, it speaks of our Lord's *majesty*. He has returned to heaven in glory. He had prayed, "Father, glorify me together with Yourself, with the glory I had with You before the world was" (John 17:5), and God did that. God the Father gave God the Son His majesty, and now He is the King–Priest in heaven. "You are a priest forever according to the order of Melchizedek" (v.4). Nowhere in the Old Testament do we find a priest on a throne, but Jesus in His majesty is both our King and our Priest. As our King, He tells us what to do. As our Priest, He gives us the strength to do it.

Psalm 110 also speaks of *victory*—He has won the battle. "Sit at My right hand, till I make your enemies Your footstool" (v.1). That's about as low as you can get. Our Savior is victorious. He has won every battle. He is the Conqueror, the King of kings and Lord of lords. There is nothing for us to fear.

This psalm also speaks about His *ministry*. Most people on thrones have others serve them. Not so with Jesus. He serves us.

Finally, the psalmist speaks of our *security*. "He ever lives to make intercession" for us (Heb.7:25). As long as He lives, we live—and that's forever.

Because Christ is the King of kings, He has won the victory. He has conquered sin and death. Because He is our High Priest, we have security, for He is interceding for us. Do you know Jesus as your Savior? Is He your King and High Priest?

Read Psalm 111:1-10

REAL WISDOM

We live in a world with a great deal of knowledge but not a great deal of wisdom. So-called smart people do stupid things. David tells us the secret of wisdom and understanding in Psalm 111. "The fear of the Lord is the beginning of wisdom; a good understanding has all those who do His commandments. His praise endures forever" (v.10) Here we have three secrets of wisdom, and a person doesn't have to go through a university to learn them.

Fear God. "The fear of the Lord is the beginning of wisdom." This is not the fear of a slave before an angry master. This is the reverence and respect of a loving child for a loving Father—showing respect for God, His Word, His presence and His will for our lives.

Obey Him. "A good understanding has all those that do His commandments." The Word of God is given to us not just to read and study but to obey. We are to be doers of the Word, not just auditors who sit in class and take notes. When we obey God, we begin to understand what He is doing. Obedience is the organ of spiritual understanding.

Praise Him. "His praise endures forever." Praise takes the selfishness out of our lives. It takes us away from idolatry, from living on substitutes.

The more we fear Him, the more we obey Him. The more we obey Him, the more we praise Him. These are the ingredients of a happy and successful life.

The world's wisdom is based on faulty foundations. Genuine wisdom begins by fearing God. You increase your wisdom as you obey His Word and praise Him. As you walk with the Lord today, do so with the Wisdom that comes from fearing Him.

Read Psalm 112:1-10

ONE LEGITIMATE FEAR

DAY **283**

Psychiatrists call the fear of certain things phobias. There are people who fear heights (acrophobia) and people who fear closed-in places (claustrophobia). There are people afraid of water, dogs and even other people. But there is one fear that drives out all other fears, and we find it in Psalm 112. "Praise the Lord! Blessed is the man who fears the Lord, who delights greatly in His commandments" (v.1).

All kinds of fears are taken care of if we fear the Lord. One is *family fears*. "His descendants will be mighty on earth; the generation of the upright will be blessed" (v.2). Commit your children to Him and you won't have to worry about their lives.

Fear of the Lord also drives out *financial fears*. "Wealth and riches will be in his house" (v.3). This doesn't mean we will all be millionaires. It means we'll always have what we need. If we fear the Lord, we can let go of our financial fears.

Some *fear the dark*. "Unto the upright there arises light in the darkness" (v.4). Fear God and you'll always have light when you need it. You will have His guidance and direction.

Some *fear the future and change*. "Surely he will never be shaken; the righteous will be in everlasting remembrance" (v.6). God says, "Don't be afraid of the changes that are going on around you or in you. I am the God of the universe. Fear Me, and I'll take care of the changes."

Finally, some people have a fear of *bad news*. But verse 7 reads, "He will not be afraid of evil tidings; his heart is steadfast, trusting in the Lord." No news is bad if you're walking in the will of God.

When you fear the Lord, every other fear is conquered. Walk today in the fear of the Lord, trusting Him with your future. He will give you peace.

Read Psalm 113:1-9

THE RESPONSIBILITY OF PRAISE

"Blessed be the name of the Lord from this time forth and forevermore! From the rising of the sun to its going down the Lord's name is to be praised" (vv.2,3).

These verses tell us that we have some responsibilities. First, we are to praise God. It's tragic when we forget to praise the Lord. Someone has said that he feels sorry for atheists and agnostics because when they want to be thankful, they have no one to talk to. How can a person really enjoy a beautiful sunrise or a sunset, a beautiful spring day or even a beautiful winter day, if he can't thank the One who creates these things? God deserves our praise, for He does so much for us.

The psalmist also tells us to *praise God all day long*, "from the rising of the sun to its going down" (v.3). Praise Him when you have to get up in the morning. Praise Him when you're tired at the end of the day. Praise Him during the day for the good things that happen and for the difficult things. Give Him thanks for seeing you through every situation.

We also should *praise Him all over the world*—as suggested by the psalmist's reference to the daily journey of the sun from the east to the west. What are we doing about those who do not know the Lord, the many who have never heard about Jesus Christ and His salvation? Let's begin by witnessing right where we are. Let's pray and give. Missionaries need our support. Perhaps God wants you to go and carry the Gospel message overseas.

God has attached responsibility to your privilege of praising Him. You never run out of reasons to praise the Lord. Your praise to Him should encompass the whole day and the whole world. Is praise part of your daily walk with the Lord?

Read Psalm 114:1-8

OBSTACLES ON THE JOURNEY

DAY 285

Have you ever seen the sea flee? Have you ever seen the mountains skip like rams or the hills run like lambs? That's the vivid description the psalmist gives of the Exodus of Israel from Egypt. "The sea saw it and fled; Jordan turned back. The mountains skipped like rams, the little hills like lambs . . . Tremble, O earth at the presence of the Lord, at the presence of the God of Jacob, who turned the rock into a pool of water, the flint into a fountain of waters" (vv.3,4,7,8).

The psalmist mentions the time God opened the Red Sea and the Israelites walked across on dry land. He talks about when the nation entered the Promised Land over the dry bed of the Jordan River. Then he refers to their experience in the wilderness, when they were thirsty and God turned the rock into a pool of water.

What are we to learn from all of these experiences? God helps us in the obstacles of life. When you turn your obstacles over to the Lord, He acts. What will He do? Sometimes He *overcomes the obstacles*. God is with us in the hopeless places. How hopeless the Israelites were at the Red Sea! The enemy soldiers were behind them; the wilderness was around them; the sea was in front of them. But God opened a way to escape.

Sometimes God *removes the obstacles*—the "hills" and the "mountains." He just makes them skip and run away like animals.

He also can *turn the obstacles into blessings*. He "turned the rock into a pool of water, the flint into a fountain of waters" (v.8). If God doesn't overcome or remove your obstacle, let Him turn it into a blessing.

Trust God with your obstacles. He can help you in the hopeless places the high places and the hard places.

DAY

286

Read Psalm 115:1-8

POINTLESS WORSHIP

Psalm 115 tells us about the blessings we have because our God is the living God. He's not one of the "idols of the nations." "Their idols are silver and gold, the work of men's hands" (v.4). How true that is today also. Many people worship silver and gold as their god. They think money can do anything. We do need money for some of the practical things in life. But what good are the things that money can buy if you don't have the things that money *can't* buy?

The psalmist describes the idols and the pointlessness of worshiping them. "They have mouths, but they do not speak [no promises]; eyes they have, but they do not see [no protection]; they have ears, but they do not hear [no prayer]; noses they have, but they do not smell [no praise]; they have hands, but they do not handle [no power], feet they have, but they do not walk [no presence]; nor do they mutter through their throat. Those who make them are like them; so is everyone who trusts in them" (vv.5-8). How unlike God. Christians have *promises*—our God talks to us. We have *protection* because He sees all that happens. We have *prayer* because His ears are open to us. We can *praise* Him. (In the Bible, the smelling of a fragrant offering is a picture of God's acceptance of our praise to Him.) We have *power* because He has an omnipotent hand.

We become like the god we worship. Those who worship silver and gold become like that—dead, lifeless and hard. Many people are making a god in their own image. But God made us in His image, and He wants us to have an active faith in Him.

Christians have a living faith and serve a living God. The more you read His Word, fellowship with Him and praise Him, the more you become like Him. You have His promises, protection, prayer and power.

Read Psalm 115:9-18

DEAD FAITH

DAY 287

Years ago there was a "God is dead" movement in theology. Of course, He is very much alive, as Psalm 115 tells us: "But our God is in heaven. He does whatever He pleases" (v.3). The problem with people is not that God is dead but that their faith is dead. They do not have living faith in the living God.

The psalmist addresses three groups of people in this passage. First, he speaks to the nation. "O Israel, trust in the Lord; He is their help and their shield" (v.9). Then he talks to the priests. "O house of Aaron, trust in the Lord; He is their help and their shield" (v.10). Then He talks to all believers. "You who fear the Lord, trust in the Lord; He is their help and their shield" (v.11).

If we are going to have the kind of relationship with God that we ought to have, if He is going to be to us the living God with living power and blessing, first of all we must *trust Him*. That means to rely on Him, to believe that what He says is right and true, that He does not lie. It means to believe that what God is doing is the best thing for us. He is our Help. He is our Shield. He is our Provision. He is our Protection and our Security. He also is our Sufficiency.

Second, we must *fear Him*. "He will bless those who fear the Lord, both small and great" (v.13). The blessing that He gives is the best blessing. To fear God means to show reverence to Him, to respect Him when He speaks and acts, to have a heart that does not tempt or test Him.

Third, we must *bless Him*. "But we will bless the Lord from this time forth and forevermore. Praise the Lord!" (v.18). We are always asking God to bless us, but the psalmist says, "We bless God."

When you fear the Lord, trust Him and experience the blessings He has for you, you cannot help but bless Him. If your relationship with Him is what it ought to be, then you will be praising Him "from this time forth and forevermore."

DAY **288**

Read Psalm 116:1-11

DELIVERED!

Whoever wrote Psalm 116 went through some difficult experiences to give us these verses. In fact, he almost died. But the Lord heard his cry and delivered him, and that's why he wrote, "I love the Lord, because He has heard my voice and my supplications. Because He has inclined His ear to me" (vv.1,2).

Picture God leaning down to His little child, getting close enough to hear. Sometimes I have to get close to people who are speaking because my hearing is not as good as it used to be. God can hear as well as He always has, but He gets close to us—not to hear us better but to help us. The psalmist tells us, "I was brought low, and He saved me" (v.6). God comes down where we are to deliver us and make us all that He wants us to be. "For You have delivered my soul from death, my eyes from tears, and my feet from falling" (v.8).

The psalmist discovered the grace of God. "Gracious is the Lord, and righteous; yes, our God is merciful. The Lord preserves the simple; I was brought low, and He saved me" (vv.5,6). God delivered him from death and stopped his tears. He strengthened and guided his feet so that he did not stumble.

We, too, have all this help through Jesus Christ. He is the source of grace and mercy. The psalmist said, "The pains of death surrounded me" (v.3), but he did not die spiritually. Jesus died in his place.

Do you need God's deliverance today? Rejoice that He hears and helps you. All you need comes from His bountiful hand. He is gracious and merciful. Call upon His name; He will deliver you.

PRECIOUS DEATH

Few people really want to talk about death. Yet verse 15 says, "Precious in the sight of the Lord is the death of His saints." This statement is often misunderstood, so let's examine it and see what it means to our lives today.

Death is the penalty of sin; God is the author of life. When God made His original creation, there was no death. But when man sinned, death came on the scene. It now reigns as a king. "It is appointed for men to die once, but after this the judgment" (Heb.9:27). Certainly God doesn't enjoy it when unsaved people die, because He knows they go to a Christless, dark eternity (Ezek.18:23). Nor does He enjoy it when His own people die. Jesus stood at the grave of Lazarus and wept (John 11:35).

The death of God's children is so precious to Him that it will not be an accident. The psalmist was brought low and almost died. "The pains of death encompassed me, and the pangs of Sheol laid hold of me; I found trouble and sorrow" (Ps.116:3). He was going to die, and then he cried out to God, who replied, "Your death is so precious to me, I will not allow you to die just by accident." The death of everyone who goes home to be with the Lord is not an accident—it is an appointment. We are immortal until our work is done. That, to me, is a real encouragement. There's a lot of danger that can come to us in this world. But God says, "Your death is too precious for me to permit it to just happen." Death for the believer is precious because Jesus bore our sins on the cross to give us eternal life.

Neither your life nor your death is an accident. Take comfort in the fact that God knew every detail about your life before you were born. You have work to do for Him, and only when that is finished will He take you to be with Himself.

DAY
290

Read Psalm 117:1-2

SHORT BUT DEEP

Psalm 117 is the shortest of the psalms—only two verses. "Praise the Lord, all you Gentiles! Laud Him, all you peoples! For His merciful kindness is great toward us, and the truth of the Lord endures forever. Praise the Lord!" What a tremendous psalm of praise this is; it's short but deep.

We don't find too much difficulty in thanking people for what they have done for us. Even when we pay someone to work for us, we still say thank you. But sometimes we take advantage of the Lord and take for granted the things He has done for us—especially the "little" things. Do we thank Him for eyes to see, for ears to hear? Recognize and thank God for His numerous blessings.

The psalmist says, "Laud Him, all you peoples." But billions of people in this world don't praise the Lord because they don't know Him. They've never been told that Jesus Christ is the Savior of the world. Unfortunately, many Christians for some reason are not concerned about this. How can all the nations praise Him until all the nations trust Him?

Praise the Lord for His merciful kindness and enduring truth. And make every effort to tell others about the One you praise.

Think of some of the blessings you can praise God for. It's easy to take His blessings for granted and overlook some of His greatest provisions. But though you praise the Lord, there are many who don't. Ask Him to use you today to reach someone who does not know Christ as Savior.

Read Psalm 118:1-9

ASSURED, CONFIDENT, DEFIANT

DAY **291**

"The Lord is on my side; I will not fear. What can man do to me?" (v.6). This is a *word of assurance.* "If God is for us, who can be against us?" (Rom.8:31). The God of the universe is on our side—Father, Son and Holy Spirit. No matter who may be against us, He is on our side.

It's also a *word of confidence.* "I will not fear." As I look at the past, I see that God has cared for me every step of the way. As I look at the present, I know He is with me. As I look to the future, I know He is ahead of me. He surrounds me. He promises, "I will never leave you nor forsake you" (Heb.13:5). I respond, "I will not fear. What can man do to me?" (v.6).

Finally, it is a *word of defiance.* "What can man do unto me?" In other words, fear God, not humans. Jesus taught this to His disciples. "And do not fear those who kill the body but cannot kill the soul. But rather fear Him who is able to destroy both soul and body in hell" (Matt.10:28).

When you fear God, you need not fear anyone else. To fear God means to love Him, revere Him and respect Him.

No matter how difficult your experiences are, the Lord is on your side. You need not fear the past, present or future or what anybody can do to you, because you fear God. You have His words of assurance, confidence and defiance.

Read Psalm 118:10-18

MEETING LIFE'S DEMANDS

"The Lord is my strength and song, and He has become my salvation" (v.14). This also is found in Exodus 15:2 and Isaiah 12:2. The Israelites sang these words when they were delivered from Egypt, as they saw their enemy drowned in the sea. And Isaiah 12 promises that Israel will sing this song in the future when God restores her and establishes His kingdom. We, too, can rejoice for what these words mean for us today.

God is our Strength. That takes care of the demands of life. Where do you look to find strength? Your experience? Your health? Your money? Your job? All these things could vanish. Only the strength of the Lord can meet the demands of life. "Those who wait on the Lord shall renew their strength" (Isa.40:31).

He is our Song. That takes care of the dullness of life. Many people have to go through boring, tedious experiences. Perhaps your job is not as exciting as you'd like it to be. Perhaps you are a shut-in, and you can't get out and do and see what others have the privilege of doing and seeing. The Lord will give you joy.

He is our Salvation. That takes care of the dangers of life. He delivers us and is always at our side. "The right hand of the Lord is exalted; the right hand of the Lord does valiantly" (v.16). That right hand is available to us today.

Believers may sing this song of praise, for God takes care of the demands, the dullness and the dangers of life. He is your Strength, your Song and your Salvation. Remember that God is ever available to deliver you from the difficult experiences of life.

Read Psalm 118:19-29

REJOICING IN EACH DAY

DAY 293

"This is the day which the Lord has made; we will rejoice and be glad in it" (v.24). When you are having one of those difficult days—a day when the storm is blowing and the battle is raging, when the burdens are heavy, when your heart is broken and your tears are flowing, when it feels like everybody is turned against you, including your Heavenly Father—that's the time to heed this verse by faith.

The psalmist was going through battles and difficulties, yet he was able to say, "If God put this day together, I'm going to rejoice and be glad in it. Even though I may not see the blessing now, eventually by faith I'll be able to say, 'It all worked together for good.' So I'll say it now."

Jews sing this psalm at Passover. Jesus also sang this song before He was crucified. Can you imagine saying on your way to Calvary, "This is the day which the Lord has made; I will rejoice and be glad in it"? That's another way of saying, "Not my will, but Your will be done." If Jesus sang this song, we should sing it also.

Perhaps your day is full of overwhelming burdens or sorrows. Jesus also suffered days like that. Accept the day God has given you and acknowledge that He is in charge. Anticipate what God is going to do for you today; rejoice and be glad in it. You may not understand His purposes now, but one day you will.

DAY 294

Read Psalm 119:1-8

THE BIBLE'S ABCs

What would your Christian life be like if you had no Bible? Would that make any difference? After all, what is the Bible supposed to do for our lives?

God gives us some answers to those questions in this Psalm. Every verse in this long psalm (except verse 4) in some way refers to the Word of God. The psalm is arranged according to the Hebrew alphabet. The first eight verses all begin with the Hebrew letter *aleph;* the next eight verses start with *beth;* the next eight, *gimel;* and so on. It's as though God were saying, "Here are the ABCs of how to use the Word of God in your life."

"Blessed are the undefiled in the way, who walk in the law of the Lord!" (v.1). *Undefiled* means "people who are blameless, those who have integrity." *Integrity* is the opposite of duplicity and hypocrisy, which is the pretense to be something we are not. If we have integrity, our whole lives are built around the Word of God.

The psalmist says, "Blessed are those who keep His testimonies, who seek Him with the whole heart!" (v.2). Are you wholeheartedly into the Word of God? In the Bible, *heart* refers to the inner person, and that includes the mind. "I will praise You with uprightness of heart, when I learn Your righteous judgments" (v.7). It also includes the will. "I will keep Your statutes!" (v.8). In other words, when you give your whole heart, mind and will to the Word of God, it starts to put your life together. Is your life or your home "falling apart" today? Turn to the Word of God.

The Bible has one author—God. It has one theme—Jesus Christ. It has one message—the salvation of your soul. And it has one blessing to bring—a life of integrity.

The Word of God is a powerful spiritual resource. Its truth feeds your soul. As you walk in the life of faith, the Holy Spirit uses the Bible to minister to you. Get into the Word and allow it to make you whole and build integrity into your life.

KEEPING CLEAN

How does a person keep clean in this dirty world? The psalmist asks this question in verse 9: "How can a young man cleanse his way?" The answer: "By taking heed according to Your word." Of course this doesn't apply only to a young man. The same is true for a young woman, a child or an older person. We are living in a dirty world, and because of the pollution around us, we have to walk in the Word of God. The psalmist gives us several instructions to follow to keep us spiritually clean.

First, *heed the Word*. We first have to read and study the Word so we know it. And if we know it, we should obey it.

Second, *hide the Word*. "Your word I have hidden in my heart, that I might not sin against You" (v.11). G. Campbell Morgan used to say of this verse, "It tells us about the best book—'Thy Word'—in the best place—'my heart'—for the best purpose—'that I might not sin' against God." Are you obeying the Word of God? Are you treasuring it in your heart?

Third, *herald the Word* by sharing it with others. "With my lips I have declared all the judgments of Your mouth" (v.13). If we have Scripture in our hearts, it has to come out through our lips, because "out of the abundance of the heart the mouth speaks" (Matt.12:34).

Finally, *honor the Word*. "I will meditate on Your precepts, and contemplate Your ways" (v.15). In other words, "I will honor God's Word. I will respect what He wants me to do. My Father is telling me what to do, and I am going to obey Him."

God's Word has a cleansing effect. But you must get into the Word before it can become effective in your life. Obey God's Word, and He will keep you clean in this dirty world.

DAY

296

Read Psalm 119:17-24

HANDLING THE CRITICS

What do you do when people criticize you? What goes through your mind when you are in the presence of people who are unkind, especially people who don't believe the Word of God? The psalmist gives one answer: "Princes also sit and speak against me, but Your servant meditates on Your statutes. Your testimonies also are my delight and my counselors" (vv.23,24).

Meditate on the Word of God. Get your mind fixed upon what God says. If we ponder and think about the things other people say, we will be agitated and anxious and uptight. But if we meditate on what God says, those things that are true and right and holy and beautiful, His peace will fill us.

Delight in the Word of God. "Your testimonies also are my delight" (v.24). Some people delight in gossip. They enjoy listening to rumors about people. But the psalmist says, "While they were gossiping and telling lies, I was meditating on the Word of God, because I delight in it."

Obey the Word of God. "Your testimonies also are my delight and my counselors" (v.24). The Hebrew text means, "the men of my counsel." Authorities, friends and even enemies may want to give you counsel. But get your counsel from the Word of God.

Whatever your difficulty today, turn to the Bible and let it counsel you. Let it saturate your mind, heart and will.

Read Psalm 119:25-32

DAY 297

OPEN, OBEDIENT, OCCUPIED

An enlarged heart, in the physical sense, is dangerous. But spiritually speaking, an enlarged heart can be a blessing. "I will run in the way of Your commandments, for You shall enlarge my heart" (v.32). If you have an enlarged heart physically, you don't do much running. But if you have an enlarged heart spiritually, you are ready to walk and run with the Lord and accomplish His purposes. When an athlete is running, he is on a path and has a goal in mind, which gives him the energy to continue. That's what God wants for us today. He has a goal for us to reach and a path for us to follow. And He gives us His strength through His Word.

What does it mean to have an enlarged heart? First, *an enlarged heart is open to God's truth*. It's a heart that's honest and says, "Lord, I want Your truth even if it hurts."

Second, *an enlarged heart is obedient to God's will*. It's a humble heart that says, "O God, what You have said, I will do. I am the servant. You are the master."

Third, *an enlarged heart is occupied with God's glory*. It's a happy heart. Some people's hearts are small and narrow. They live in their own little world and have their own narrow view. What a wonderful thing it is to grow in grace and the knowledge of truth (II Pet.3:18)! Our horizons are expanded. We can see what we haven't seen before. We can hear what we haven't heard before. God gives us an enlarged life because we have an enlarged heart.

Open your heart to God's truth and be obedient to His will. Every step of obedience expands your horizon of blessing and ministry. Most of all, be occupied with God's glory.

Read Psalm 119:33-40

You Become WHAT YOU SEE

Outlook determines outcome. What you are seeing helps to determine what you are becoming. So you'd better be careful what you look at. It's no wonder that the psalmist prays, "Turn away my eyes from looking at worthless things, and revive me in Your way" (v.37). *Worthless things* here literally mean "vanity." Much of what we see every day in the media, for example, is worthless and false. It doesn't come from God, who is Truth; it comes from Satan and the world. And it doesn't last; it's all vanity. The word for vanity means "emptiness"—what is left after you break a soap bubble.

Look at the Word of God. It is truth. It is God's treasure. It will endure forever. "Forever, O Lord, Your word is settled in heaven" (Ps.119:89). When we fill our lives with the Word of God, we fight vanity. When we turn our eyes upon the pages of the Bible, we grow in truth and value and are in touch with eternity. It's an interesting coincidence that we find the letters "T" and "V" in verse 37 (in the words *turn* and *vanity*). I think a lot of people need to put this verse on their television sets. You may say, "TV is just harmless entertainment." But so much of what you see goes right into your mind and heart, making you cheap, false, worthless and temporary. The Bible tells us that "he who does the will of God abides forever" (I John 2:17).

So much of what the world offers is trivial, false and worthless. Don't build your life on the world's foundations. Build your life instead on the Word of God, for it endures forever.

Read Psalm 119:41-48

REAL FREEDOM

DAY 299

Many people have the strange idea that God's Law and man's liberty are enemies. They say, "I want freedom. I want to do my own thing." How wrong they are. God's Law and your liberty go hand-in-hand, and verse 45 makes this clear. "And I will walk at liberty, for I seek Your precepts." Now, the world would write that verse like this: "And I will walk at liberty, for I reject and break Thy precepts. I'm going to do my own thing, my own way."

Let's get down to basics. What is freedom? Some may say freedom means the privilege of doing what you want to do. But that is not freedom. In fact, that's the worst kind of slavery in the world—to be controlled only by your impulses and inclinations. Real freedom is a life controlled by God's truth and motivated by His love.

This is true in every area of life. If we obey the traffic laws, we have the freedom to drive on the streets and highways. If we obey the laws of truth, we have the freedom to speak, and people will believe us. If we obey the laws of science, we won't blow up the laboratory. If the airplane pilot obeys the laws of aerodynamics, he will be able to fly his plane. You see, we have the freedom to enjoy the power of the Law when we have yielded to the commandment of the Law. So when I submit myself to the will of God, I am taking my first step toward freedom. As Charles Wesley wrote, God "breaks the power of canceled sin; He sets the prisoner free." He says, "If you submit to me, together we will enjoy truth and love."

Are you enjoying real freedom in your Christian life? If not, you may have real freedom by submitting to the will of God. He gives us His Word so that we may know His will. Submit to Him and take your first step toward freedom.

SING THE LAW

I enjoy classical music. I often tune my radio to classical music while I'm studying. I also enjoy going to concerts. Before a concert begins, I browse through the concert program to see what will be played. I might read that the orchestra is going to play Tchaikovsky's "Pathetique." Or perhaps I will hear a Bordin string quartet. But what if, right in the middle of the program, I read that the choir is going to sing the local housing code? I'd ask, "What is going on? Choirs don't sing the law. What musician would waste time putting the housing code to music?" Look at verse 54: "Your statutes have been my songs in the house of my pilgrimage." The psalmist says, "I sing the Law."

This verse presents three different attitudes toward life. To a, *child*, life is like a prison, with nothing but rules. "Don't do this. Don't do that. Don't go there." We have to protect children so they can grow up and live their own lives. To *adolescents*, life is a party. They don't want statutes. "Don't tell me what to do," they say. They just want the songs. But when we become *mature adults*, we realize that life is not a prison or a party. It's a pilgrimage. We make this pilgrimage in obedience to God's Word. I don't know where I would have been during all these years of my life without the guidance of the Bible. God's Word is not a burden; it's a blessing. Duty becomes delight when you are yielded to the will of God.

I hope you are not trying to run away from the will of God and turn life into one continual party. Realize that your life is a pilgrimage and that, as a pilgrim and a stranger in this world, you need the guidance of Scripture.

Are you having difficulty today on the pilgrim road? Take the mature view—yield to God's will and seek guidance in His Word. Without it, you will lose your way.

CHOOSING YOUR FRIENDS

All of us enjoy having friends. We need them. The psalmist says that the Word of God pertains to our friendships. "I am a companion of all who fear You, and of those who keep Your precepts" (v.63). He let the Word of God guide him in his choice of friends and associates. We have many acquaintances but few real friends. A friend is someone you don't have to talk to all the time. You can be together for long periods without saying a word, yet your hearts are united. At the other extreme, a friend is someone you aren't afraid to talk to. You can unburden your heart, and you are a better person for having been with him.

God is our best friend. Abraham was called the friend of God and we can be His friends also. Jesus said to His disciples, "I'm not going to call you slaves. I'm going to call you friends" (see John 15:15). Friends talk to each other. And if we talk to God and let Him speak to us through His word, we will be a companion of those who fear Him and keep His commandments.

One of the most important tests of friendship is what my friend's attitude is toward the Bible. Does he accept it? Does he receive the Word of God as truth? Does he fear God with a reverential awe and love for Him?

If I am in a right relationship to God through His Word, I will be in a right relationship with people. My friends will be God's friends. The Bible calls this separation—not isolation, but separation. It's the blessed by-product of a life lived in Scriptures.

Choose your friends carefully. Do they fear God? Do they receive the Word of God in their hearts? Use your friends' attitudes toward the Bible as an important test of friendship. Relationships are investments of our time and other resources. Make them count for eternity.

Read Psalm 119:65-72

TRUE RICHES

"The law of Your mouth is better to me than thousands of coins of gold and silver" (v.72). Can we honestly say that we would rather have God's Word than money?

Many people in the Bible had that testimony. For example, Abraham led his army to a great victory. He brought back all of the captives and all the spoil. The King of Sodom showed up and said, "Abraham, you can have all this spoil. Just give me the people." But Abraham said, "Before this battle started, I lifted my hand to the Lord and said, 'When I win this battle, I'm not taking one thing from these people.' I would rather have the Word of God than have thousands of shekels of gold and silver" (see Gen.14). Abraham kept his testimony clean.

But I also think of Achan in Joshua 7. God had commanded that no spoil be taken from Jericho. But Achan stole some silver and gold and clothing and buried them under his tent. He thought no one knew, but God knew. Achan wanted riches rather than God. Judas made the same mistake. He sold Jesus Christ, the greatest Treasure in the universe, for 30 pieces of silver.

If we love the Word of God, we'll read it, meditate on it and seek to obey it. If the Bible does not change our values, it will not change our lives. Jesus was the poorest of the poor. He made Himself poor to make us rich. We, in turn, should make ourselves poor to make other people rich, for we have the riches of the Word of God.

You have a choice to make today: you can seek the kingdom of God and His righteousness, or you can bow down to the kingdom of man and seek riches. Would you rather have the temporal possessions of this world or the spiritual riches of God's Word?

Read Psalm 119:73-80

CONSULT THE MANUAL

DAY 303

Whenever my wife and I purchase a new appliance, we add another instruction manual to our collection. We have instruction manuals for the various appliances in our home, for the automobile and for office equipment, such as tape recorders, computers and copying machines.

Someone may say, "I wish we had a manual of instruction for life." We do. It's called the Bible, the Word of God. "Your hands have made me and fashioned me; give me understanding, that I may learn Your commandments" (v.73). God made and fashioned us in His image. According to Psalm 139, He had plans for each of our lives before we were born. He gave each of us a unique mind and genetic structure. He wrote into His book the days that He assigned to us, and He planned the best for us. He also wrote a manual to help us live the way we ought.

He gives us the Bible and says, "I want to give you understanding. The better you understand this Book, the better you will understand yourself. You are made in My image. I want to reveal to you from My Word how to use your hands, your feet, your eyes, your ears and your tongue. I want to tell you how My Word can make your heart work the way it is supposed to work." The psalmist says, "Your hands have made me and fashioned me"—that's our origin. "Give me understanding, that I may learn Your commandments"—that's our operation. The Bible is the operation manual for life.

How strange it is that people try to live their lives without an instruction book. They wonder why their marriages fall apart, why their bodies are in trouble and why they've gotten themselves into a jam. Before all else fails, read the Word of God, the instruction manual for everyday living.

The Word of God covers the spectrum of life and provides guidelines for living in faith. When life presents new challenges and problems, refer to God's operation manual for life. It will help you align with His plans for your life.

DAY

304

Read Psalm 119:81-88

REVIVING POWER

Some days everything seems to go wrong. Every phone call brings bad news. The mail is nothing but bills. The children come home from school with some kind of injury or a bad report. Work is frustrating. What do you do when you have one of these days?

"My soul faints for Your salvation, but I hope in Your word. My eyes fail from searching Your word, saying, 'When will You comfort me?' For I have become like a wineskin in smoke, yet I do not forget Your statutes. . . . The proud have dug pits for me, which is not according to Your law" (vv.81-83,85). Here's a man who was fainting and failing. He was like a wineskin in the smoke. Wherever he walked there was a pit for him to drop into. What did he do? He turned to God. His source of hope was His Word.

If you hope in circumstances, you will be disappointed, because they change. The psalmist hoped in the Word and trusted in God's faithfulness, and God comforted him.

People will fail you, but God never will. "All Your commandments are faithful" (v.86). The psalmist clung to the comfort, hope and faithfulness of God, and as a result he experienced revival. "Revive me according to Your lovingkindness" (v.88). God came with a Breath of fresh, heavenly air—the Holy Spirit—and revived him.

Thank God for His faithfulness. If you are having a rough day, remember that you can depend on Him. He is your Hope and your Comfort, and He's always faithful. He'll give you the reviving power you need to rise above your circumstances and continue.

SETTLED QUESTIONS

Have you ever noticed that very little gets settled in this world? Few things are resolved politically. We sign treaties and contracts, and then they're broken or reinterpreted. Nothing seems final. Your life may be unsettled because of a situation or person. If that's the case, consider verse 89: "Forever, O Lord, Your word is settled in heaven."

My word—or anyone's, for that matter—is not settled. I've changed my opinions and my beliefs on certain things. I hope that when I give my word it is trustworthy. But God's Word is always *true*. We can trust it. We don't have to worry about Him lying to us. He can't.

God's Word is *eternal*. I often go to used bookstores and find bestsellers from years ago being sold for 25 cents each. Not so with God's Word. Jesus said, "Heaven and earth will pass away, but My words will by no means pass away" (Matt.24:35).

God's Word also is *changeless*. God is not a diplomat who argues endlessly. He simply says, "This is the way it is going to be." If you want to find out how He has settled things, read His Word.

I'm glad that when I open my Bible, I find that things are settled. God tells us how to stop wars, how to solve problems, how to take care of sin. Best of all, He tells us how we can go to heaven. That's all settled. The Lord Jesus Christ died for us on the cross, rose again and will save all who will come to Him by faith.

The strength and stability of God's Word stand out as a beacon in the instability and unsettledness of life. Because it is true, eternal and changeless, we may trust it and live by its truths. God has settled the questions of sin, death, salvation and eternal life. Do you need to settle these questions for yourself? Read and study His Word.

DAY **306**

Read Psalm 119:97-104

SWEETER THAN HONEY

How well I remember the day my doctor looked at me and said, "Reverend, you will not eat any more sweets." I've learned to do without desserts, but there's one sweet I cannot do without—God's Word: "How sweet are Your words to my taste, sweeter than honey to my mouth!" (v.103).

Is the Word of God like honey or medicine to you? The way some people treat it, you'd think it is castor oil. True, there are times when we need the healing medicine of the Scripture. But the Bible is much more than medicine. It also is honey. Having an appetite for God's Word is one sign that a person is truly born again, for the Bible is food for the soul. Job said, "I have treasured the words of His mouth more than my necessary food" (Job 23:12). Jeremiah said, "Your words were found, and I ate them, and Your word was to me the joy and rejoicing of my heart" (Jer.15:16). Jesus said, "Man shall not live by bread alone, but by every word that proceeds from the mouth of God" (Matt.4:4). And Peter urges us to "desire the pure milk of the word" (I Pet.2:2).

When people are sick, their appetites change—in fact, they often lose their appetites completely. Likewise, sin in our lives robs our spiritual appetite, and we lose our desire for the Word. May we always have an appetite for the sweetness of the Word of God, even when we have to read things that convict us. That first bite of Scripture may taste sour sometimes, but it will turn sweet.

It's important to feed your soul a proper diet. Do you feed and nourish on God's Word? The Bible is sweet to those who love it, learn it and live it.

A LIGHT IN THE DARKNESS

You probably know the following verse well, but read it aloud as though you were hearing it for the first time. "Your word is a lamp to my feet and a light to my path" (v.105). What lessons can we learn from that statement?

The world is dark. It is in a constant state of moral and intellectual darkness. We have more education today and less wisdom. People make foolish decisions. The world is also dark spiritually. Satan has numbed people's minds. They don't want to see the light of the glory of God in Jesus Christ.

The way is definite. How do we make it through this dark world? God has marked out a definite path for each one of us, and we don't have to be afraid of where it leads. It is a path of life, blessing and righteousness.

Our walk is deliberate. As we take each step, we see more of what God has for us. Sometimes I would like to have a spotlight that shines for miles down the road. But God says, "You're going to learn to walk by faith. You're going to learn to walk by patience, by My promise."

The Word is dependable. That lamp of the Word will not go out, and it will not lead us astray. When you read your Bible and let its truth shine on your path, God will show you what He wants you to do.

Because your walk is by faith, you can see ahead only a step at a time. Be encouraged that the way is definite and deliberate and that God's Word is dependable. Let it be the light of life that guides you as you walk through this dark world today.

DAY 308

Read Psalm 119:105

HOW THE LIGHT WORKS

What does it mean to have the Word of God as light? Verse 105 gives us four statements that answer that question. First, *the Word is a light that shines from above*. It is revelation. We know that God is Light (I John 1:5). He gave us the Word, just as He gave us the sun. The sun is at the center of our solar system; if it ever burned out, we would die. Likewise, God is the center of our universe through His Word. The Word is a necessity, not a luxury. Like a ray of light going into a prism, the Word of God gives us a multicolored exhibition of His grace. It provides whatever kind of light we need. But if you turn your back on the Word, you'll walk in darkness.

Second, *the Word is a light that shines within* (II Cor.4:3-6). Paul uses the Old Testament story of creation to illustrate the new creation (Gen.1:1-3). God formed that which was formless and filled that which was empty. That's a picture of salvation. The light shines in our hearts, and then God begins to form and fill our lives. He works on us through His Word and the power of His Spirit (Ps.119: 130). He has given the Holy Spirit and the gift of teaching to help us understand His Word. The devil tries to confuse us. How tragic it is that some people radiate darkness! Everything they touch is made dark. It's so important to study and read the Word, because the unfolding of the Word brings light and understanding to the simple.

Third, *the Word is a light that shines around* (v.105). The life of the believer is dangerous. Satan is a roaring lion and a deceiving serpent. He, the world, the flesh and other pitfalls surround us. We need God's Word (Ps.43:3), for it guides us (Prov.6:23; Eph.5:8). Don't walk in this world without a lamp. And remember that human teachers are fallible. Depend ultimately on the Spirit of God (John 16:13; I John 2:20). The Author of the Bible lives inside you!

Finally, *the light shines ahead* (II Pet.1:19). We can see what is coming: Jesus will return for His Church. Only in the Bible do we have assurance about the future, so walk in the light of His Word.

The Word of God is indispensable to the believer. It shines from above, within, around and ahead of you. Avoid the hidden snares and pitfalls of the world. Improve your vision—use the Word as a lamp to your feet and a light to your path.

Read Psalm 119:113-120

INVENTORY TIME

DAY 309

Let's take time for a spiritual inventory and ask there simple questions: What do you hate? Where are you hiding? In what do you hope? The best answers to those questions are found in verses 113 and 114. "I hate the double-minded, but I love Your law. You are my hiding place and my shield; I hope in Your word."

What do you hate? The psalmist hated vain thoughts (Ps.119:37). *Vanity* means that which is empty, false and temporary. Thoughts are important, because what you think is ,what you become. "As he thinks in his heart, so is he" (Prov.23:7). Thinking leads to doing, and doing leads to being. Sow a thought and you reap an action. Sow an action and you reap a habit. Sow a habit and you reap a character. Sow a character and you reap a destiny. If we love God's Law, we will hate the things that are contrary to His will.

Where are you hiding? "You are my hiding place and my shield." Are you hiding in the Lord? Is He your Shield? Christians have enemies who want to rob us of the blessing of God. Maybe you are hurting today. Run and hide in Jesus Christ.

In what do you hope? "I hope in Your word." If your hope is anywhere other than in God, your future is hopeless. But If you are hoping in the Word of God, the future is secure, because God is preparing the way for you. What a glory it is to be able to hope in the Word of God.

Spiritual inventories force you to see if you are aligning with God's will and Word. Today, ponder the three questions found in these verses. Stay aligned to God's Word.

Read Psalm 119:121-128

A PERFECT BOOK

I have a large library, and I've written a few books myself, but I cannot point to the books I've written or collected and say that everything in them is absolutely right. In fact, I've been embarrassed to find typographical, factual or other kinds of errors in the ones I've written. Only one book can carry an unqualified endorsement, and that is the Word of God. That's why the psalmist writes, "Therefore all our precepts concerning all things I consider to be right; I hate every false way" (v.128). All of the Bible is *inspired*. That means it is God-breathed. "All Scripture is given by inspiration of God, and is profitable" (II Tim.3:16). Inspiration is a miracle. The Spirit of God spoke through Moses, Isaiah, Matthew, Mark, Paul and others, and each put his own fingerprints on what he wrote. Yet this is God's Word.

Remember also that all of God's Word is *inerrant*. It is absolute truth. What the Bible says about history is correct. What the Bible says about prophecy is correct. Even what it says about science is correct, although it's not a science book. We don't test the Bible by the wisdom of men. We test the wisdom of men by the Bible. This means that we should live by all of Scripture. Jesus said we must live "by every word that proceeds from the mouth of God" (Matt.4:4). Every word. Oh, what you might be missing if you are not reading the whole Word of God! Because the Bible is inspired and true, we can go to it and say, "Lord, what should I do?" He has an answer for us.

The Bible is a miracle, for it is inspired by God. Live by its wisdom and truth. It leads to a miraculous life when you accept and obey it.

Read Psalm 119:129-136

THE ANSWER BOOK

DAY **311**

Have you ever faced the problems of dullness, darkness and dryness? Certain days come to us that are simply dull. There may be sameness and tameness about them. And sometimes we have to go through periods of darkness, and we wonder what in the world God is doing. Or we experience dryness—we are so spiritually dry, hungry and thirsty.

What is the answer to *dullness*? The Word of God. "Your testimonies are wonderful; therefore my soul keeps them" (v.129). Life cannot be dull when we read and obey the Bible. It has a way of taking the ordinary things of life and making them wonderful. When our minds and hearts are filled with Scripture, everything we see appears different.

What is the answer to *darkness*? "The entrance of Your words gives light; it gives understanding to the simple" (v.130). *Entrance* means the opening up, the expounding, the unfolding of God's Word. As Scripture is explained to us, it illuminates us. If you find yourself in darkness today, read your Bible, and it will give you light.

What is the answer to *dryness*? Sometimes we feel so dry and needy. "I opened my mouth and panted, for I longed for Your commandments" (v.131). The Word of God is like fresh air when we feel smothered, like water when we are parched, like food when we are famished.

If you are having a dull, dark or dry day, turn to the Word of God. Its truths will brighten your soul, and its promises will encourage you. God designed the Bible to meet your needs. So when the discouraging days come, feed your mind and heart with the Word.

DAY 312

Read Psalm 119:137-144

TRIED AND TRUE

Whenever we buy appliances, we want a guarantee that they're going to work efficiently. So we look for those special seals of approval that indicate the product has been tested. Similarly, when we buy food at the store, we want to be sure that the ingredients are safe for consumption.

God's Word has been tested and found true. It is guaranteed. "Your word is very pure [refined]; therefore Your servant loves it" (v.140). It has gone through the furnace. Gold ore is put into a furnace to be tested. The assayer wants to know if it's really gold; likewise with silver. As we read through the Bible and through Church history, we find that the Word of God also has been through the fire. Abraham tested it and found that it was true. He left his home without knowing where he was going, but he had the Word of God, and God saw him through. Moses also tested the Word of God during those 40 years in the wilderness. Furthermore, when we read the Psalms, we see the furnaces that David went through. What was he doing? Testing the Word of God.

The Bible has been tested and has passed the test. Therefore, it can be trusted. It's pure, void of falsehoods. All the people who have trusted the Lord throughout history can say, "You can lean upon the Word of God."

Have you tested the Word of God in your own life? You may be going through the furnace right now. If so, remember that one reason you endure such difficulties is so you will discover that the Word of God is pure, refined and trustworthy. Test the Word for yourself and find that it is true.

Read Psalm 119:145-152

SACRIFICING SLEEP

DAY 313

Would you rather have the Word of God than sleep? Don't misunderstand me. We need sleep. In fact, the Bible makes it clear that God expects us to take care of our bodies, and sleep is part of that care. But the psalmist says that he would rather have the Word of God than sleep. "I rise before the dawning of the morning, and cry for help; I hope in Your word. My eyes are awake through the night watches, that I may meditate on Your word" (vv.147,148).

Imagine being married to a person who gets up early in the morning to cry out to God and hope in His Word. Then late at night he's still awake, reading and meditating on the Scriptures.

Jesus also was up early in the morning, praying and meditating on the Word. And on the Mount of Transfiguration, Jesus, Moses and Elijah were discussing Christ's plan to die in Jerusalem. Peter, James and John were there, but they were asleep (Luke 9:32). They slept through perhaps the greatest Bible conference ever held on earth!

I'm afraid some of us have done the same thing. We've slept through the blessing. For God to bless us through His Word, we have to start each day with it. Do you set your alarm clock early enough in the morning to read the Bible? Sure, that extra half hour in bed would be pleasant. But like the psalmist, we need to say, "I'm going to anticipate the dawning of the morning. I want to spend time with God and meditate in His Word."

Sacrificing sleep to meditate in the Word of God is not a loss; it's an investment in your spiritual life. The Bible contains blessings you can use the rest of the day. Let it be the key that opens and locks your day.

DAY

314

Read Psalm 119:153-160

"PLEAD MY CASE"

Nobody enjoys going to court. I once was a character witness in a court case, and it wasn't fun. How much worse it must be for the accused. But if you must stand trial, it's good to know that somebody is there to plead your case. This is what the psalmist talks about when he says to the Lord, "Plead my cause and redeem me; revive me according to Your word" (v.154).

The greatest Advocate we have is God. "If God is for us, who can be against us?" (Rom.8:31). During the week we may go through difficulties. People may lie about us, and uncomfortable situations may arise because people don't like us. Sometimes we are misunderstood and criticized. You may be going through such an experience today. But God is with you in the trials of life. When you and I are on trial, He pleads and defends our case.

He can handle the dispute. When we pray to God and say, "Plead my case," He goes to work. He also can accomplish our redemption, our deliverance. We are not going to be found guilty, and we are not going to be put in jail. God sets His people free in the difficulties of life.

God can overcome your discouragement. When you've been through a tough experience, you feel discouraged and let down. But God lifts you above discouragement with His reviving power.

Today, Jesus is pleading your case in heaven. He is your Heavenly Advocate and your High Priest. He gives you the grace to stay away from temptation and sin. But if you sin, you can go to your Advocate. He will forgive you, cleanse you and plead your case.

When others create difficulties for you, let God handle your dispute. He will deliver you and lift you above your discouragement. Likewise, Jesus will plead your case before the Father and forgive you.

Read Psalm 119:161-168

DAY 315

A TREASURE TO WIN

"I rejoice at Your word as one who finds great treasure" (v.162). When do we find great treasure or spoil? Usually after a battle. Thus, this verse indicates that Bible study involves a battle or conflict that starts with our own flesh.

The flesh and the natural mind don't want to be disciplined enough to read and study the Word of God. Of course, the world doesn't want this either. The world wants us to ignore Scripture and believe its own lies and vain thoughts. And Satan hates the Bible. He will do anything he can to keep us from reading, studying, meditating on and obeying the Word of God.

So the Bible can become an arena for conflict. Sometimes I'll be reading it and think of something that needs to be done, or I'll see a book out of place on my shelf and want to get up and fix it. The Devil puts distractions all around me to keep me from winning the battle of studying the Word of God.

Scripture is indeed a treasure to win. And sometimes there is a battle that must be fought first to win it. But there is also a joy to experience. "I rejoice at Your word as one who finds great treasure." It's beautiful to think your way through a portion of Scripture, to meditate, study and pray and then see the treasure that is revealed. Bible study enriches our lives. It not only helps you understand the Word but also enables you to become more like the Author.

The Devil rages a battle against believers who read and study the Bible. Why? Because when you study the Word, you become more like Jesus. If you win the battle, you will gain the spoils. Let the Word enrich your life. Win the treasure and experience the joy of Bible study.

DAY 316

Read Psalm 119:169-176

A CHAIN REACTION

Let me tell you about a spiritual chain reaction that has the power to transform our lives. It begins in verse 169: "Let my cry come before You, O Lord; give me understanding according to Your word." *Prayer leads to understanding.* This is the first part of the chain reaction. Do you pray for understanding as you read your Bible? Do you pray, "Open my eyes, that I may see wondrous things from Your law" (119:18)?

Next, *understanding leads to freedom.* "Let my supplication come before You; deliver me according to Your word" (v.170). The psalmist asks for the freedom that comes from the truth of God. Jesus said, "You shall know the truth, and the truth shall make you free" (John 8:32). The greatest bondage in the world is the bondage to lies. If you believe a lie, you are in slavery; but if you believe God's truth, you live in freedom.

The third stage in this spiritual chain reaction is found in verse 171: "My lips shall utter praise, for You teach me Your statutes." *Freedom leads to praise.* When we understand the statutes of God, we can sing: Knowing His Word makes us want to praise Him.

Finally, *praise leads to witnessing.* "My tongue shall speak of Your word, for all Your commandments are righteousness" (v.172). As a result of our witness, people may come to know Jesus Christ as their Savior.

Read the Word of God and pray, and let the Spirit begin this life-transforming chain reaction in your life.

PEACEMAKERS

Jesus said, "Blessed are the peacemakers" (Matt.5:9). But not everybody in this world is a peacemaker. Some people are troublemakers. They enjoy making trouble, and sometimes we have to live or work with them. That's the kind of situation the psalmist found himself in when he wrote Psalm 120. "In my distress I cried to the Lord, and He heard me. Deliver my soul, O Lord, from lying lips and from a deceitful tongue" (vv.1,2). He continues, "My soul has dwelt too long with one who hates peace. I am for peace; but when I speak, they are for war" (vv.6,7). That sounds like a description of Jesus when He was on earth. He was the Prince of Peace and came to bring peace to the hearts and lives of people, yet people did not want to follow or trust Him.

Ever since Cain killed Abel, we've had conflict in this world. Nations war against one another; families fall apart; and even Christians don't get along with each other. David went through conflict. Jesus went through it. And we experience it also.

Still, we are to be peacemakers—not peace breakers. After all, we have the peace of God in our hearts, and we have peace with Him—we are not at war with Him the way unsaved people are. So wherever we are, we will experience conflict but also the opportunity to bring peace.

"I am for peace," the psalmist says. Literally, the Hebrew text means, "I am peace. They are war." Each of us is either a battlefield or a blessing. Each of us is either declaring war or declaring peace. Some people enter a situation, and peace comes in with them. Other people walk in, and war follows. Let's ask God to help us in this wicked, conflicting world to be people who promote peace, not war.

God's people are to be peacemakers. This world of never-ending conflict affords many opportunities for you to make peace. However, peacemaking often is not easy. Are you quick to promote peace when you confront conflict? Strive to be a blessing to others—be a peacemaker.

DAY **318**

Read Psalm 121:1-8

OUR HELPER AND KEEPER

This psalm is special to my family. When our children were young and we were all in the car ready to leave on a trip or a vacation, we often read Psalm 121 and then prayed. The children became accustomed to hearing the words, "I will lift up my eyes to the hills—from whence comes my help? My help comes from the Lord, who made heaven and earth" (vv.1,2). God is our *Helper*. You don't have to go on a vacation or drive on a busy highway to know that.

Where does your help come from? The psalmist lifted his eyes to the hills. The most stable, secure thing the Jews knew were the mountains around Jerusalem. Then the psalmist lifted his eyes higher and said, "No, I don't get my help from the hills. I get my help from the heavens. God is my Helper." Whatever your need or task is today, your help will come from the Lord, the Creator of the heavens and the earth. A God big enough to make this world and keep it going is big enough to help you with your problems today.

God is also our *Keeper*. "He will not allow your foot to be moved; He who keeps you will not slumber. Behold, He who keeps Israel shall neither slumber nor sleep" (vv.3,4). This is a dangerous world we live in. Enemies would like to attack and destroy us. But as we walk in the will of God and depend on His power, He is there as our Keeper and Preserver. "The Lord shall preserve you from all evil" (v.7). This verse doesn't say we won't have pain. It doesn't say we will never suffer or sorrow. Though we may be hurt, we won't be harmed. "He shall preserve your soul. The Lord shall preserve your going out and your coming in from this time forth, and even forevermore" (vv.7,8). God will be your Guide even unto death.

God is your Helper and Keeper. No matter where your path in life leads, if you walk in His will, He will preserve you. Walk with confidence today. You have a Helper, a Keeper and a Preserver, who will see you through.

Read Psalm 122:1-9

DAY
319

A Place of
PRAYER AND PRAISE

Are you glad when it's time to go to the house of God to worship? Are you really happy when, on the Lord's Day or any other day, you can go to church? The psalmist was. "I was glad when they said to me, 'Let us go into the house of the Lord'" (v.1). We worship the Lord privately as well. I trust that every day you read His Word and pray and worship Him. But Christians belong to each other. We are the sheep of God's flock. We're the children in His family, and we should want to worship Him together.

The house of God is *a place for praise*. Verse 4 talks about the tribes of Israel going up to give thanks to the name of the Lord. We also go into the house of God to praise Him, and how much we have to praise Him for! Charles Spurgeon used to say that Christians are prone to write their complaints in marble and their blessings in the sand. How soon we forget what God has done for us. The next time you go to church, praise Him for all He has done.

God's house is also *a place for prayer*. In verse 6 the psalmist says to pray for the peace of Jerusalem. I hope you are praying for God's people, Israel, and for peace in Jerusalem. I hope you also are praying for peace in your congregation, in your community and for those who are in authority. We are also to pray for prosperity—the riches of grace and spiritual blessing. "May they prosper who love you" (v.6). The psalmist also prays for God's people. "For the sake of my brethren and companions, I will now say, 'Peace be within you'" (v.8). We should be praying for God's people and seeking good for them. "Because of the house of the Lord our God I will seek your good" (v.9).

Do not take your privilege of worship for granted. God's people should gather to praise Him and to pray to Him. When you do this, you become a vehicle through which God can give His peace to others.

Read Psalm 123:1-4

LIFT YOUR EYES

If the outlook in your life is disturbing, try the uplook. That's what the psalmist did. "Unto You I lift up my eyes, O You who dwell in the heavens" (v.1).

What does it mean to lift your eyes to the Lord? First, it means to *acknowledge His sovereignty*. We lift our eyes because He is higher than we are. Isaiah focused his eyes on the throne of God and saw Him "high and lifted up" in the temple (Isa.6:1). He is sovereign. He is the Master; we are the servants. He is the Creator; we are the creatures. He is the Heavenly Father; we are the children.

Second, *we admit His sufficiency*. "Behold, as the eyes of servants look to the hand of their masters, as the eyes of a maid to the hand of her mistress, so our eyes look to the Lord our God, until He has mercy on us" (v.2). We look to Him because of His sufficiency. Whatever we need, He is able to provide. "My God shall supply all your need according to His riches in glory by Christ Jesus" (Phil.4:19).

Third, when we lift up our eyes to the Lord, we can *accept His generosity*. "Have mercy on us, O Lord, have mercy on us!" the psalmist prays in verse 3. God is generous, the Giver of every good and perfect gift. "If you then, being evil, know how to give good gifts to your children, how much more will your Father who is in heaven give good things to those who ask Him!" (Matt.7:11).

Acknowledge the sovereignty of God today. He is in control. Recognize His sufficiency. He can give you what you need for this day. Then accept His generosity. He enjoys giving to those who trust Him and glorify Him in all that they do.

Read Psalm 124:1-8

HE BREAKS THE SNARE

DAY 321

"If God is for us, who can be against us?" Paul asked in Romans 8:31, and we know the answer. No one can be against us if God is for us. That's the theme of Psalm 124. "If it had not been the Lord who was on our side, when men rose up against us, then they would have swallowed us alive, when their wrath was kindled against us" (vv.2,3).

Because God is on our side, men cannot devour us. The psalmist compares his enemies to ferocious lions or bears who might come down upon him and eat him. There are people who would like to "eat us up" also. When men are determined to devour you, remember that God will stop them.

But it may not be that men are devouring you. Perhaps circumstances are drowning you. "Then the waters would have overwhelmed us, the stream would have gone over our soul; then the swollen waters would have gone over our soul" (vv.4,5). Life seems to drown us and sink us as the waters rush over our souls. But because God is for us, circumstances cannot drown us.

The psalmist changes the picture from swallowing and drowning to escaping from a trap. "Our soul has escaped as a bird from the snare of the fowlers; the snare is broken, and we have escaped" (v.7). God not only keeps us from drowning and being devoured, He keeps us from being deceived and trapped by the Devil. He doesn't just set us free; He breaks the snare. In other words, the Devil can't trap us again as long as we are following the Lord.

Don't let life devour you. Don't let life drown you. Don't let the Devil deceive you. If God is for you, who can be against you?

On those days when you feel overwhelmed by people or circumstances, you must never forget the truth that God is on your side. You have the promises of His Word. Look past your circumstances and place your confidence in God alone. He will protect you.

DAY

322

Read Psalm 125:1-5

LIKE A MOUNTAIN

"As the mountains surround Jerusalem, so the Lord surrounds His people from this time forth and forever" (v.2). We don't have to know much about geography to understand what the psalmist is saying. It's a declaration we can believe and put to work in our own lives today. God is compared to many things in the Bible. For example, "our God is a consuming fire" (Heb.12:29). Or, "God is our refuge and strength, a very present help in trouble" (Ps.46:1). Here the psalmist says God is like the mountains surrounding Jerusalem. That was the most special city to God and the Jewish people, and it still is. And when the psalmist looked at the mountains surrounding the city, he said, "That's the way God is."

How is God like a mountain? First, a mountain has *stability*. When the psalmist was a little boy, he saw the mountains surrounding Jerusalem. When he became a young man, those mountains were still there. When he grew older, the mountains were there, and the mountains are still there today. Likewise with God. He is stable, dependable. He doesn't change. God is the same yesterday, today and forever (Heb.13:8).

Second, a mountain offers *security*. God surrounds and guards us. He is like Mount Zion to us. Verse 1 says, "Those who trust in the Lord are like Mount Zion." In other words, God can make you to be like a mountain also"—stable and secure because He is your Refuge and Strength.

Therefore, we should trust Him. Those who trust in the Lord have stability and security. They have all they ever will need. "Do good, O Lord, to those who are good, and to those who are upright in their hearts" (v.4).

The next time you need a refuge, remember that God has a special way of caring for His people. The strength and security God gives His people is solid and unchanging. Trust Him.

REAP IN JOY

Did you know that each one of us is a sower? Each of us today is sowing seed that will produce a harvest. Some people are sowing to the flesh. Paul tells us in Galatians 6:8 that those who sow to the flesh will reap corruption. Some are sowing discord among the brethren. Some are sowing lies. Psalm 126 tells us to be careful what and how we sow, because we're the ones who will reap the harvest.

Notice what the psalmist says: "Those who sow in tears shall reap in joy. He who continually goes forth weeping, bearing seed for sowing, shall doubtless come again with rejoicing, bringing his sheaves with him" (vv.5,6). God's people weep as they sow, but they will reap in joy. As a Christian, you are to sow the seed of the Word of God by sowing good deeds, truth and His love. You plant the seed that produces the fruit of the Spirit—love, joy, peace, long-suffering, kindness, goodness, faithfulness, gentleness and self-control.

Life is often serious and difficult. That may cause us to sow with tears, but we will reap in joy. Non-Christians are not like that. The Devil's crowd goes out and sows with laughter. Oh, they have a good time. But when the harvest comes, they will reap in sorrow.

Each of us has a decision to make: Are we going to get pleasures now or wait until the harvest of the Holy Spirit? "Do not be deceived, God is not mocked; for whatever a man sows, that he will also reap" (Gal.6:7). In fact, we will reap more than what we've sown, because seed multiplies.

If today you are living for the pleasures of sin, the harvest will bring weeping. But if you're living for the will of God, the harvest will bring joy. What kind of harvest will you have? Ask God to help you sow the seeds that will bring His fruit in your life and in the lives of others.

Read Psalm 126:1-6

HAPPY HARVESTERS

The context of this psalm is II Kings 19 and Isaiah 37, when Hezekiah, king of Judah, was attacked by Sennacherib and the Assyrian forces. The enemy forces surrounded Jerusalem, so the Jews had to protect their food supply. They already had lost an entire season of sowing and reaping. Grain was precious. When the people went back to their farms after being delivered, they had to make a decision. Should they use the grain to feed the children, or should they sow it? The farmer wept because his sustenance had to go into the ground (v.6).

All of us are sowers and reapers. What must we sow to be happy harvesters? First, *sow the seed of the Gospel.* The Bible contains many pictures of witnessing (II Cor.5:20; Zech.3:2; Matt.4:19; 5:14). Reaching people with the Gospel is like farming. It requires cooperation, because one sows and another reaps. Are you a part of the harvest? We need to pray for the harvesters. You may be weeping today over unsaved loved ones, but one day you will rejoice (Gal.6:9). Those who sow the Gospel will be happy harvesters.

Second, *sow your wealth to the glory of God.* The way we use our money is like sowing seed. We reap in the measure that we sow (II Cor.9:6-11). Many people are wasting money on foolish things, while missionaries are waiting for support, and churches are waiting to be built or expanded. Paul says we can be a happy harvester if we sow the seed bountifully.

Third, *sow to the Holy Spirit of God* (Gal.6:6-8; 5:16-23). How do we do this? We take the things of the Spirit and put them into our hearts. When we memorize and meditate on the Word of God (Ps.119:11), we cultivate a spiritual harvest. The heart is like a garden, so we must weed it. That's repentance. Take time to be holy, to pray, to meditate on the Word and to plant the seed in your heart.

You are sowing today in all you do; be sure you sow the right seed.

INHERITANCE FROM GOD

I feel like weeping when I think about the tragedy of more than 1.5 million babies murdered in their mothers' wombs in the United States every year. Abortion has turned the womb into a tomb.

I wonder what those presiding doctors and nurses would think if they read Psalm 127. "Behold, children are a heritage from the Lord, the fruit of the womb is His reward. Like arrows in the hand of a warrior, so are the children of one's youth. Happy is the man who has his quiver full of them; they shall not be ashamed, but shall speak with their enemies in the gate" (vv.3-5). The psalmist tells us that children are wealth—a heritage and inheritance from the Lord.

What are we to do with wealth? First, we *accept* it. When our children come to us, we accept them. They are God's gift to us, a treasure. We protect our wealth, and we ought to protect our children. It's so wrong that many are not protected before they are born.

Then we are to *invest* it. We train our children, teaching them to live righteously. Their lives become as invested money, and the dividends start to return. One of the great delights of getting older is seeing those godly dividends. Children enrich our lives.

But children are also weapons—"like arrows in the hand of a warrior" (v.4). Who's going to fight God's battles if Christians don't bring children into this world and raise them to know the Lord? Whenever God wanted to do something great, he brought a baby into the world—Moses, Samuel, David, John the Baptist and our Lord Jesus Christ. In this world of sin, when truth is being attacked on every side, we need to raise our children to be able to stand with authority and say, "Thus says the Lord."

Children are God's blessing but also a great responsibility. Ask God for wisdom as you invest in and train your children or other's children. Prepare them for the ministries He has for them and rejoice at the inheritance He has given you.

DAY
326

Read Psalm 128:1-6

THE BLESSINGS OF FEAR

We don't hear much these days about the fear of the Lord. All too often the Lord is looked upon only as a heavenly friend, someone who walks with us and smiles on us constantly. But verse 1 says, "Blessed is everyone who fears the Lord."

What does it mean to fear the Lord? It means to be in reverential awe of Him. It means we don't tempt Him. We don't jest with Him. We don't try to make Him do things He will not do. The Israelites did not fear the Lord. They tempted Him. They played with His Law and tried to see how close they could get to the world. So God had to discipline them.

God blesses us in three areas of our life when we truly fear Him. First, He will bless us in *our walk*. "Blessed is everyone who fears the Lord, who walks in His ways" (v.1). This means that our conduct and our character become holy.

Second, God blesses us in *our work*. "When you eat the labor of your hands, you shall be happy, and it shall be well with you" (v.2) Some people are unhappy in their work. But if we are obedient to God, we are doing His work no matter what our occupation is and therefore can rejoice in it. When we fear the Lord, we can go to work and be happy.

Third, God blesses us in *our homes*. "Your wife shall be like a fruitful vine in the very heart of your house, your children like olive plants all around your table" (v.3). This does not mean that everybody is going to have a family, let alone a big family. It does mean that you'll be a blessing to your family. "Behold, thus shall the man be blessed who fears the Lord" (v.4).

Never become so "familiar" with God that you lose your reverence for Him. He is your personal God, but He deserves your awe and respect. The fear of the Lord is the key to His blessings. Fear Him. Walk in His ways and receive His blessings.

PLOWS OF PAIN

Verse 3 is a vivid description of personal suffering: "The plowers plowed on my back; they made their furrows long." Many other pictures of personal suffering are found in the Word of God: going through the storm, going through the furnace, going through a battle and carrying a burden. Why would the psalmist use plowing as a picture of personal suffering?

For one thing, he felt as if people were treating him like dirt. They were saying, "You're just like a dirty field, and we're going to plow right up this field, and we don't care how you feel." If we live for Jesus, we can expect people to treat us the way they treated Him. They treated Him like dirt.

The central truth in this picture is that plowing is preparation for a harvest. When people are treating you like dirt, when the plows of criticism and accusation dig in your back, remember: God is preparing you for a harvest. What kind of a harvest? That depends on the kind of seed you plant. If you plant seeds of revenge and hatred and malice, saying, "I'll get even with them someday," the harvest will be bitter. But if you plant the seeds of the Word of God, letting love and peace and patience reign in your heart, you can say with the psalmist that the Lord is righteous—He will resolve this problem. Then the harvest will be one of blessing, as in verse 8: "The blessing of the Lord be upon you; we bless you in the name of the Lord!"

If you want a harvest in your life, you must plow, plant and water. When people treat you like dirt, when the trials of life go right through your life like a plow, get ready for the harvest. God has a harvest of blessing for you today, so remember to plant the right seed.

DAY
328

Read Psalm 130:1-8

WAITING AND HOPING

The next time you feel at rock bottom, read Psalm 130. "Out of the depths I have cried to You, O Lord" (v.1). Three basic requests in this psalm echo the concerns in our hearts today.

First, the psalmist says, "Lord, hear my voice!" (v.2). Why? "I can't swim; I am in the deep waters, and they are coming over my head. I am drowning, and I'm afraid I can't make it." No matter how far down you may go or feel, God always hears you.

Then he says, "If You, Lord, should mark iniquities, O Lord, who could stand? But there is forgiveness with You, that You may be feared" (vv.3,4). We can't stand before God in the courtroom of His justice; we are helpless. Only Jesus Christ can stand there, because only He is perfect. But He stands with us; He's our Savior. God not only hears us when we are down, but He holds us. He says, "I forgive you. You've trusted my Son; you've confessed your sin; and now you can stand before Me." The psalmist expresses his confidence in this truth: "I wait for the Lord, my soul waits, and in His word I do hope. My soul waits for the Lord more than those who watch for the morning" (vv.5,6).

Next he asks, "O Israel, hope in the Lord; for with the Lord there is mercy, and with Him is abundant redemption" (v.7). We are sometimes like soldiers in the watchtower, waiting for the light. We can't see, but God can see, and there is a future hope for His people.

Place your confidence in the promises of God's Word. No matter how down you may feel, God hears you, holds you and helps you. Turn to Him; He'll see you through.

A METHOD FOR MATURITY

One day King David was walking through the palace, and he heard a child crying. What was going on? The child was being weaned. The mother was saying, "Now, my child, you are growing up, and it is time for you to be weaned." The child was saying, "You don't love me; you hate me. If you loved me, you wouldn't do this." Then David went to his desk, got his pen and wrote Psalm 131.

The problem with too many of us is that we have grown old without growing up—we still need to be weaned. The weaning process is important. God's goal for your life is maturity, and His method for maturity is weaning. He has to wean us away from things we think are important.

How do you convince a child that he doesn't want to be attached to his mother for the rest of his life? Love him? Yes! But he must grow up, step out and be a man. And so it is with us. God has to wean us away from the things of the world, from the cheap toys that we hold on to. He wants to give us the best, and His desire in weaning is our submission. The weaned child of Psalm 131 was not losing; he was gaining. He was moving out into a larger life. Likewise, God has to take things away from our lives, not because they are bad, but because they are keeping us from the best.

The next time you whimper and cry because God takes something away from you, remember: He might be weaning you. He might be saying, "Get closer to me. Step out into a life of maturity and let's go together."

God wants His children to grow into mature believers and eventually to become like His Son. When He decides to wean you from something in your life, be an obedient child. Let Him prepare you and develop you for what He has in store for you.

DAY

330

Read Psalm 132:1-10

THE NEXT BEST THING

What is the consuming ambition of your life? What is the dream that fills your mind and heart? King David's dream was to build a temple for the Lord. He tells us about it in this psalm. I wish more people had this same wonderful ambition—to be builders, not destroyers.

During much of his life, David was a soldier. He defended Israel from her enemies and brought about peace in the land. But then he wanted to turn from battling to building. He wanted to exchange the sword for a trowel. He said, "I am not going to have any sleep until I find a place for God to dwell."

But God did not allow David to fulfill this high and holy ambition. Solomon, his son, built the temple instead. David was disappointed at first but then said, "If this is the will of God, I'll accept it." Then he did the most wonderful thing: he helped the next generation build the temple. David provided the plans and millions of dollars in gold, silver, precious stones, bronze and iron.

We may not fulfill all of our plans and ambitions, but we can do the next best thing. If God doesn't let us accomplish our goals, let's help somebody else meet his goals. Let's pay the bill. Let's give our wisdom. Let's encourage. We can't do everything, but we can do something.

If your dreams are not fulfilled in the will of God, help fulfill someone else's dreams by sharing your talents and resources. When you're concerned more with God's glory and not with who gets the credit, He can use you in more ways to accomplish His purposes. Let God use you in the ways He sees best.

A HOUSE FOR DAVID

God did not permit King David to build Him a house. Instead, He did just the opposite; He built a house for David. God said, "David, I am not going to build you a physical house but a house made of people. There will always be one of your descendants on the throne of Israel."

He also said some things about David's children. "If your sons will keep My covenant and My testimony which I shall teach them, their sons also shall sit upon your throne forevermore. For the Lord has chosen Zion; He has desired it for His habitation" (vv.12,13).

There is an application here for God's children. He chose us in Christ before the foundation of the world (Eph.1:4). Jesus said, "You did not choose Me, but I chose you" (John 15:16). What a high and holy privilege! We were chosen to be God's children. "Beloved, now we are children of God" (I John 3:2). What a wonderful calling! Paul tells us we also reign in life (Rom.5:17). God wants us to reign as kings, even as David's children did. We reign through obedience and holiness.

God wants us to reign in righteousness for His glory. Because we are His children through faith in Jesus Christ, we are seated with Christ in the heavenlies. Therefore, let's be clothed with salvation. Let's shout for joy!

Someday believers will reign with Christ in His kingdom. But today He wants you to reign in life. Do you reign in life with Christ? As you obey the Word of God and keep your heart pure, you become a king. Don't live beneath your spiritual station in life. Be a king!

Read Psalm 133:1-3

THE UNITY OF THE SPIRIT

"Behold, how good and how pleasant it is for brethren to dwell together in unity!" (v.1). This is as true today as when it was written centuries ago. We would expect brothers and sisters to dwell together in unity. After all, they share the same nature because they have the same parents. Until they move out, they live at the same address and eat at the same table.

We also would expect God's people to dwell together in unity—but not uniformity. My wife and I currently have seven grandchildren. We can tell that they all belong to the same family, but each is an individual. Similarly, God does not want uniformity among His children; He wants unity.

The psalmist gives us two descriptions of spiritual unity. "It is like the precious oil upon the head, running down on the beard, the beard of Aaron, running down on the edge of his garments" (v.2). Over his chest, his heart, Aaron wore a breastplate that had twelve stones—one for each of the tribes of Israel. The oil bathed all of those stones, and they all became one in that anointing oil. That's a picture of the Holy Spirit of God, who baptizes us into the Body of Jesus Christ and gives us spiritual unity. Unity is not something we create; it's something God gives us.

Spiritual unity also is fruitful like dew. "It is like the dew of Hermon" (v.3). With the mountain dew comes God's blessing.

We should strive to maintain the unity of the Spirit. Ask God to help you be a part of the answer, not a part of the problem.

As a believer in the Body of Christ, you must do your part to dwell in unity. The Holy Spirit helps you live in unity with your brothers and sisters in Christ. Pray for the fragrant oil and fruitful dew of spiritual unity in your life today.

Read Psalm 134:1-3

NIGHT SHIFT

DAY 333

Years ago when I was attending seminary, I worked the night shift on occasion. It paid a little more money than the day shift, but I was a bit lonely. If you've ever had to work the night shift, you will appreciate Psalm 134.

God never slumbers or sleeps. Therefore, we can serve and praise Him any time of day. The psalmist says there were priests who prayed and praised God in His temple at night. There was a constant repetition of praise and prayer from the temple.

We can bless the Lord in the night seasons. It's not easy when we are going through the nighttime experiences of life to lift our hands and bless the Lord. But He does give us songs in the night. Paul and Silas were able to lift their hearts in praise to God while in the Philippian jail (Acts 16). They were on the night shift. They knew that God was awake, so they blessed Him, and He sent deliverance. We can get some strange blessings in the night seasons, for God speaks to us in different ways. Others may not see your praise at night, but God sees and hears.

Whether you are in the sunshine or in the darkness, whether you are serving on the day shift or the night shift, remember that you are serving the Lord. Because He never slumbers or sleeps, He hears your prayer and praise at all times, and He will bless you.

DAY

334

Read Psalm 135:1-12

GREAT GOVERNMENT

"Praise the Lord! Praise the name of the Lord; praise Him, O you servants of the Lord!" (v.1). That's the way Psalm 135 begins. It's strange that the psalmist has to instruct us to shout hallelujah, but he goes on to tell us why.

First, *we should praise God because of His goodness.* "Praise the Lord, for the Lord is good; sing praises to His name, for it is pleasant" (v.3). We sometimes take God's goodness for granted. He is good, and His goodness is unsearchable. God shows us His goodness in both material and spiritual blessings.

Second, *we should praise the Lord for His grace.* "For the Lord has chosen Jacob for Himself, Israel for His special treasure" (v.4). Israel was not a treasure before God chose her. After He chose her, she became precious. God also chose us. Jesus said, "You did not choose me, but I chose you" (John 15:16). God showed His grace by choosing us to be His children.

Third, *we should praise Him for His greatness.* "For I know that the Lord is great, and our Lord is above all gods" (v.5). What god is like our God?

Finally, the psalmist tells us *we should praise God for His government.* "Whatever the Lord pleases He does, in heaven and in earth, in the seas and in all deep places" (v.6). He then describes God's sovereignty in creation and in history.

Whatever your situation, you can stop and praise the Lord for His goodness, His grace, His greatness and His government. He is managing all of creation and all of history to bring about His purposes. Let God use you to do His work.

Read Psalm 135:13-21

DAY 335

THE COST OF IDOLATRY

Some things in the Bible are so important that God repeats them. The last verses in Psalm 135 parallel Psalm 115. These two psalms describe the dead idols of other nations. The psalmist says, "The idols of the nations are silver and gold, the work of men's hands. They have mouths, but they do not speak; eyes they have, but they do not see; they have ears, but they do not hear; nor is there any breath in their mouths. Those who make them are like them; so is everyone who trusts in them" (vv.15-18). Here we see the folly of idolatry—worshiping silver and gold, the work of men's hands. But that's going on today, isn't it? Many people worship the works of their hands.

How do you know what you are worshiping? The thing you work for, sacrifice for and live for is your god. For some people, it's money. For others, it's possessions. With still others, it's ambition or people. The psalmist shows us how foolish this is. Idols have mouths, yet they can't make promises. But our God speaks to us, and He gives us promises in His Word. Idols have eyes, but they cannot see. They offer no protection. But "the eyes of the Lord are on the righteous" (Ps.34:15). God's eyes are watching us every moment of the day. He never goes to sleep. He cares for His children. Idols have ears, but they cannot hear your prayers. If you talk to an idol, you are talking to yourself. But God's ears are open to our cries. He says, "Call to Me, and I will answer you" (Jer.33:3).

The saddest thing about idolatry is that we become like the god we worship. "Those who make them are like them; so is everyone who trusts in them" (v.18). But if we worship the true and living God, we become like Him. We are transformed into the image of Jesus Christ.

Be careful what you worship. Satan wants you to substitute many idols for the Lord. Place no gods before Him; worship Him only. Today, get rid of any idols that might prevent your worship of the Lord.

DAY

336

Read Psalm 136:1-9

ENDURING MERCY

Psalm 136 magnifies the mercy of God. Every verse ends with the refrain, "For His mercy endures forever." I would like to have heard this psalm sung in the Jewish temple. One group of priests would say, "Oh, give thanks to the Lord, for He is good!" (v.1). Then the priests on the other side of the court would answer, "For His mercy endures forever."

Mercy and grace go together. God, in His grace, gives me what I don't deserve, and God, in His mercy, does not give me what I do deserve. His mercy endures forever, and our response should be thanksgiving and praise.

Praise the Lord for His wonders. "To Him who alone does great wonders, for His mercy endures forever" (v.4). "His name will be called Wonderful" (Isa.9:6). Jesus Christ said and did wonderful things. When God touches a life, it becomes filled with wonder. I think of Peter, Andrew, James and John—men who would have remained ordinary fishermen had they not met Jesus. They went to a wedding at Cana, and wonders happened. They went to funerals, and wonders happened.

Praise God for His wisdom. "To Him who by wisdom made the heavens" (v.5). The God who created the universe has the wisdom to run it, and He has the wisdom you need for your life. "If any of you lacks wisdom, let him ask of God" (James 1:5). He'll guide you.

Praise Him for His works. "To Him who laid out the earth above the waters" (v.6). Let's worship God today because of His wonders. Let's seek His guidance because of His wisdom. Let's enjoy all that He gives to us through His manifold creation.

You would not be saved were it not for God's grace and mercy. Never take those two gifts for granted. Do you devote time to praising and thanking Him for what He does in your life?

A COMPLETE HISTORY

Israel is the only nation for which we have a complete history. We know how it started, how it grew, where it is today and where it will be for the rest of history—thanks to the Word of God.

In Psalm 136 the psalmist reviewed Israel's history. As he looked, he saw the mercy of God. He performed three marvelous ministries for the Israelites: He brought them out; He brought them through; and He brought them in. God wants to care for us in the same way today.

God brought Israel *out of the slavery* and the bondage of Egypt (vv.10-12). That's redemption. He then brought them *through* the Red Sea and the wilderness. Finally, He brought them *into the Promised Land.* The old generation died off in their unbelief, but the new generation entered in with great glory and power and claimed their inheritance.

God wants to do this for us today. He wants to free us from sin's slavery. He wants to bring us through the deep water and wilderness experiences of life, that He might bring us into the inheritance that He has for us. Our history is already complete with God.

Today you might be facing some seemingly impossible situation in your life. Trust God to open the way for you. Let Him bring you out of your bondage and through your difficulty and bring you into your inheritance.

Read Psalm 137:1-9

FINDING YOUR SONG

One test of your spiritual condition is whether or not you really have a song. Psalm 137 tells us about people who lost their song. They lost it because they lost their sanctity—they repeatedly sinned against the Lord.

Here's the record: "By the rivers of Babylon, there we sat down, yea, we wept when we remembered Zion. We hung our harps upon the willows in the midst of it. For there those who carried us away captive required of us a song, and those who plundered us required of us mirth, saying, 'Sing us one of the songs of Zion!'" (vv.1-3). Can't you just picture the Babylonians taunting the Jews? The Jews responded, "How shall we sing the Lord's song in a foreign land?" (v.4).

It can be done. They were there because of their disobedience, and they had lost their song. But even in a foreign land, we can have a song to the Lord. Jesus came down to earth from heaven, and He had a song. In fact, the night on which He was betrayed, He sang a song of Zion in the upper room (Matt.26:30).

When you are not walking with the Lord, you lose your song and start living on memories. "If I forget you, O Jerusalem, let my right hand forget her skill! If I do not remember you . . . if I do not exalt Jerusalem above my chief joy" (vv.5,6). Are you living on memories, or are you daily receiving blessings from the Lord?

In verses 7-9 we find the Jews looking for revenge. This is understandable from a human perspective, for they had seen their babies dashed against the stones. So they pray, "Lord, render to them what they deserve. You are the Judge. You remember them." But as Christians, we must think first of forgiveness.

If you are without your song, living on memories and looking for revenge, you are not walking closely with the Lord. Your first task is to get that song back by confessing your sins to the Lord. God will restore the joy of your salvation.

Read Psalm 138:1-8

DAY
339

A PERFECT PURPOSE

"The Lord will perfect that which concerns me" (v.8). God has a purpose for each of our lives. We are not numbers in a computer; He knows our names. In fact, He has numbered all the hairs on our heads (Matt 10:30). God knows our needs today. We are His personal concern, the work of His hands.

When does God perfect that which concerns us? When can we expect Him to work in our lives? First, *when we praise Him*. Verse 1 says, "I will praise You with my whole heart." Verse 2 reads, "I will worship toward Your holy temple, and praise Your name." When we take time to worship and praise God, He can perfect that which concerns us. But if we go our own way, we lose that special blessing from God.

God also perfects that which concerns us *when we pray to Him*. "In the day when I cried out, You answered me, and made me bold with strength in my soul" (v.3). It doesn't say God changed the outside circumstances. Instead, He changed the psalmist on the inside. When we worship and cry out to the Lord, He can work on our behalf.

Finally, God perfects that which concerns us *when we glorify Him*. "All the kings of the earth shall praise You, O Lord, when they hear the words of Your mouth. Yes, they shall sing of the ways of the Lord, for great is the glory of the Lord" (vv.4,5). Praising Him to others should be a natural part of our conversations.

The God of the universe desires to work personally in your life. When you worship the Lord by praying to Him, glorifying Him, witnessing for Him and submitting to Him, He works on your behalf. If you need a reviving blessing today, turn to Him. He will give it.

Read Psalm 139:1-24

RIGHT THOUGHTS

Some people never think about God. They live and die as strangers in His world. Others think wrong thoughts about Him. They live and die in the shadows of superstition and confusion. Still others think right thoughts about God, but somehow it makes no difference in their lives. They live and die disappointed and defeated. Psalm 139 was written by a man who had right thoughts about God that made a difference. He lived with confidence, security and fulfillment. He submitted to God. Let's look at the four discoveries David made as he thought about God and the difference He made in his life.

God knows everything (vv.1-6). Theologians call this God's *omniscience*. God knows you personally. We find nearly 50 personal pronouns throughout the psalm. He knows your name, nature, needs and even the number of hairs on your head. He knows you intimately, including your actions and your thoughts. He knows you sovereignly.

God is everywhere (vv.7-12). You cannot flee from Him. This is a beautiful description of His *omnipresence*. "Where shall I go to get away from God?" Jonah asked this and never got an answer. You cannot hide even in darkness. God is in all places at all times (v.11).

God can do anything (vv.13-18). *He is omnipotent.* David says the greatest marvel of all is human birth. God can make life. He gives each baby the genetic structure He wants him or her to have. If you leave God out of your life, you will never fulfill what you were born for.

God can guide your life (vv.19-24). You dare not fight against Him. David said he was going to serve God—a decision that led to dedication (vv.23,24). When we put the whole psalm together, we discover a man who knows God. You, too, can know God through Jesus Christ (John 14:9; 17:3).

God knows everything about you. Be open and honest with Him, and He can lead and bless you. Strive to do His will. God made you and wants to fulfill in your life that for which He made you.

Read Psalm 139:1-6

INTIMATE KNOWLEDGE

DAY 341

Psalm 139 is a short course in theology, the science of God. In the first six verses the psalmist says, "God knows everything; don't try to fool Him."

"O Lord, You have searched me and known me" (v.1). In these first six verses we find 13 personal pronouns. God knows us *personally*. Few people can recognize us in a crowd, but God does. With Him there are no crowds, only individuals. At times you may feel lonely and say, "Nobody knows me. Nobody cares about me." But God knows you intimately. He knows your every action and thought. "You know my sitting down and my rising up; You understand my thought afar off" (v.2). He also knows your words. "For there is not a word on my tongue, but behold, O Lord, you know it altogether" (v.4). The psalmist is saying, "He's behind me. He's before me. He's laid His hand upon me. He is sovereign."

What should be our response to this? Simple. "Praise the Lord!" I am glad that my Father in heaven understands me personally and intimately and that His hand is upon me. This doesn't make me afraid; it gives me confidence. What an encouragement to know that our Father in heaven knows all about us—where we are and what we're doing. Of course, we don't want to be in the wrong place, doing the wrong thing. But if the child of God is walking in the will of God, he has the confidence that His Father in heaven is caring for Him and knows his every need.

God has a thorough knowledge of you. That gives you all the more reason to pray honestly to the Lord and walk uprightly before Him. His knowledge of you ought to encourage you and make you confident. Thank Him that His intimate knowledge of you leads to His complete care for you.

Read Psalm 139:7-12

Here, There, EVERYWHERE

Have you ever tried to run away from God? Don't try; it can't be done. "Where can I go from Your Spirit? Or where can I flee from Your presence? If I ascend into heaven, You are there. If I make my bed in hell, behold, You are there. If I take the wings of the morning, and dwell in the uttermost parts of the sea, even there Your hand shall lead me, and Your right hand shall hold me" (vv.7-10).

No matter where we go in the will of God, He is there. Why should we flee from Him? Why should we try to find height or depth, east or west, darkness or light? "If I say, 'Surely the darkness shall fall on me,' even the night shall be light about me; indeed, the darkness shall not hide from You, but the night shines as the day; the darkness and the light are both alike to You" (vv.11,12). Sometimes I've found myself in dark places and have wondered, "Does God know?" He indeed knows. If we sin, we go out into the darkness, but God sees us. And sometimes when we are walking with the Lord, we still find ourselves in darkness. But that darkness is as light to God.

God is everywhere and sees everything. Rather than flee *from* Him, we should flee to Him. "God is our refuge and strength, a very present help in trouble" (Ps.46:1). Nothing can separate us from the love of God—neither height nor depth, east nor west, darkness nor light (Rom.8:38,39).

God promises to "never leave you nor forsake you" (Heb.13:5). The next time you go through dark days, remember that God knows your problems and needs. You may take refuge in Him; He will see you through.

FLEE TO GOD

Years ago, A. W. Tozer wrote, "The essence of idolatry is the entertainment of thoughts about God that are unworthy of Him" God is much greater than we are, and our thoughts of Him must be great thoughts. David's thoughts of God in this psalm center on His omnipresence. As we read his words, we can answer three simple questions.

Can we flee from God? The psalmist says no. Height and depth will not enable us to run away from God. Life has its ups and downs. God is there when we're up, and He's there when we're down. In essence, David says in verse 9, "If at sunrise, I could jump on one of the sunbeams, if I could fly across the sky from east to west at 186,000 miles per second, when I got there, You'd be there already, Lord." The word *dwell* means "to arrest." Even if we try to run away, God's hand is going to catch us and lead us.

Who would flee from God? Those who are afraid of Him. Among those in the Bible who tried to flee Him are Adam and Eve, Jonah and Judas Iscariot. No true believer would ever try to run away from God. As believers, we have fled to God, and we are hiding in Him.

What are the blessings of fleeing to God? If you have problems, difficulties and sin, run to God. The Lord's presence kept Paul going during difficult times. Like the apostle, we need to discover that no matter how difficult a situation is, the Lord is with us. When we hide in the Lord, we receive courage, encouragement, comfort and strength for the battle. Respond to God's invitation: "Come to Me, and I will give you rest" (Matt.11:28). Hide in the Lord. He's the only place of safety and satisfaction.

God's omnipresence is a blessing to those who hide in Him. Perhaps you have tried to run from the Lord. Return to Him; He is always ready to receive you when you've gone astray. Whatever difficulty you may be facing, don't hide from life—hide in the Lord. He will give you strength to fight the battle.

DAY
344

Read Psalm 139:13-18

WONDERFULLY MADE

"I will praise You, for I am fearfully and wonderfully made" (v.14). The psalmist is talking about the miracle of conception and birth. It's an amazing story. "For You have formed my inward parts; You have covered me in my mother's womb. . . . Marvelous are Your works, and that my soul knows very well" (vv.13,14).

Someone defined a baby as something that gets you up at night and gets you down during the day. That may be true, but so are the words of poet Carl Sandburg: "A baby is God's opinion that the world should go on." When we contemplate human birth, our first response ought to be *reverence*. The God of the galaxies is the God who is concerned about the color of a baby's hair and the genetic structure of a yet unborn child. We ought to bow in reverence before God and worship Him, because each individual child is a part of His handiwork. We don't understand why some children are born handicapped or exceptional in some areas. But God knows.

Our next response should be *confidence*. We can trust God because He made us as we are. Instead of complaining about what we're not, we can gratefully accept from God what we are. He knew all about each of us before we were born.

Finally, we should respond with *obedience*. We can take what God has given us and use it for His glory. Instead of searching for something you can't have, invest what you do have to serve Him.

When you contemplate the miracle of birth, praise God. As you respond in reverence, confidence and obedience, determine to be a good steward with the personal resources and talents He gave you. Good stewardship honors God.

Read Psalm 139:13-18

THE MARVEL OF LIFE

DAY 345

The greatest evidence of God's power is human birth. When a baby is born, there is promise, potential and excitement. David considered babies to be miracles from the hand of God. Eugene Peterson has said, "In the presence of birth we don't calculate, we marvel." As we ponder these truths, what should be our response?

We worship God. The word *fearfully* means "I am shuddering with astonishment; I am trembling with awe" (v.14). I fear that today people have taken sex, conception, birth and babies and turned the process into something functional instead of miraculous. Some people think of sex as animal excitement, but David thought of spiritual enrichment. No wonder we are aborting babies today; we don't see anything holy about sex, conception and birth.

We show confidence in God. What we are is God's gift to us. What we do with our lives is our gift to Him. He accepts us as we are. He's not going to judge us on the basis of what He has given someone else, but on the basis of what we have done with what He has given us. Never be discouraged by what you don't have. Having confidence in God about your life brings eager expectation.

We obey God. The more we glorify God, the more we enjoy Him. We can take the miracle of life He gave us and wreck it, or we can present our bodies to the Lord as a living sacrifice.

To leave God out of your life is simply to exist, not really to live. Jesus died that you might be saved from your sins and one day go to heaven. But while you're here on earth, God wants you to fulfill all that He has built into you. Are you responding to His power for your life? Worship Him, place your confidence in Him and obey Him.

DAY **346**

Read Psalm 139:13-18

Interrupting A MIRACLE

Since the 1973 Supreme Court decision *Roe v. Wade*, more than 21 million babies have been killed. These verses are an amazing statement about conception, growth and birth. When a baby is aborted, what really happens?

First, *a miracle is interrupted* (v.14). *Fearfully* means "I am trembling with astonishment." By thinking about birth, David also was contemplating God's attributes. The world has cheapened sex, conception and birth to the point that it treats pregnancy as a nuisance, not a miracle. God made us and has covered (protected) us. The baby in the womb is covered by God. Let's not turn the womb into a tomb!

Second, *a real person is murdered.* Today, medical science calls the fetus a P.O.C. (a product of conception)—a mass of tissues or a collection of cells. But God calls it a human being, and we had better be careful how we treat the child.

Third, *a divine law is broken* (Ex.20:13). Dr. Gleason Archer, commenting on Exodus 21:22-25, says that if a fight occurred and it resulted in a baby being born dead, then the assailant had to pay with his life. God protected the unborn by His Law. But today it is legal to kill them.

God gives and takes life—not man. An even greater tragedy awaits us in this country. Abortion leads to infanticide, which leads to mercy killing. In some parts of the world, voluntary euthanasia is legal.

God's people need to take a strong stand to protect the miracle of human life.

God loves children and wants to protect them. Rejoice in the miracle of birth and protect the sanctity of the womb and the lives of unborn babies. What can you do in your community to take a stand against abortion?

Read Psalm 139:17, 18

GOD'S THOUGHTS

PART 1

DAY 347

A.W. Tozer used to say, "The only real world is the Bible world." Nothing is more unsure than the world, for it is passing away. But the will and Word of God will abide forever (see Mark 13:31). As we consider the character of God's thoughts, we will want to do His will.

God's thoughts are *personal* (v.17). They concern you and me. He makes the individual and then plans for him. He knows all about us. Paradoxically, the sovereignty of God is the basis for our freedom. If He were not on the throne, this world would be run by chance. But the psalmist tells us that life is not a gamble. God put your substance together and ordained your genetic structure (vv.13,14). We must use what He has given us for His glory. And our obedience to His will reaches beyond this life, for our future is wrapped up in God's plan for us (Jer.29:11).

God's thoughts are *precious* (v.17). *Precious* means "weighty, valuable." His thoughts toward us are unique, tailor-made, and that makes them valuable. When we accept God's plan for us and exercise believing faith, then He can work out His perfect will in our lives. Remember, His thoughts are deep (Ps.92:5); they are higher than ours (Isa.55:8).

God's thoughts about you are more than mere "thoughts." They include His purposes and His care. As you meditate on His thoughts, renew your commitment to know and do His will for your life.

DAY 348

Read Psalm 139:17, 18

GOD'S THOUGHTS

PART 2

Yesterday, we learned that God's thoughts are personal and precious. They are full of His purpose and care. Let's consider three additional characteristics of God's thoughts.

God's thoughts are *practical.* Paul said, "none of these things [tribulations] move me; nor do I count my life dear to myself, so that I may finish my race with joy, and the ministry which I received from the Lord Jesus, to testify to the gospel of the grace of God" (Acts 20:24). Paul was living to do one thing—finish his course. As we run the race of life, following God's thoughts leads to fulfillment, courage and the strength to continue.

God's thoughts are *vast* and *inexhaustible* (v.17). How great is the "sum of them." The Hebrew word for sum is plural. Thus, His thoughts just keep growing. People who don't want to do the will of God live their lives in a little bucket of water. But when we accept His will for our lives, we launch out on an ocean of possibility. God said to Abraham, "You walk before Me and do My will, and I am going to give you horizons like you've never seen before" (see Gen.15:5). If you want to be a stagnant Christian, reject the will of God. You will not grow, and you will miss what He has for you. He wants to do great things in your life.

God's thoughts are *unfailing* (v.18). He works out His plans even while we sleep. Adam went to sleep, and God gave him a wife. Abraham went to sleep, and God worked out His covenant to him. God already has revealed things about our daily living to us by His Spirit in the Scriptures.

Are you discouraged by events in your life or weary of the day's routine? Think God's thoughts by reading His Word and obey His thoughts by doing His will. He will work in your life. He will open horizons of blessing and help you along your pilgrimage.

Read Psalm 139:19-24

DAY 349

THE PENETRATING PRAYER

There is no higher occupation than the contemplation and the worship of God. David says, "My God knows everything; I can't fool Him. My God is everywhere; I can't flee from Him. My God can do anything; I can't fight Him. What should I do?" We find his answer in verses 23 and 24. "Search me, O God, and know my heart; try me, and know my anxieties; and see if there is any wicked way in me, and lead me in the way everlasting." That's one of the most penetrating prayers found in the Bible.

If we can't fool God, flee from Him or fight Him, the only thing for us to do is surrender to Him—in awe, reverence and worship. Notice the psalmist's request: "Search me, O God, and know my heart." God knows our hearts. He knows us from top to bottom, inside out. But we don't know our own hearts. Jeremiah said, "The heart is deceitful above all things, and desperately wicked; who can know it?" (Jer.17:9). Only God can know it. The Hebrew word for *search* used in verse 23 means to dig in a mine and find ore. "Search me, O God; I am like a mine. I am deep, but dig out the potential that is in me. Dig out all the treasure you have put into me, even before I was born." It also means to explore a land. How broad and wide are the horizons of possibility in life. "Search me, O God; bring out of me all that is there for your glory."

Then David says, "Try me, and know my anxieties." *Try* means to test metal in a furnace. That's why we suffer sometimes. "See if there is any wicked way in me, and lead me in the way everlasting" (v.24).

Here, then, are three penetrating requests: search me, try me and lead me. Are you asking God to lead you in His will today? If you do, He will bring out of the mine of your life treasures that will glorify His name.

Can you echo David's prayer? If not, perhaps you need to surrender to God's will or ask Him to forgive some sin in your life. Remember, He knows you intimately. Ask Him for the grace to stand up to His scrutiny.

Read Psalm 139:19-22

CONFRONTING EVIL

Many people are bothered by the problem of evil. They say, "If God is a loving and good God, why does He allow evil?" David did not ignore this problem, nor did he give in to it. Instead, he made a decision and took his stand with God. Only our God can permit evil and be able to overrule it to accomplish His purposes. As David confronted the problem of evil in the world, he did so in stages.

Stage one: He evaluated (v.22). David looked at the wicked, violent, blasphemous, deceitful and rebellious crowd. He showed courage and honesty in taking his stand against them. When we start asking ourselves, *Is it safe?* or, *Is it popular?* we have moved away from biblical ethics and integrity.

Stage two: He grieved (v.21). God the Father grieves (Gen.6:6); God the Son grieves (Mark 3:5); and God the Holy Spirit grieves (Eph.4:30) over sin. We also ought to grieve over sin. When Nehemiah heard that the walls of Jerusalem were destroyed, he sat and wept (Neh.1:4). Today, we need people who will sit down long enough to weep over sin.

Stage three: He hated (vv.21,22). We could use a little more holy anger today. Christians sometimes are too bland, too complacent and too comfortable. Edmund Burke said, "All that is required for evil to triumph is for good men to do nothing." Love and hate are not contradictory when dealing with sin. Jesus showed both compassion toward sinners and hatred of sin.

Stage four: He decided (v.19). David decided to separate himself from evil (Ps.119:115). We need to stand among sinners as the salt of the earth and the light of the world, but we need to have contact without contamination.

Stage five: He trusted (v.19). We must leave vengeance with God; He will punish the wicked (Rom.12:19). Our job is to give ourselves to Him and do the work He wants us to do.

If you fail to make a decision, the world will make it for you. Take your stand with God and use David's experience as a guide for confronting the problem of evil. Determine to live a holy life that honors the Lord.

Read Psalm 139:23, 24

NOTHING TO HIDE

DAY 351

The most important knowledge in the world is the knowledge of God. The second most important is the knowledge of yourself. To know God, we must know Jesus Christ as our Savior (John 17:3). In his prayer, David makes two basic requests that should also be our prayer.

Our prayer should be that *we want God to know us*. This doesn't mean we want God to get information about us; it means that we have nothing to hide from Him. We hide from God with our words. When we lie to other people, we're lying to ourselves, and we are lying to God.

God has purposes for us to fulfill. He wants us to explore new territory and expand the horizons of our lives. Let God put you through the furnace (if He needs to) to remove the dross from your life. Let Him prepare you for what He has planned for you.

Our prayer also should be that *we want God to guide us*. We can't flee from God or fight Him, so we might as well follow Him. Jeremiah said, "O Lord, I know the way of man is not in himself; it is not in man who walks to direct his steps" (Jer.10:23).

When we are willing to obey, God is more than willing to reveal His way to us. He guides us through His *word* and through *prayer*. Don't be stingy with God, giving Him only a minute or two of your time every day. He also guides us through the *prompting of the Holy Spirit,* through *circumstances* and through His *people*. How glorious it is to have Christian friends with whom you can pray and to have a pastor who prays for you and ministers to you.

If you want God to know you and guide you, He will. You'll know yourself better and know Him better. And then He will guide you and lead you in an everlasting way.

Read Psalm 140:1-13

OUR DELIVERER

King David was going through another battle. He needed deliverance from an attacking enemy. "Deliver me, O Lord, from evil men; preserve me from violent men, who plan evil things in their hearts; they continually gather together for war. They sharpen their tongues like a serpent; the poison of asps is under their lips. Keep me, O Lord, from the hands of the wicked; preserve me from violent men" (vv.1-4). David's enemies had hidden snares to trap him.

What do you do when you face this situation—when evil, violent, lying people are busy setting traps for you? Remember that *God hears you.* "I said to the Lord: 'You are my God; hear the voice of my supplications, O Lord'" (v.6). *God also strengthens you.* "O God the Lord, the strength of my salvation, You have covered my head in the day of battle" (v.7). If you have to do battle against the Enemy today, let God outfit you in the armor you need. Finally, *God vindicates you.* David prayed that God would vindicate him and that his enemies' own sins would destroy them.

David concluded by giving thanks to the Lord. "I know that the Lord will maintain the cause of the afflicted, and justice for the poor. Surely the righteous shall give thanks to Your name; the upright shall dwell in Your presence" (vv.12,13). The battle over, he said, "One day I am going to dwell in Your presence, where there will be no more lying, slandering, battling, fighting or sinning." We will enjoy the peace of God forever.

If you are a believer, God has already delivered you from the penalty of sin. Today He works to deliver you from sin's effects. Perhaps enemies are slandering your reputation. Call upon the Lord for help. He will hear you, strengthen you and vindicate you. Let Him give, you the victory today.

Read Psalm 141:1-10

MIXED PRAYERS

DAY 353

One of the greatest privileges we have as children of God is prayer, yet so often we take it for granted. As the gospel song goes, "O what peace we often forfeit, O what needless pain we bear, all because we do not carry everything to God in prayer!"

In Psalm 141 David pictures prayer in a beautiful way that will help us appreciate it more. "Lord, I cry out to You; make haste to me! Give ear to my voice when I cry out to You. Let my prayer be set before You as incense, the lifting up of my hands as the evening sacrifice" (vv.1,2). The Jewish priest would go to the altar of incense in the holy place and offer a special incense that no one was allowed to duplicate. As the smoke of the incense rose from the altar, it was as though prayer were going up to God. David was not in the temple; he was a king, not a priest. He may well have been out somewhere in the battlefield when he wrote this. But he says, "I am going to lift up my hands to you as the evening sacrifice. My prayer is going to come to you as incense."

The incense at the altar was mixed together carefully; it was well prepared. Likewise, let's mix our prayers carefully. Our prayers should contain adoration and confession to the Lord, petition, thanksgiving and submission to Him. Let's allow the Holy Spirit to ignite the altar of our souls. Do not pray from a cold heart. David goes on to say, "Set a guard, O Lord, over my mouth; keep watch over the door of my lips. Do not incline my heart to any evil thing" (vv.3,4). After we pray to the Lord, let's make sure that our lips and hearts do not sin.

Are your prayers a good mix rather than a series of petitions? When you pray from the heart, you can't help but praise God and thank Him for His grace and generosity. Make your prayers like fragrant incense that brings joy to the heart of God.

Read Psalm 142:1-7

LOOK AHEAD

I do not like caves. When I visited Mammoth Cave in Kentucky, I could hardly wait to get out. Thus, I somewhat understand David's distress as he wrote this psalm while hiding from Saul in a cave. In his distress, he looked in four directions.

First, *David looked within.* "I cry out to the Lord with my voice; with my voice to the Lord I make my supplication. I pour out my complaint before Him; I declare before Him my trouble. When my spirit was overwhelmed within me, then you knew my path" (vv.1-3). He looked within and said, "Look, I'm in trouble; I'm complaining; I'm overwhelmed." Introspection sometimes can be good for you, but don't spend too much time looking within, or you will get discouraged.

Then *David looked around,* hoping to find help. "Look on my right hand and see, for there is no one who acknowledges me; refuge has failed me; no one cares for my soul" (v.4). Do you ever feel like that? Do you look around and say, "Nobody even cares—everyone is bearing his own burdens, and nobody wants to share mine"? Perhaps in those situations you should take time to bear other people's burdens—then they might be interested in your concerns.

After looking within and around and finding only discouragement, *David looked up.* "I cried out to You, O Lord: I said, 'You are my refuge, my portion in the land of the living'" (v.5). In other words, "God, you're going to hear my cry. You're going to deliver me from my persecutors; they are stronger than I am."

Finally, *David looked ahead.* "Bring my soul out of prison, that I may praise Your name; the righteous shall surround me, for You shall deal bountifully with me" (v.7). After you have seen the glory and the blessing of the Lord, you can look ahead with confidence.

Perhaps you are in a cave of discouragement today. Your hope lies not within yourself or with your circumstances. Look to the Lord and obey His Word. Then look ahead with confidence, for God's promises are sure and His Word is true.

WILLING TO LEAD

How should we pray when we are going through trouble? We find several requests in David's prayer, and if we follow his example, God will lead us through our difficulties into blessing.

First, he says, "Hear my prayer" (v.1) and "answer me speedily, O Lord; my spirit fails!" (v.7). We don't have to shout to God; we don't have to argue with Him. We simply can come to Him and say, "Lord, hear me." When a child comes to his father or mother, the parent has his ears open. "The eyes of the Lord are on the righteous, and His ears are open to their cry" (Ps.34:15). Have you prayed to God about what worries you today?

David's second request is, "Cause me to hear Your lovingkindness in the morning, for in You do I trust" (v.8). In other words, "Speak to me, Lord." Each morning David meditated on the Word of God, and God guided him. Have you taken time to read the Bible and let its Author speak to you? He'll show you the way you ought to go.

David's next request is, "Deliver me, O Lord, from my enemies" (v.9). God can do that if we are walking in the way He wants us to walk. In verse 10 David asks for instruction and guidance. "Teach me to do Your will, for you are my God; Your Spirit is good. Lead me in the land of uprightness." Oh, how willing He is to do this!

Finally, David says, "Revive me, O Lord, for Your name's sake!" (v.11). Why do we want God to bring us out of times of difficulty? Sure, we want relief, but we also should want Him to be glorified. We want Him to deliver us for His name's sake, that He might receive all the glory.

Your spirit can begin to fail when you go through extended trials. Ask the Lord for help, and He will lead you through difficult times. Always stay open to the guidance and instruction of God's Word. God will speak to you through Scripture as He leads you through your trial. Keep trusting Him, and He will accomplish what is best for you and what glorifies Him.

Read Psalm 144:1-8

JEHOVAH'S COVENANT

Why should Almighty God pay attention to us? Who are we that we should receive His mercy? David asks these questions in verse 3. "Lord, what is man, that You take knowledge of him? Or the son of man, that You are mindful of him?"

What are we that God should pay any attention to us? Are we smart? I don't think so. Are we strong? Some animals are much stronger than we are. Are we righteous? No, we have sinned against God. Are we faithful? Too often we disobey Him. From the human point of view, there is no reason why God should pay any attention to us. "Man is like a breath; his days are like a passing shadow" (v.4). Compared to eternity, our lives are just a puff of smoke. They appear, and then they are gone.

Why should God pay any attention to us? Because God, in all of His mercy and grace, loves us. The word David uses for God in this psalm means Jehovah God, the God of the gracious covenant. He has made promises to us, and we can trust Him. David describes Him as "my lovingkindness and my fortress, my high tower and my deliverer, my shield and the One in whom I take refuge" (v.2).

This is a mystery too deep for us to explain, but it's not too deep for us to experience. We may not understand why God should pay any attention to us, but we know that His Son came to be a servant for us. He died on the cross, a sacrifice for us, and now He lives in heaven, interceding for us.

God pays attention to you because He loves you and wants to be glorified through your life. Walk with Him and glorify Him with your life.

The Joys of
GOD'S PEOPLE

"Happy are the people whose God is the Lord!" (v.15). That's the way David concludes Psalm 144. In the first half of this psalm, he cries out to God for help. In the last half, he sings praises to the Lord because of the help He gave him.

"I will sing a new song to You, O God; on a harp of ten strings I will sing praises to You, the One who gives salvation to kings, who delivers David His servant from the deadly sword" (vv.9,10). This shows David's *personal joy* in the Lord. We can picture him laying down his sword, picking up his harp and composing a new song to praise and glorify God. We ought to have personal joy in our hearts also. We have many reasons for praising God, but too often we remember only the sorrows of life and forget the blessings.

Then there is *national joy*—"the One who gives salvation to kings" (v.10). David was the king, and when God delivered him, it was for the good of the nation. How we need national righteousness and national repentance to have national joy!

Finally, there is *family joy*. David talks in verse 12 about his sons being like plants and his daughters like cornerstones that are polished for a palace. What a joy it is in the home to praise the Lord and see family members growing in Him.

God's people ought to be joyful—expressing personal, national and family joy. Our joy is founded on what God does and who He is. Rejoice in the Lord today for all of His goodness, grace and mercy toward you in Christ Jesus.

DAY **358**

Read Psalm 145:1-13

GREATLY TO BE PRAISED

This psalm has special meaning for me. Several years ago a drunken driver hit me going 80 or 90 miles an hour. When I woke up in the intensive care ward of a hospital with broken bones and lacerations, this is the verse that went through my mind: "Great is the Lord, and greatly to be praised; and His greatness is unsearchable" (v.3).

Let's praise God for His *greatness*. The psalmist says His greatness is eternal. "I will extol You, my God, O King; and I will bless Your name forever and ever. Every day I will bless You, and I will praise Your name forever and ever" (vv.1,2). We will spend all eternity praising the greatness of God. His greatness also is unsearchable. We can't begin to measure it. We can't know its depth, its height or its breadth. And the greatness of God is memorable. "One generation shall praise Your works to another, . . . I will meditate on the glorious splendor of Your majesty" (vv.4,5). We must tell the next generation of the greatness of God.

Then the psalmist praises the *goodness* of God. Verse 7 says, "They shall utter the memory of Your great goodness, and shall sing of Your righteousness. . . . The Lord is good to all, and His tender mercies are over all His works" (vv.7,9). Verse 8 expounds the *grace* of the Lord: "The Lord is gracious and full of compassion." Aren't you grateful that He is slow to anger?

All of this leads to the *glory* of the Lord. "They shall speak of the glory of Your kingdom, and talk of Your power" (v.11).

As finite beings, we can scarcely comprehend God's attributes. But we can certainly praise Him for who He is and what He has done in our lives. Thank God for saving you. Praise Him for His greatness, His goodness, His grace and His glory.

Read Psalm 145:14-21

GOD IS NEAR

DAY 359

"The Lord is near to all who call upon Him, to all who call upon Him in truth" (v.18). Isn't that a great promise? It's one you can put to work today. Let's look at it more closely.

First, God *is near to those who are stumbling*. "The Lord upholds all who fall, and raises up all those who are bowed down" (v.14). You may have stumbled and fallen. Perhaps you just didn't do what you should have. Maybe you stumbled in your job, and you are embarrassed and worried about it. Perhaps you have stumbled into sin.

Second, God *is near to those who carry burdens*. Those who are bowed down with the weight of care can find rest if they will call upon Him.

Third, God *is near to those who are hungry*. "The eyes of all look expectantly to You, and You give them their food in due season" (v.15). Verse 16 shows how simple it is for God to answer prayer: "You open Your hand and satisfy the desire of every living thing." All God has to do is open His hand to meet our needs today. The problem is, we often don't open our hearts and cry out to Him.

Fourth, God *is near to those who call upon Him*. We have this great promise: He will fulfill the desire of those who fear Him; He also will hear their cry and will save them" (v.19).

Finally, God *is near to those who love Him*. "The Lord preserves all who love Him, but all the wicked He will destroy" (v.20). Follow the advice of James: "Draw near to God and He will draw near to you" (James 4:8).

God is not far from you. He's waiting for you to take that first step, to cry out to Him and say, "Lord, I want to draw close to You. Here I am." Have you stumbled? Are you carrying a burden, or are you needy? He promises to be near to all those who call upon Him.

DAY 360

Read Psalm 146:1-10

THE GOD OF JACOB

"Happy is he who has the God of Jacob for his help, whose hope is in the Lord his God" (v.5). This tells us that God is all we need for today—and for tomorrow. When you know God, you have happiness, help and hope: happiness in walking with Him, help for the burdens of the day and hope for the concerns of the future. What more could you want?

Who is the God of Jacob? First, *He is the Creator.* Verse 6 says He is the One "who made heaven and earth, the sea, and all that is in them; who keeps truth forever." Any God great enough, wise enough and strong enough to create and sustain and run this universe can take care of our problems today.

Second, *He is the Judge* "who executes justice for the oppressed" (v.7). God knows when you have been wrongly criticized. He knows when others have tried to make life difficult for you. Leave the judgment with Him. Don't waste your time and energy trying to fight battles that only God can fight for you. He's with all of His people, and He does what is right.

Third, *He is the Father.* Verse 7 offers a picture of the Father feeding the hungry. God's Word always assures us of His provision. "My God shall supply all your need according to His riches in glory by Christ Jesus" (Phil.4:19).

Fourth, *He is the Redeemer.* "The Lord gives freedom to the prisoners. The Lord opens the eyes of the blind; . . . The Lord loves the righteous" (vv.7,8).

Finally, *He is the King.* "The Lord shall reign forever" (v.10). Sometimes you may feel like saying, "I don't deserve to have a God like this." That's true, but He's the God of Jacob. Jacob stumbled and made mistakes, but God remained his God. The eternal God is our Refuge.

God is your greatest Refuge. But He doesn't simply shelter you; He provides for you and strengthens you. Is the God of Jacob your God? If so, call upon Him, and He will be your help, hope and happiness.

Read Psalm 147:1-11

THE GOD OF YOUR HEART

DAY 361

The God of the galaxies is also the God of the brokenhearted. That's what David tells us in verses 3 and 4: "He heals the brokenhearted and binds up their wounds. He counts the number of the stars; He calls them all by name."

The contrast we see in these two verses—between the heavens and the broken heart—ought to encourage us. God made the heavens. He spoke and it was done. His creation stood steadfast. The God who made the heavens is concerned about your broken heart. Others may not be concerned, but God is. He's not so far away that He doesn't know your heart is hurting. He's not so great that He can't stoop down to you when you are pained, weeping and looking for help.

Yes, the God of the heavens is the God of your heart. The God who numbers and names the stars knows your needs. He knows all about you, and thus He is able to meet your every need. The God who controls the planets in their orbits is able to take the pieces of your broken heart and put them together again. He will heal your broken heart, provided you give Him all the pieces and yield to His tender love.

"Great is our Lord, and mighty in power; His understanding is infinite" (v.5). His love and understanding are limitless. His power is great. He can do what needs to be done.

The One who set the galaxies in motion is the same One who addresses your needs. There is no limit to God's love, His understanding or His power. Perhaps you have a broken heart today. Give Him the pieces and let Him heal your heart.

Read Psalm 147:12-20

PRECIOUS TREASURE

I wonder if the Old Testament people of Israel realized how privileged they were. This is what the psalmist addresses in today's passage. He's telling the Jewish people to praise the Lord because of all He had done for them. "For He has strengthened the bars of your gates; He has blessed your children within you" (v.13). He gave peace in their borders. He fed them. He gave them His Word and His Law. He gave them land. "He has not dealt thus with any nation; and as for His judgments, they have not known them" (v.20). God deposited with Israel the precious treasure of His Word.

Notice what the psalmist says about the Word of God. Verse 15 tells us that *God's Word runs*: "He sends out His command to the earth; His word runs very swiftly." When God speaks, that Word goes out like a rapidly running messenger and accomplishes His purposes. God runs the universe by His Word. He decrees things, and they happen.

God's Word also melts obstacles. "He sends out His word and melts them" (v.18). God's Word can melt the cold, hard heart. Are you facing an impossible situation? The Word of God can melt any bars or walls and open the way for you.

Finally, *God's Word blesses.* "He declares His word to Jacob, His statutes and His judgments to Israel. . . . Praise the Lord!" (vv.19,20). Read the Word of God. It's a great treasure that, when invested in your life, bears fruit.

God's Word runs and accomplishes His will. It melts and opens the way. And it blesses all who will receive it, obey it and trust it. God desires that you spend time daily appropriating the riches of His Word. Do you invest God's Word in your life?

Read Psalm 148:1-14

RUN BY DECREE

DAY

363

When I was a young pastor in my first church, we had to build a new sanctuary. My friends know that I don't know the first thing about construction. I can't read blueprints. I can't even make a birdhouse. But we began the project. Construction went slowly, and it was difficult. Then winter came.

I recall standing by that piece of property, looking at those snowcovered arches and wondering, "Lord, why is it taking so long?" Then the Lord led me to Psalm 148 and showed me that when we complain about the weather, we should remember that He is in control. He gave me a great word of assurance from verse 8: "Fire and hail, snow and clouds; stormy wind, fulfilling His word."

All of Psalm 148 tells us that the Word of God is in control. When He speaks in heaven, things happen on earth. In verses 1-6 the heavens praise the Lord. In verses 7-10 the earth praises the Lord. And in verses 11-14, all people, young and old, praise the Lord, including kings, princes, judges and ordinary people. Why? Because His Word is creative. Verse 5 tells us He commanded, and they were created. He also has "established them forever" (v.6).

God does not run this world by consensus but by decree. His Word is sufficient to guide our lives.

God's Word creates, establishes and fulfills His will. The next time you find yourself in a storm, don't complain; instead, surrender. Remember, the stormy wind as well as the calm wind fulfills the Word of God. Submit to God's control and to His creative Word in your life.

DAY 364

Read Psalm 149:1-9

SINGING IN STRANGE PLACES

"Praise the Lord! Sing to the Lord a new song" (v.1). We have a tendency to want to sing the same songs in church, and there's nothing wrong with that. The psalmist isn't telling us to buy a new hymnbook. He means we should have a new experience with the Lord so that we will have a new song of praise to give to Him.

Every new valley that we go through, every new mountaintop we climb, every experience of life ought to be writing on our hearts a new song of praise. When we face a difficulty, we have an opportunity to have renewed faith and see God do new things.

In verse 1 the psalmist tells us to sing in the congregation. I can understand that command. I enjoy congregational singing when people sing to the Lord. "Let Israel rejoice in their Maker; let the children of Zion be joyful in their King" (v.2). I am glad when God's people gather in a congregation of celebration, rejoicing in the goodness and the glory of the Lord.

But he also tells us we should be joyful on our beds. "Let them sing aloud on their beds" (v.5). This could be while we're resting or recuperating from an illness. Perhaps you're lying in bed right now, and you don't feel well. Sing praises to the Lord upon your bed and worship Him. Then the psalmist says, "Let the high praises of God be in their mouth, and a two-edged sword in their hand, to execute vengeance on the nations" (vv.6,7). This is a picture of warriors on the battlefield, singing in the midst of the battle.

It is easy to sing in the congregation, not quite so easy to sing on our beds and difficult to sing on the battlefield. But if we sing, we'll glorify the Lord, and we'll grow. "He will beautify the humble with salvation" (v.4). We'll be happier and holier and more beautiful if we sing to the Lord.

God brings you through different experiences so you may learn new dimensions of His love and grace. What difficulty are you facing today? Don't simply endure or waste it. Use it as an opportunity to find a new song of praise to God.

Read Psalm 150:1-6

AN ORCHESTRA OF PRAISE

DAY 365

The hymn book of the Bible is the Book of Psalms, and the last psalm summarizes what God wants us to know about praise and worship. The Christian faith is a singing and praising faith. No other religion has praise and singing such as we have, because we have the song of the Lord in our hearts. The psalmist answers some important questions about praise in this psalm.

Who is it that we praise? "Praise the Lord" (v.1)—not the church, not the preacher, but the Lord. Our problem is that we often don't see the Lord. We look at gifts or lack of gifts from God. We say, "Why didn't the Lord do this, or why wasn't it done differently?" We don't really see Him. Let's get beyond the gift to the Giver. Let's get beyond the blessing to the Blesser. Let's praise the Lord. "Rejoice in the Lord," Paul said. "Again I will say, rejoice!" (Phil.4:4).

Where do we praise Him? "Praise God in His sanctuary; praise Him in His mighty firmament" (v.1). What an interesting combination. When we praise God in church, it's just like the praise of the angels in heaven. In the sanctuary or wherever we are, let's praise Him.

Why do we praise Him? "Praise Him for His mighty acts; praise Him according to His excellent greatness!" (v.2). We praise Him for what He is and for what He does.

How do we praise Him? With the sound of the trumpet, with the psaltery, the harp, the timbrel, the dance, the stringed instruments, the flute and the loud cymbals. The psalmist is saying, "Get the whole orchestra together. Find every instrument you can, and let's praise the Lord." Some people don't like that kind of praise, but we are commanded here to praise Him and to make a loud song to His glory.

All of nature is praising God today, but His people are prone to forget to praise Him. Ask yourself these praise questions of Psalm 150 and then meditate on the psalmist's answers. You have much for which to give praise. Bring joy to God's heart by praising Him.

MORE USEFUL BOOKS

BLESSINGS ALL MINE WITH 10,000 BESIDES!

by
George Verwer

PAGES 394
ISBN 978-81-7362-725-5

CONVERSATION WITH THE SOVEREIGN LORD

by
Pauline Deborah

PAGES 376
ISBN 978-81-7362-961-7